Threatened Identities

Threatened Identities

Edited by
Glynis M. Breakwell
Department of Psychology
University of Surrey

JOHN WILEY & SONS
Chichester · New York · Brisbane · Toronto · Singapore

Library of Congress Cataloging in Publication Data
Main entry under title:

Threatened identities.

Includes indexes.
Contents: Formulations and searches/Glynis M. Breakwell—Identity projects/Rom Harré—Breakdown of personal relationships and the threat to personal identity/Steve Duck & Martin Lea—Negativism and identity/Michael Apter—[etc.]
1. Identity (Psychology)—Addresses, essays, lectures. 2. Threat (Psychology)—Addresses, essays, lectures. 3. Social groups—Psychological aspects—Addresses, essays, lectures. I. Breakwell, Glynis Marie.
BF697.T55 1983 155.2 82-8451

ISBN 0 471 10233 4 AACR2

British Library Cataloguing in Publication Data:

Threatened identities.
1. Identity
I. Breakwell, Glynis M.
155.2 BC199.14
ISBN 0 471 10233 4

Photosetting by Thomson Press (India) Limited, New Delhi and
Printed at Vail-Ballou Press Inc., New York

To H. B.

Acknowledgements

I would like to acknowledge my debt to Nuffield College, Oxford, for its material and intellectual support during the time that this book was being compiled.

List of contributors

MICHAEL APTER	*Dept. of Psychology, University College, PO Box 78, Cardiff, CF1 1XL*
SHIRLEY ARDENER	*Queen Elizabeth House, University of Oxford, Oxford*
GLYNIS M. BREAKWELL	*Dept. of Psychology, University of Surrey, Guildford, Surrey*
STEVE DUCK and MARTIN LEA	*Dept. of Psychology, Fylde College, Bailrigg, Lancaster, LA1 4YF*
FAY FRANSELLA	*Centre for Personal Construct Psychology, 132, Warwick Way, London SW1V 4JD*
ROM HARRÉ	*Sub-Faculty of Philosophy, 10, Merton St., Oxford, OX1 4JJ*
PETER HITCH	*School of Applied Social Studies, University of Bradford, Bradford, West Yorkshire*
TOM KITWOOD	*School of Science and Society, University of Bradford, Bradford, West Yorkshire*
JUDITH A. MATTHEWS	*Dept. of Geography, Rolle College, Exmouth.*
PETER WEINREICH	*School of Psychology, Ulster Polytechnic, Shore Rd., Newtown Abbey, Co. Antrim, BT37 OQB*

Contents

Preface xiii

PART I: FORMULATIONS AND SEARCHES

Formulations and Searches 3
Glynis M. Breakwell

PART II: REFORMULATIONS AND RESEARCHES

SECTION A: THREATS TO INDIVIDUAL IDENTITY . . 29

Identity Projects 31
Rom Harré

Breakdown of Personal Relationships and the Threat to Personal Identity 53
Steve Duck and Martin Lea

Negativism and the Sense of Identity 75
Michael J. Apter

Threat and the Scientist 91
Fay Fransella

SECTION B: THREATS TO THE INDIVIDUAL AS GROUP MEMBER 105

Social Identity and the Half-Asian Child 107
Peter Hitch

Self-conception among Young British–Asian Muslims: Confutation of a Stereotype 129
Tom Kitwood

Emerging from Threatened Identities 149
Peter Weinreich

SECTION C: THREATS TO THE IDENTITY OF GROUPS 187

Identities and Conflicts 189
Glynis M. Breakwell

Environmental Change and Community Identity 215
Judith A. Matthews

Arson, Nudity and Bombs among the Canadian Doukhobors: A Question of Identity 239
Shirley Ardener

Author Index 267

Subject Index 271

Preface

This book is about the identity of individuals and groups. More specifically it is about threatened identities. The contributors seek to describe what constitutes a threat to identity, the effects of such threats and the responses generated by threats.

The contributions originate from a variety of disciplines: philosophy, social and clinical psychology, sociology, anthropology, and human geography. It is therefore not surprising that a range of theoretical perspectives are represented in the way in which the problem of threats to identity has been examined by the contributors. They approach the problem from different levels of analysis and explanation. Some take as the target for analysis the identity of the individual and these contributions from, Rom Harré, Steve Duck and Martin Lea, Michael Apter, and Fay Fransella, have been grouped together in Section A of Part Two of the book. Some, Peter Hitch, Tom Kitwood, and Peter Weinreich, are specifically concerned with how group membership affects the identity of the individual and these are presented in Section B of Part Two. Section C of Part Two comprises chapters by Glynis Breakwell, Judy Matthews, and Shirley Ardener and their prime focus of concern is the identity of groups.

Nevertheless, all of these contributions have to be seen against a common backdrop of general questions about the nature and functioning of identity. The purpose of Part One, Formulations and Searches, is to provide this backdrop by outlining some of the central debates about identity.

Oxford GLYNIS M BREAKWELL

PART ONE

Formulations and searches

Threatened Identities
Edited by G. Breakwell

Formulations and Searches

GLYNIS M. BREAKWELL

The purpose of this chapter is to set the scene for the chapters in Part II of this book. The chapters in Part II present current reformulations of the concept of identity and contain recent researches on the nature and consequences of threats to identity. The object here is to examine some of the formulations and searches from which these derive.

This chapter is, therefore, concerned with five areas:

1. Debates surrounding the concept of identity for the individual.
2. The nature of threats to identity.
3. Types of responses to threat to identity.
4. The identity of groups.
5. Threats to group identities.

The treatment of these areas cannot be comprehensive given the constraints of space. Issues which illuminate the chapters in Part II have been selected for special attention.

1. THE CONCEPT OF IDENTITY FOR THE INDIVIDUAL

Four central questions surround the concept of identity for the individual:

(a) How should identity be defined?
(b) Why study identity?
(c) Is the individual autonomous or an automaton?
(d) In what ways are personal and social identity distinct?

Some of the considerations important in answering these questions are considered below. Harré, in this volume, offers a further perspective that supplements this review.

(a) How should identity be defined?

'Definitions of identity vary with overall definitions of reality' (Berger *et al.*, 1974).

Where the concept of identity is concerned there are simultaneously problems of terminology and definition. The terms identity, self, character and personality are all used as labels for that uniqueness which differentiates one individual from the next. Clear and universally applicable distinctions between the terms are difficult to establish. Where one theorist talks about identity another will call it personality or the self-concept, yet they seem to be referring to the same thing. Despite their disparate terminology they seem to be reaching out to understand the same processes and phenomena.

The term they choose to label these processes is dependent upon the philosophical and methodological foundations of their particular theory. The theorist whose work emanates from acceptance of behaviourism and the use of factor analytic methods is more likely to employ the term 'personality' than 'the self-concept'. More importantly, in the long run it is the theory which they adopt or evolve which determines how they define the term or label they choose. The abstract and operational definition of the concept will depend upon the role it has to play in their theory. It will also depend upon why that theory has been developed.

The fact that the concept, of identity for instance, is dependent upon its theoretical context for its definition least to further difficulties. It means that the same term can be used by two different theorists who define it in totally different ways. Making direct comparisons across theories consequently has nightmare qualities.

It is not the purpose of this chapter to summarize the multitude of different theories that have been constructed about identity, the self, personality or character. There are many books which do this (for example, Bavelas, 1978; Burns, 1979; Cattell and Dreger, 1977; Fransella, 1981; Hall and Lindzey, 1978; Harré, 1976; and Holland, 1977). Nor is it the purpose of this chapter to rehearse the many definitions of identity, the self, personality and character found in these theories. The purpose is to consider issues which cut across definitions and theories and are important in some way to all.

One such issue concerns the inherent duality in the use of identity and similar terms. Theorists see identity simultaneously in two ways. Firstly, identity is something to be explained—the fact that individuals have an identity must be explained. Psychologically and socially, identity is a phenomenon and theories can be constructed to account for its development and changes over time. Secondly, identity is something which can be used to explain why other things occur. Used in this way, identity becomes a theoretical construct which can be used to explain why an individual behaves in a particular fashion. For instance, a person's actions may be said to be the result of the need to act in accordance with his or her self concept.

Confusion of these two aspects of identity is frequent and needs to be avoided: identity as a psychological phenomenon cannot be equated with identity as a theoretical abstraction. The distinction is particularly important when considering the reasons why identity is studied.

(b) Why study identity?

The primary reason for studying the nature of identity is simple. If one is interested in explaining and predicting an individual's behaviour, the notion of identity is useful. Many theorists have explained behaviour in terms of personality traits: people act in an aggressive fashion because they *are* aggressive, others behave in a humble way because they *are* humble. Inherent in this type of explanation is the assumption that people behave consistently across situations. So that, if someone is aggressive they are likely to act aggressively in many different situations. Studying identity or personality types was thus considered important because once a person was classified as a member of a 'type', it was believed that their behaviour could be predicted. Many ways of measuring personality traits and types have been evolved with this ultimate objective of prediction in mind.

Recently, these assumptions about the neat correlation between personality and behaviour have been severely challenged (Mischel, 1968; Argyle, 1976). The challengers contend that behaviour is never merely a function of personality. They suggest that it is invariably a function of the interaction between the individual's personality and the situation in which the behaviour is exhibited. Mischel (1977) states 'the idiosyncratic organization of personality makes behaviour largely situation-specific so that personality characteristics, which have been central to psycho-dynamic and other forms of personality theory, have little scientific value for the prediction and explanation of behaviour'.

Since this attack on the traditional use of concepts of personality and identity to explain behaviour has been supported by considerable empirical research, the reason for their study has begun to change. There is growing emphasis upon the analysis of identity or personality in its social context. The focus is upon the analysis of 'social situations' (Argyle *et al.*, 1981). There is a growing concern, exemplified in this book, with the dialectical relationship between identity and its social context. This work has emphasized the need there is to understand the processes of growth and change in identity. It testifies to the fact that identity is not a static, measurable structure which will predict behaviour.

The desire to predict behaviour may still ultimately motivate the study of identity. But naïve assumptions about the primacy of identity in the determination of behaviour are currently thin on the ground. Instead, the label identity or personality or whatever is used to signify a series of complex processes that orient the individual in the social world; the operation of these processes can only be understood in context, and, with situational variables, they are deemed to determine behaviour.

(c) Is the individual autonomous or an automaton?

The recognition of the importance of situational constraints upon the genesis of behaviour leads naturally to the third question which hovers around this concept of identity. This concerns the issue of free will. Is the individual's behaviour determined by circumstances or does the individual have a choice in the matter? It is an old debate and receives extensive and beautiful coverage in a collection of primarily philosophical readings edited by Mischel (1977). Repetition of that coverage seems superfluous. Most of the contributors to the present volume would concur with Harré's analysis.

Harré (1979) argued that people have 'relative autonomy' that is to say their conduct is not wholly determined by their immediate context. People have the power to shift from 'acting according to one principle, impulse, sentiment or whatever, to acting according to another, whatever the original principle might be' (Harré, 1979, p. 253). This is, of course, a hazardous *via media* between proclaiming people automata or autonomous. It fails to explain how they come to move from one principle to another or from one impulse to another. Presumably, such moves could be explained in terms of the operation of complex conceptual processes which are themselves a product of experience. If this is correct then the doctrine of relative autonomy is very similar to that weak form of determinism adopted by James (1890): seen in historical perspective the behaviour of the moment is understood to be determined and the individual is seen to have no lattitude for choice; seen at the moment of execution, the behaviour cannot be said to be determined by situational constraints.

(d) In what ways are personal and social identity distinct?

Consideration of this question needs to be broken into three parts:

(i) What are the constituent parts of identity?
(ii) Do both personal and social identity exist?
(iii) What is the genesis of personal identity?

These questions will be considered in turn.

(i) *The constituent parts of identity*

Writers on the concept of identity and the concept of self have sought to understand these entities by specifying their constituent parts. Interestingly, they have not sought to specify the dynamic relationship of these parts. To put it another way, it has been traditionally the case that the structure of identity or the self is discussed without considering the processes involved.

The nature of the constituent parts has been said to be relatively simple. William James (1890) assimilated what had already been voiced in philosophical writings (Descartes, Hume, Locke, Kant, and Schopenhauer) when he distinguished between the self as subject (I) and the self as object (me). James recognized that his 'I' and 'me' were merely 'discriminated aspects of the singularity of the process of experience' which comprises the 'global self'. Yet he went on further to differentiate four aspects of the self:

the spiritual self: entails thinking and feeling
the material self: entails those 'material possessions' we have
the social self: entails reference to those individuals and groups about whose opinions we care
the bodily self: entails the physical organism

It can be seen that James is listing those features of an existence which differentiate one person from the next: the way he or she thinks about the world; the possessions he or she has; the social connections he or she prizes; and the shell he or she occupies. These are the aspects of the self and seem to comprise what Allport (1955) called the 'proprium' 'all the regions of our life that we regard as intimately and essentially ours' (p. 38).

For James, the process of knowing or experiencing these distinguishing features of the self is inextricably tied to the process of evaluating them. The value, according to James, of any characteristic is related to the individuals 'pretensions'. Only deficiencies perceived to be relevant to pretensions have the power to lower self-esteem.

In James' writings, all the fundamental distinctions drawn by his successors in their descriptions of the self are visible. Largely these centre upon a series of distinctions or oppositions:

self-concept vs. self-evaluation
self-as-object vs. self-as-subject
social-self vs. spiritual-self
real-self vs. ideal-self

Different writers emphasize different aspects of these oppositions. However, their conceptions revolve around the idea that the self is both knower and known; evaluator and evaluated; personal and social; and actual and potential. The paradoxes entailed in the self encompassing all these states of being simultaneously are of course overwhelming. They are so overwhelming that they seem to encourage theorists to take the Taoist path where contemplation of the paradox is its own answer and resolution of the paradox is unnecessary. For instance, Cooley (1902) faced with the problem of the origin of the self answered:

> 'self and society are twin born . . . and the notion of a separate and independent ego is an illusion'

Cooley proposed the concept of the 'looking-glass self' to describe the development of the self-concept. People, he suggested, see themselves as others see them because they learn about themselves from others. Others effectively act as mirrors in which a person sees himself or herself. His description entails an infinite regress of mirror reflecting mirror: each acts as a mirror for others and responds to the mirrors that others are for them. Cooley is actually describing the growth of the self-concept through an elegant but nonsensical metaphor. In reality, it is a striking fact that if two mirrors are arranged face to face, neither can produce an image. All too frequently, having specified their paradox (e.g. self and society are twin born), writers resort to metaphor (e.g. the looking glass imagery) without any delineation of how their metaphor can be translated into practical operations (whether social processes or not). The 'looking-glass self' only becomes meaningful if the processes whereby the feedback from others is subsequently subjectively interpreted are explained.

After James, Mead (1934) must be the most renowned writer on the self. The distinction between 'I' and 'me' was taken as a given by Mead but he went on to try to describe the processes involved in the evolution of this distinction. According to him, the self develops as a result of its relations to the 'generalized other'. The reactions and expectations of those who are important to us are the template for our behaviour. The 'generalized other' is composed of one's apprehension of those around one. Mead's basic argument is that everyone learns to interpret the world as others do in order to act as expected.

Mead differentiates between 'I' and 'me' by giving them different contexts in which to operate. 'Me' is focal in interchanges involving group membership, status, roles and other people. 'I' is focal when the individual asserts himself or herself against the situation, emphasizing his or her unique capacities. Mead's analysis, although not invested with concepts of the unconscious, is akin to that of Freud. The 'I' represents the impulsive, undisciplined, unorganized potential of the individual. As it becomes controlled by societal constraints, a behaviour will move from the domain of 'I' into the domain of 'me'. In the same way, in the Freudian framework, the id is translated into action only through interaction with the ego and superego which are oriented to the reality principle and acceptance of socitey's restraints. In Mead's analysis, 'me' is essentially a social construction. It is eminently compatible with James' 'social self'.

Goffman (1959, 1967), together with many role theorists (e.g. Biddle, 1979), takes this distinction between components of identity to its logical extreme. They argue that people can adopt short-term selves, they put them on as roles and they can shed them again. They see the individual as an actor in a drama where, for the duration the role dictates the appropriate actions. The drama having ended the actor moves on. Goffman is not concerned to explain what it is that the actor is, what state of being he or she resides in, during periods where no role is available. It is assumed that no such moratoriums occur. The individual always has a role to perform. It would be excusable if one were to conclude that the individual is nothing but the role or the conglomeration of roles occupied. Many have done so (see McCall and Simmons, 1966; Stryker, 1964; Turner, 1970). Certainly, it seems that for Goffman the self is always social. This leads to the next question.

(ii) *Do both personal and social identity exist?*

> 'The problem is to make personal identity personal and social identity identity' (Hollis, 1977).

This distinction between social and personal identity has become central to theorizing about the self. At its simplest, the distinction is clear. Social identity is that part of the self-concept derived from the individual's group memberships and interpersonal relationships and social position and status. Personal identity is that part of the self-concept which is free of role or relationship determinants. But the problem, pinpointed so eloquently by Hollis, is immediately evident. It is difficult to see how personal identity can be defined except in terms of its social history and context. Moreover, it is difficult to see how social identity says anything about identity since it is merely the crystallization of a series of social roles and relationships: anyone occupying those positions might be attributed with that social identity; it has no power to distinguish between unique individuals.

This has led to questions about whether both social and personal identity exist. These questions can be answered at two levels: the theoretical and the phenomenological. The first is unproblematic: theoretically the existence of both personal and social identity is merely a definitional trick. A semantic boundary is drawn between personal and social identity and both spring into existence and that is that. For the purposes of theory-building, both personal and social identity exist because they are defined as such.

The second sort of answer is more interesting: do both social and personal identity exist phenomenologically? Do people actually experience both a social and a personal identity? This is a relatively simple empirical question. In fact, there is evidence to suggest that people do experience both aspects of identity. Turner (1976) found that people distinguished between times when they behaved according to the precepts of their 'real self' and other times when they behaved out of character or purely because of social constraints. For some people, Turner found that the 'real self' was deemed to be in control only when they acted in accordance with impulse; for others, it was only when they acted according their social role that they felt they were their 'real selves'.

It seems that the perception of both social and personal identity is most likely to occur when they are in conflict with each other. When a person finds his or her social role demands one course of action and his or her personal feelings call for another course of action, the individual becomes aware of both personal and social identity. The interesting thing is that at other times the distinction is not made. When conflict does occur, however, the dualism is immediately evident.

The form of conflict between personal and social identity is often quite complex. A hypothetical example can illustrate this complexity. Take the case of the mayor of a small town which has been occupied by foreign soldiers. The mayor is faced with an ultimatum from the invaders: she must hand over to them a resistance fighter or they will execute many of the townsfolk. As mayor, as occupant of a specific social role, the woman has obligations to her electorate which dictate one course of action. As a pacifist, as an adherent of a specific moral doctrine, the woman has obligations to her beliefs which prescribe that she should take another course of action. But her position is further complicated: she is the mother of the resistance fighter. As a mother she has obligations to her child which demand yet another course of action. The predicament of this woman serves to illustrate a series of things.

Firstly, it emphasizes the fact that a person may occupy several social roles simultaneously (mayor, pacifist, and mother). All of these roles have a contribution to make to the individual's social identity. Moreover, the nature of the roles in the example points to the fact that social roles originate in both public (being a mayor) and the private (being a mother) realms. Being mayor and being a mother are both social roles, they simply tend to operate in different spheres. Both are tied to the occupation of a particular social position and both have prescriptions for behaviour bound around them. This distinction between public and private roles is a qualification to the broader dichotomy between social and personal identity.

Secondly, all aspects of identity are tied to belief systems and to value systems since these are central defining properties of any social niche. A particular social role can thus be derived from adherence to a specific ideology or doctrine (like pacifism).

Thirdly, where personal and social identity come into conflict, this is often because a clash of value systems has occurred. McCall (1977) argues that in fact personal identity can only be revealed in the context of moral decisions: where the person chooses between moral routes, that person discloses his or her 'real self'. The mayor who decides to save the resistance fighter rather than the townsfolk reveals what she truly values.

Fourthly, any or all of the social roles which form subsets of social identity can come into conflict with the demands of personal identity. Consequently, there can be a series of different but simultaneous battles going on for control of behaviour.

The case of the mayor fails to illustrate what can be a vital feature in the clash between personal and social identity. In her case the conflict was acute, a decision required immediately which—for good or ill—would resolve the conflict. Often the conflict is chronic. For instance, the lesbian who passes as heterosexual for long periods is likely to experience a chronic state of incompatibility between what she knows or thinks herself to be and what she can be in her society. Hollis (1977) argues that this experience constitutes a crisis of identity which:

> 'strikes when what I am no longer accounts for who I am, because what I do is no longer the rational acting out of what I have chosen to become. The reasons for action supplied to me no longer function as my own good reasons. The threat to my identity is then both subjectively painful and objectively real' (Hollis, 1977, p. 106)

The important thing to realize, of course, is that though this chronic state of incompatibility may be long-lived it is rarely static. Either social or personal identity has to change in such a situation. The importance of change to identity leads on to the next question.

(iii) *What is the genesis of personal identity?*

All of this talk of conflict indicates that at a given time, for a given person, both a social and a personal identity may be discerned. They are thrown into relief by their conflict. They can only be captured if the moment of their conflict is frozen, that is only if they are examined as if they were a still life. Life is, however, not still; it entails continual change. If examined from a realistic dynamic standpoint personal and social identity are not distinct entities, they are merely different points in the process of development. This is the process whereby conceptions of the self are learnt, actively used and transformed through contact with new experiences, and then act to filter future impacts of the social expectations surrounding the individual.

The person actively accommodates to and assimilates conceptions of himself or herself which are provided by the social world (Gergen, 1977). The important thing is that social identities or social roles provide templates for self-conception: providing a structure (a set of dimensions for description) and an evaluation of that structure (via moral and social norms). To this extent, personal identity, being that residue of the accommodation to and assimilation of social identities, is the product of social identities.

This suggestion that personal identity evolves through social identity is not meant to imply that crude social determinism is involved. The model is not of a 'plastic man' (Hollis, 1977) destined to move with every gust of the social wind and to move for no other reason. Perceptions of social pressures and adaptation to them is a selective and active process. The personal identity may be said to be the residual product of this active process but it is also an inherent part of this process; it should be remembered that even the principles of selection which guide adaptation are the consequences of past experiences.

In real time, the evolution of identity entails this continual and truly dialectical relationship between personal and social identity. Current personal identity is the product of the interaction of all past personal identities with all past and present social identities. But the reverse is also true: current social identity is the product of the interactions of all past social identities with all past and current personal identities.

When this evolutionary perspective is adopted it is the processes of adaptation, change and influence which come to seem important rather than the dichotomy between personal and social identity. After all, they are merely labels for grossly delineated aspects, or products, of these processes.

This process notion of identity also overcomes the paradoxes associated with distinctions between the knower and the known, the evaluator and the evaluated, the subject and the object. If identity is a process, a selective, active, adaptive process, there is no need to assume these distinctions. It is the parameters of the process which come to matter. The 'knower' is superfluous to the self-process. These processes may be intrinsically evaluative; postulations of the homunculus evaluating and directing the self are unnecessary.

In practice, this sort of conclusion is hardly new. Social psychologists, having found the paradoxes inherent in the categorical distinctions within the self-concept to be unproductive, have been exploring these processes for many years. Certainly in examining the nature of threatened identities, the contributors to this book have been concerned the internal and external processes which generate threat and intervene when it is dealt with. Consequently, much of the second part of this book is devoted to exploring identity *processes* and not static identity *structures*.

2. THE NATURE OF THREATS TO IDENTITY

Threats to identity take many forms and examples of them are given in Part II of this book. However, there are a few general comments which can be made about the nature of such threats before considering specific examples. These general comments concern:

(a) The types of threat.
(b) The origins or sources of threat.
(c) The perspectives on or perceptions of threat.

They will be considered briefly in turn.

(a) The types of threat

Any experience can potentially constitute a threat to an individual's identity. Any thought, feeling, action or experience which challenges the individual's personal or social identity is a threat. The challenge can be at one or both of two levels:

(i) It may query the content of the personal or social identity.
(ii) It may query the evaluation of the personal or social identity.

(i) *Queries about the content of identity*

In content terms, identity is comprised of the labels one would use to describe oneself. Over the years, a man may come to think of himself as middle class, handsome and intelligent. A threat which attacked the content of identity might query whether these labels were apt. So that for our handsome, intelligent, middle-class male, such a threat might come when he loses his money, or wrecks his good looks in a car accident, or destroys his intellect by excessive drinking. Equally, he may be just as threatened if he does not change but others claim that they no longer think him handsome, intelligent, or middle class.

Effectively, the propriety of self-description can be challenged either because the individual concerned actually changes and the old labels are no longer valid *or* because society changes the meaning or usage of the labels. Either way, identity is threatened.

(ii) *Queries about the evaluation of identity*

There is another type of threat which does not challenge the content of identity but questions its value. In this case, the fact that the chap is middle class, handsome and intelligent would not be queried. Instead, it would be argued that being any or all of those things is bad and to be avoided. Imbuing the characteristics an individual claims to be his own with negative connotations is a fundamental threat to identity—so long as the individual accepts the legitimacy of those connotations.

The potency of these two types of threat seems to rest upon the importance which people place upon being consistent and upon being able to maintain self-esteem. People seek to be consistent. They seek to act consistently. Cohen and Taylor (1972) claim that men in prison who are removed from their normal social setting try to maintain their identity by acting in accordance with the prescripts of their 'historical self' or 'true self', maintaining as far as possible the rituals and habits of their life outside of prison. Anything which prevents such consistency across time or indeed anything which simply claims that it is not there represents a real threat to identity.

Similarly, people seek to maintain their self-esteem. They seek to feel positive about themselves. The need for self-esteem has been shown to be a strong motive force (Gergen, 1971, reports much empirical evidence for evidence for this). Anything which attacks self-esteem is consequently a serious threat to identity.

Threats to self-esteem and consistency operate on at least three levels:

I. Attacking the individual.
II. Attacking the individual's group memberships.
III. Attacking the individual's group.

I. *Attacking the individual.* Such attacks insist that the individual is not what she or he thinks she or he is. So they come in the form: 'you might think you are compassionate but you aren't really, you are hard hearted and mean'. They challenge whether the individual possesses prized personal qualities. Such attacks can, of course alternatively take place on the evaluative plane. Their form would be: 'yes, you are compassionate—so what? Compassion is an outmoded response, not worth the tears its written in'. Content and evaluative attacks can sometimes be combined: 'you are hard hearted and mean and that is a truly terrible thing to be'.

II. *Attacking the individual's group memberships.* These types of attack are really always upon the content plane. The individual is told that they are not or should not be a member of a group whose membership they prize. The chapter by Hitch in Part II considers what happens to people in this situation. He is particularly concerned with marginals—people who find themselves caught between two groups.

III. *Attacking the individual's group.* These types of attack do not challenge the individual's membership of a particular group, instead they berate and decry the group to which the individual belongs. Such denigration of the group acts as a threat to identity in so far as identity is derived from group memberships. Belonging to groups which have a good social standing and which others consider valuable acts to inflate and support the self-esteem of the individual. When the group is attacked, the individual's self-esteem is also attacked. The chapters by Breakwell, Ardener and Matthews in Part II are devoted to an examination of what happens when the group is attacked.

(b) The origins or sources of threat

Given the multitudinous forms of threat it is hardly surprising that it can emanate from many sources. There are as many sources as there are origins for new information relevant to identity. But these sources can be divided into three categories:

(i) The individual.
(ii) Other people.
(iii) The material world.

(i) *The individual*

The individual may threaten his or her own identity. This is most common where disease or accident causes changes in bodily functions. The most disruptive of these sort of changes are probably those associated with illness. For instance, hallucinations and delusions often centre upon a change of identity—the person comes to believe that he or she is someone else, perhaps Helen of Troy or Christ.

(ii) *Other people*

This is perhaps the most obvious source of threat and all of the examples so far have relied upon other people as the originators of the threatening information or judgements. In order to calculate the impact of threats, however, the precise standing of these other people is important. The person threatened has to believe that those who threaten have a legitimate right to make comments and pass judgements before their threats will have any direct influence and even then it will be difficult to trace. Suffice it to say here that the social position and moral standing of others who threaten is important in determining the consequences of their threats.

(iii) *The material world*

It is important in cataloguing the sources of threat to identity not to ignore the material world. Features of the material world which have little to do with the individual or other people can have dramatic impact upon identity. Take for example the case of the businessman whose empire crashes and wealth vanishes because the stock exchange folds; his social and personal identity is threatened by material change. An even more totally asocial example is typified by the case of the cross-channel swimmer who believes in her ability to reach the other shore but who is prevented by unprecedented storms. That part of her identity founded in her ability to conquer the elements is threatened.

An interesting feature of the way in which people deal with threats emanating from the material world seems to be the ease with which they can ignore them. Research on attribution processes has shown that people who can, for instance, attribute a failure to material circumstances refuse to admit that their failure in those circumstances indicates anything about them as people or about their identity. This denial revolves around the question of how threats are perceived.

(c) The perspectives on or perceptions of threat

The nature of threats needs to be understood from at least two perspectives: the internal and the external. This distribution echoes the fact that a threat has a subjective and an objective existence. The internal perspective consists of the threatened person's subjective understanding of the threat. The external perspective rests in the understanding that other people have of the threat. In a sense, the external perspective is the objective understanding of the threat. At least, it is objective in so far as observers have a consensual understanding of the nature of the threat.

It is obviously important to recognize that the internal and external perspectives on the threat are not always compatible. Sometimes, the individual will feel threatened when others can see no reason for it. At other times, the individual will feel no threat even though others consider them to be in a threatening position. There is undoubtedly a very important *distinction to be made between the experience of threat and the threatening position* since a person can occupy the latter without feeling the former.

Whether a threat in the objective sense is perceived to be a threat in the subjective sense will depend upon the construal system of the individual involved. In other words, it will depend upon the prior state of that person's identity.

3. RESPONSES TO THREATS TO IDENTITY

Since the study of responses to threats to identity is the focus for much of Part II of this book, it seems superfluous to produce more than an outline for their classification here. Three types of responses to subjectively experienced threat seem common:

(a) Reconstrual.
(b) Mobility or change.
(c) Inertia.

The exact pattern of responses in these three categories is dependent upon the source of the threat and the level at which it operates (attacking the individual, the individual's group memberships, or the individual's group). Nevertheless, something can be said about the general properties of these types of responses to threat.

(a) Reconstrual

This response can involve either or both of the following targets for reconstrual: the threat or the identity. Reconstrual of threat as a strategy for coping with it is exemplified by the chapters in Part II by Duck and Lea, and by Fransella. The purpose of such reconstrual is to devalue or invalidate the threat. It may be achieved through reinterpretation of the information contained in the threat—e.g. the information may be deemed incorrect, partial, or simply not as damning as it originally appeared. Alternatively, the threat may be dismissed because its source can be considered beneath respect. Either way, the threat is translated into something less harmful through purely cognitive machinations.

Secondly, the individual may respond to threat by reconstruing his or her identity. In such cases, the impact of the threat is such that the individual cannot ignore it or translate it and his or her understanding of his or her identity is changed as a result of the new information or evaluation. The chapters by Weinreich and Kitwood in Part II exemplify this process. This type of response to threat is not easy. Changing the self-concept is difficult because consistency is too highly valued.

(b) Mobility and change

Mobility and change are really two quite distinct responses to threat but they are grouped together here because, unlike reconstrual, they require action from the threatened person. The type of acts they involve are, however, quite different.

(i) *Mobility*

This involves the individual moving to evade the threat. It may simply mean moving physically so that the threat no longer has access. For instance, if your image of yourself as a courageous fellow is threatened daily because your next door neighbour intimidates you, one way of evading the threat is to change house. But mobility may be more complex since it may involve attempts to change one's social position or social group in order to avoid threats which centre upon the individual's group membership or the individual's group. This form of mobility is purely social but it is a frequent response to threat.

(ii) *Change*

Instead of seeking to move oneself, change entails seeking to move other people. The threatened person adopting the change strategy would not move house when faced with a truculent neighbour but rather would train the neighbour to more peaceful manners. Similarly, the change strategy would entail reasserting one's membership of a group and perhaps changing its norms and rules rather than relinquising membership if that were threatened. It would demand efforts to assert the superiority of one's group if the origin of threat lay in attacks upon the group's status. Essentially, the change strategy seeks either to eradicate the source of the threat or to expunge its justification.

(c) Inertia

The third sort of response is really an anti-response. It consists of doing nothing: neither reconstruing nor taking action. The person understands that the attack is being made but simply refrains from response. People can live with this chronic threat for years without responding. The forces which preserve a consistency of identity prevent material or psychological change. So the person is caught as if suspended in a spider's web: trapped in a single system of construal; immobilized; and incapable of generating social change. Such people often compartmentalize their experiences in such a way as to minimize the experience of threats. The precise extent of the disparity between their self-concept and the threatening information about their self-concept is never perceived because the direct comparison is never made. Compartmentalization of this sort is of course hardly adaptive. It reduces the individual's chances of correctly interpreting the social world and responding to it appropriately. Inertia is probably the least effective response to threat.

4. THE IDENTITY OF GROUPS

There are many difficulties facing anyone who wishes to define the concept 'group' let alone the notion of 'group identity'. Bearing this in mind it seems sensible to divide the task into two parts:

(a) The substance of group identity.
(b) The origins of group identity.

(a) The substance of group identity

Groups come in all forms and sizes. As a result, all of the abstract generalized definitions of the concept 'group' have weaknesses; there is always one group which can be shown to be an exception to their rules. They differ in their omissions but they all have them. Instead of seeking for a comprehensive definition of 'group' it may be more productive to understand the dimensions along which groups tend to differ from one another. At least in this way one gains some feel for the vast range of human conglomerations which are all labelled 'groups'.

There are at least eight salient dimensions along which groups differ:

(i) *Size*

Groups differ in size, ranging from two to millions.

(ii) *Length of Life*

The length of a group's lifetime may range from a few minutes to millenia.

(iii) *Permeability of boundaries*

This refers to the ease with which people can enter and leave the group. Entry and exit rules can vary independently. Therefore, in some groups both entry and exit are easy (for instance, in a social group around a bar); in some entry is easy but exit difficult (for example, the armed forces); in others entry is difficult but exit simple (as in the case of an elitist social club) and, finally, in some both entry and exit is difficult (secret societies may be a case in point).

(iv) *Origin of membership*

An individual's membership of a group may be ascribed or achieved. Where membership is ascribed, individuals have no choice in the matter; their membership is imposed upon them by fate or chance or the insistence of others with power. For instance, membership of a racial group is not a matter of choice, it is 'fated'. The chance occurrence of travelling through a car's windscreen and becoming blind may push a person into membership of a disabled persons' group. Being 'sectioned' under the mental health legislation and incarcerated in a psychiatric hospital may mean a person joins a group of the 'mentally ill'. In each of these cases, the group membership is ascribed not chosen. Where membership is achieved the individual makes a conscious decision to join the group. Most transient memberships fall into this category.

Ascribed and achieved membership leads to very different types of group structure and purpose.

(v) *Degree of bureaucracy and extent of status differentials*

Although these are quite separate dimensions of difference, they tend to covary: low levels of bureaucracy being tied to low levels of status differentials.

(vi) *Cohesiveness*

This concerns the extent to which members like each other and how far they act as a single entity. Cohesiveness of this sort seems to be closely attached to how far individuals identify with the group (how far they derive their self-concept from their membership of the group). Some groups are highly cohesive and members feel strong allegiance to the group and lose some of their sense of their independent identity. Other groups motivate minimal allegiance and possess little cohesion.

(vii) *The nature of intra-group communication*

Groups differ in the frequency, form and patterns of communication between members. These differences are important since the nature of communication has fundamental influences upon all features of group life.

(viii) *The type of goals*

Most, though not all, groups have goals. These goals vary in their complexity, duration, and their origin. These variations in goal structure are important in shaping group structures. Greater goal complexity is associated with greater bureaucracy, more status differentials, etc. Short-term goals are likely to lead to less bureaucracy and greater permeability of group boundaries. Some goals are established by the group members, others may be imposed by outsiders. Goals chosen by group members are likely to lead to greater cohesiveness.

It is fairly obvious that *the substance of a group's identity will depend upon it's position along these eight dimensions*. Moreover, it should be remembered that positions on these dimensions tend to covary. In fact, covariations indicate a continuum of group 'types' running from the *concrete to the conceptual group*. Concrete groups are the most common. They have clearly specified goals, defined status hierarchies and extensive bureaucracies, well-used communications networks, members who identify with the group and know each other, and a sense of their own history. Conceptual groups on the other hand have no clear goals, no status hierarchy or bureaucracy, no communication between members, ascribed membership and no group history. Examples of the pure conceptual group are rare (they exist in groups created in the laboratory, (Tajfel, 1981), and in groups created by advertising (Breakwell, 1978)). Such groups essentially exist almost solely, at least initially, in the concept systems of so-called group members. The membership believes the group exists and shows allegiance to it and it motivates their behaviour. Once established, the conceptual group may become a concrete group in the fullness of time since those who believe in its existence are likely to evolve social structures for it. By doing so, they transform its realm of operation from the subjective to the objective. It is also worth mentioning that this process can operate in the opposite direction: concrete groups may wither in the objective sense and become conceptual groups, remaining alive only in the concept system of members. This is simply to state that the dissolution of the social structures in which a group is embedded need not necessarily kill allegiance to the group. Communication between members may cease, its organization may be eradicated, and its goals may become redundant, but the group membership may be retained and sustained in the cognitions of the people who had been concerned.

The substantive identity of a group can be characterized in terms of the eight dimensions described above but there are other aspects which cannot be ignored. A group expresses what it sees to be its own character in its rules and norms. Moreover, compliance with these prescriptions is the key to maintaining one's membership and they dictate the means whereby the newcomer should be socialized into a role within the group. Obedience to the rules and conformity with the norms is what differentiates the member from the nonmember. Rules and norms thus circumscribe the substantive identity of the group.

The substantive identity of the group also finds expression in the symbols used by the group. Symbols employed by groups to express their uniqueness and continuity over time vary widely. Basically, anything can come to be used as a symbol of a group's identity and as a means of differentiating it from all others. Symbols can be simple (a flag) and they can be extremely complex (a language can become a symbol for a group). Symbols can be public and they can be kept a secret available only to group members. Elitist symbols (for example, the Masonic handshake) often remain private means of signalling membership.

Both the structure and the expression of substantive identity varies across different groups, nevertheless, the processes involved in their genesis are shared.

(b) The origins of group identity

The origins of the substantive identity of any group have to be examined at two levels:

(i) The social.
(ii) The psychological.

(i) *The social origins of group identity*

Every group occupies a social niche, it exists within a network of intergroup relations. In this network, the identity of each group is relative to that of each of the others. Identity for a particular group is the product of a negotiation process. It is rare in this process for all concerned in the negotiation to have equal power. The relative power of a group depends upon many variables—for instance, the material resources it possesses and their social value; its historical position; its ability to enter coalitions; the persuasiveness of its ideology; the numerical and psychological strength of its members; and so on. Relative power, therefore, is subject to massive fluctuations. But the important point here is that in negotiating an identity, power (from whatever source) is vital. Moreover, it is, of course, evident that once some semblance of identity has been established for a group it becomes both a determiner and an expression of the group's power. However, in saying this, it should be remembered that identity is merely the label for the product of a range of processes. The concept of identity cannot be used to explain group activities, but the processes involved in erecting identity can be used to explain intragroup and intergroup dynamics.

The negotiation of identity for the group within the power matrix is very complex. One of its complexities arises from the fact that the negotiation is rarely explicit and may be conducted in an indirect way. For instance, one group may wish to damage the established identity of another. Let us say for the sake of argument that they are two political groups. The tactic used by the attacker may be to consult a member of a third group (for example, the press) and suggest a certain member of the other group has a questionable financial deal in the offing. The press publish details of this supposedly illicit deal; the name of the attacker is suppressed. The interesting feature of this sort of attack is that the group is attacked through one of its members. The identity of the group is challenged through association. Moreover, the attackers remain hidden. The negotiation of identity in this situation is very complex. It is certainly not an explicit affair and the introduction of intermediaries intensifies the convolutions necessary in order to redress the effects of the attack.

(ii) *The psychological origins of group identity*

Within the overall process of negotiating a social niche for the group, the way in which members conceptualize the group is important. This is largely because the group may have one identity in the eyes of the world and a somewhat different identity in the eyes of the membership. This discrepancy typically arises in two sorts of ways.

Firstly, it occurs when society at large delineates a number of people who possess some common characteristic (physical, psychological or social) and then labels them a group. Initially at least, those people may feel no affinity with the group, indeed for them it may not exist. They distinguish between being a group and being a category sharing some common characteristic. For instance, deeming all immigrants to be a single group might suit people of particular political persuasions but is hardly a grouping acknowledged by those ascribed to it. In such situations, those outside the so-called group may argue it has certain identity characteristics but those supposed to be in it effectively deny it has any identity at all. Under such circumstances, the 'group' is hardly likely to behave as a group. However, it should be added that these circumstances often lead to the creation of a group because the people involved cannot evade the ascriptions and attributions of the wider society. Postulation of the group may be a self-fulfilling prophecy: the people ascribed to it may become conscious of shared interests and begin to evolve a subjective group identity. It has been argued that it is only when the individuals concerned are consciously aware of a group identity that they can be called a group. Up until then, they are merely a social category (Tajfel, 1981).

Secondly, this discrepancy between internal and external definitions of a group's identity can become important when the content or value of identity is at issue. In this situation, the members of the group believe the group has an identity based on certain characteristics and that these have specific values. The outsiders either argue that the group does not possess those characteristics or that they should not carry that value; or sometimes both these assertions are made. Under these circumstances, the identity of the group is threatened at least at the subjective level. Simultaneously, it is very likely that the identities of the individuals in the group will be threatened if their positive social identity is based upon that group membership. The response of the group to threat may in fact be predicated upon the extent to which its individual members feel threatened. Revision of their subjective image of the group's identity is more likely to occur if it is not perceived as personally threatening. In a sense, the individual's identity needs will predicate the perceived identity of the group. They may have been the reason internal and external representations of the group's identity came to be discrepant in the first place. If the group had no social standing, and could not provide kudos on which a positive social identity could be built by individual members, there is every chance that those who could not vacate the group would engage in subjective revisions of their conceptualization and appraisal of the group. The subjective and objective definitions of the group's identity would thus become discrepant.

Thus the origin and substance of a group's identity lie at both the social and psychological levels. This becomes central to understanding the nature of threat to a group's identity.

5. THREATS TO GROUP IDENTITIES

This section is very brief since these issues are taken up extensively in later chapters. But something of the forms of threat and types of responses to them can be profitably outlined. Since the identity of a group originates simultaneously from two sources (the social niche it negotiates and how it is conceptualized by its members) it is hardly surprising that threats may emanate from both. However, the question of *what constitutes a threat* is far from simple to answer. In the case of individual identity it is possible to say that anything which challenges self-esteem is a threat. But in the case of group identity, a parallel formulation is not possible or at least it is tenuous. The problem arises from the fact that no single person is the sole determiner of weather a group's esteem, status, or whatever, has been changed. The group is made up of many people and their judgements about changes in the group's esteem need not be homogeneous. It is not always clear, therefore, when a group has lost esteem. Changes which one subgroup sees as a threat to esteem may be seen by another subgroup as bolsters to that esteem. Identifying what is a threat becomes rather difficult. Of course, in practice the difficulty can be resolved arbitrarily by adopting a dictum, such as 'if the majority in a group consider a change reduces the group's standing then that change is a threat to identity'. This sort of formulation does not overcome the real problem. As a rule of thumb it may work but it should be remembered that numerical superiority is not always equated with dominance in influence.

Any objective challenge to the power of the group can be regarded as a threat to identity, if only because a change in power will result in a changed capacity to control the social processes whereby identity is negotiated. Of course, this relationship can operate in reverse. A challenge to the content or appraisal of identity can result in objective changes in social power. The feedback loop between power and identity is inevitable.

The form that threats take can therefore be either material or symbolic or both. Material threats would involve changing the resources available to the group. The symbolic threats could involve changing the conceptualization of the group primarily through rhetoric, propaganda, etc. Breakwell's chapter in Part II examines the use of rhetoric both to attack and defend an identity.

In understanding *how a group responds to threat* one thing seems to be salient above all else: direct comparison with how an individual responds when threatened is misleading. Simply because the group is composed of many individuals its response will be qualitatively different. An individual who is threatened may need to change his or her identity but the physical organism will remain—unless suicide is the chosen response to threat. The group which is threatened is likely to dramatically change its physical structure. It will lose members and may even be eradicated because it loses all its members. Where the group remains to fight, the means it has available to it are very different from those accessible to the individual. The group can mobilize its membership and its resources to renegotiate its identity. It can evolve new polemics and rhetorics and because of the sheer impact of numbers has a greater chance of these being persuasive than an argument generated by the individual. In fact, the individual wishing to use such methods in renegotiating an identity normally has to join or create a group in order to make them viable.

Though the group which is threatened undoubtedly has more chance of maintaining its identity intact than the individual, since it has more wide ranging methods at its disposal; nevertheless, groups also sometimes fail in fending off the threat. If that happens, then the members who remain in the group will revise their group image and their personal social identities derived from membership. Resolution of the threat through revision at the group level may thus result in further threats at the individual level to the members of the group. In fact, *threats to the identity of a group and threats to the identity of its members are never independent.* The irony is that resolution of one threat may simply generate another at the other level. Not surprisingly, responses to threat to the group identity will take place simultaneously at the group and individual levels. Most of the contributions in Part II illustrate this point forcefully.

6. CONCLUSION

The chapters in the remainder of this book chronicle the weird dance of individual and group identities under threat. They put flesh on the skeleton that has been wired together here. They illustrate the issues and questions which have been formulated, and the research they report queries many of the received truths about the consequences of threat, whether to the individual identity or to the individual as group member or to the group identity.

REFERENCES

Allport, G. W. (1955). *Becoming: Basic Considerations for a Psychology of Personality*. New Haven, Yale University Press.

Argyle, M. (1976). Personality and social behaviour. In: R. Harré (ed.) *Personality*. Oxford, Blackwell.

Argyle, M., Furnhan, A. and Graham, J. (1981). *Social Situations*. Cambridge, Cambridge University Press.

Bavelas, J. B. (1978). *Personality: Current Theory and Research*. California, Brooks Cole.

Berger, P. L., *et al.* (1974). *The Homeless Mind*. Harmondworth, Penguin.

Berger, P. L. and Luckman, T. (1974). *The Social Construction of Reality*. Harmondsworth, Penguin.

Biddle, B. J. (1979). *Role Theory*. New York, Academic Press.

Breakwell, G. M. (1978). Groups for sale. *New Society*, **45** (823), 66–68.

Burns, R. B. (1979). *The Self Concept*. New York, Longman.

Cattell, R. B., and Dreger, R. M. (1977). *Handbook of Modern Personality Theory*. New York, Halsted Press.

Cohen, S., and Taylor, L. (1972). *Psychological Survival*. Harmondsworth, Penguin.

Cooley, C. H. (1902). *Human Nature and the Social Order*. New York, Scribner's.

Fransella, F. (1981). *Personality*. London, Methuen.

Gergen, K. (1971). *The Self Concept*. New York, Holt, Rinehart & Winston.

Gergen, K. (1977). The social construction of self-knowledge. In: T. Mischel (ed.) *The Self*. Oxford, Blackwell.

Goffman, E. (1959). *The Presentation of Self in Everyday Life*. New York, Doubleday Anchor.

Goffman, E. (1967). *Interaction Ritual*. Chicago, Aldine Press.

Hall, C. S., & Lindzey, G. (1978). *Theories of Personality*. New York, Wiley.

Harré, R. (Ed.) (1976). *Personality*. Oxford, Blackwell.

Harré, R. (1979). *Social Being*. Oxford, Blackwell.

Holland, R. (1977). *Self and Social Context*. London, MacMillan.

Hollis, M. (1977). *Models of Man*. Cambridge, Cambridge University Press.

James, W. (1890). *Principles of Psychology*. New York, Holt.

Mead, G. H. (1934). *On Social Psychology*. Chicago, Chicago University Press.

McCall, G. J. (1977). The social looking-glass: a sociological perspective on self-development. In: T. Mischel (ed.) *The Self*. Oxford, Blackwell.

McCall, G. J., and Simmons, J. L. (1966). *Identities and Interactions*. New York, Free Press.

Mischel, T. (ed.) (1977). *The Self*. Oxford, Blackwell.

Mischel, W. (1968). *Personality and Assessment*. New York, Wiley.

Stryker, S. (1964). The interactional and situational approaches. In: H. T. Christensen (ed.) *Handbook of Marriage and the Family*. Chicago, Rand McNally.

Tajfel, H. (1981). *Human Groups and Social Categories*. Cambridge, Cambridge University Press.

Turner, R. H. (1970). *Family Interaction*. New York, Wiley.

Turner, R. H. (1976). The real self: from institution to impulse. *American Journal of Sociology*, **81**, 989–1016.

PART TWO

Reformulations and Researches

Section A: Threats to individual identity

Threatened Identities
Edited by G. Breakwell

Identity Projects

Rom Harré

1. CONCEPTS OF IDENTITY

The basic distinction that will be deployed in this chapter is that between the fact of personal identity—what it is that makes a human being this or that particular person—and the sense of personal identity—how people experience their unique selfhood. Clearly there is no necessary coordination between these aspects of personal identity. The former could be well established in a species: for example, members might have no difficulty in recognising each other as different and distinct and treating each other differentially without any member of that species having a sense of their own personal identity. One might imagine this to be the case among chimpanzees. We know that they treat each other as individuals, but we are by no means so sure each chimpanzee experiences their lives as developing autobiographies.

What is required for someone to have a sense of personal identity?

(i) Clearly, one necessary condition is that the individual should be self-conscious, that is be aware of their experiences as constituting a personal unity. A miner, hewing at the coalface, can attend not only to the things which he is doing, the plans which he is entertaining, but see them as his, by virtue of his capacity to identify himself as a unique person among others. In the sections below, I shall be bringing out what is involved in experiencing one's personal life as a unity.

(ii) If experiencing matters as one's own were only an ephemeral or momentary phenomenon, then this would not yield the full sense of personal uniqueness. There has also to be some kind of experiential continuity. In some way or other an individual woman, for example, must treat most of her actions as developments of and connected with her past personal experience and as attributes of one being herself. In short a person's present actions must be located in an autobiography.

In order to keep these complex matters under control it will be necessary to introduce some basic philosophical distinctions among the kinds of identity with which we might be concerned. These reflect two major senses of sameness. These senses of identity are well established in traditional philosophy.

(i) In one sense of 'same', two individuals are the same when they have closely similar properties, that is are qualitatively identical. They remain, however, numerically different and distinct, and there are two of them.
(ii) But sometimes by sameness we mean numerical identity. 'This is the same person' implies that there is only one individual even though some of its properties at different times are different. The notion of numerical identity raises some interesting philosophical problems about what attributes or properties of an individual must remain the same for it to count as one and only one individual of a given kind. Clearly, some kinds of change, for instance changes in fatness, can be tolerated within a continuous numerical personal identity, whereas others such as extreme changes in personality may incline us to talk of one individual or person changing into another. Some of the more difficult conceptual problems in the area of personal identity arise at just exactly this point.

A simple way of setting up the distinction between qualitative and numerical identity can be worked out by relating it to spatio-temporal considerations. If individuals exist at the same time and have all their properties in common except their spatial location, then they are numerically distinct. Sometimes an observer notices, at different times, apparently very similar individuals, at the same place. Provided the differences between the apparently distinct individuals do not breach the criteria for identifying an individual of that kind and temporal continuity can be assumed, then we can say that there is one and only one individual persisting in that place. Consider a third possible case, in which there are apparently two individuals, some of whose properties are the same and some different, and the properties that are the same are appropriate for the identity of an individual of that category. But we find these seemingly distinctive individuals at different places at different times. Only if a spatio-temporally continuous path from one place at one time to the other place at the other time can be assumed, are we justified in claiming that we have truly one and only one distinct individual. So by reference to the spatio-temporal system and the grid it lays over the world, we are able to set up criteria which can be used to make coherent judgements of identity.

In the human case, considerations of spatio-temporal location and continuous translation point to the body as the source of the fact of identity. But the sense of identity seems to involve subjective and psychological matters like memory, consciousness and so on. However, bodily identity and continuity plays a role in both the fact and the sense of identity; and the following considerations make this clear.

The distinctiveness of one's body serves as the basis of the identification of one's self by others. One can be reidentified from time to time and in different places through one's distinctive physical qualities and a corporeal body is surely spatio-temporally continuous. Once an individual has been identified, say from an old sepia regimental photograph, as having been present at a particular time and place, say Allahabad (1927), then further questions of identity are usually settled by reference to spatio-temporal continuity from that place and moment to the place and moment at which the allegedly identical individual appears to us now, for example, in the dock at the Old Bailey.

But it seems clear that the basis of one's personal sense of identity has also to be, at least in part, referred to bodily considerations. Several philosophers have recently argued for the importance of two associated continuities in human experience (Strawson, 1959; Hampshire, 1959). There is the continuity of one's location in space and time relative to one's point of view. One sees the world from a particular place, relative to which particular aspects and perspectives are disclosed to the perceiver. A moment's reflection on one's autobiography suggests that this way of triangulating one's existence forms a large part of one's sense of a permanent self. Spatio-temporal location is also required to understand where and when one can act. For normal human beings, one's point of action in the spatio-temporal system, defined by one's relations with other material bodies, is closely related to one's point of view. Even with the help of causal processes by means of which one can bring about changes at other places and times from those at which one initiated an action, one is nevertheless required to find the sensitive triggers that initiate causal processes near where one is standing oneself. These general considerations will allow us to proceed to more detail in considering the two aspects of personal identity we have identified, the fact of identity and the sense of identity.

2. THE FACT OF IDENTITY

The problems that are raised by the fact of human identity turn on the way in which the two main kinds of criteria which seem to be at work in deciding whether an individual with whom we are presented is or is not the same person, are related to one another. Consider the case of the Tichbourne claimant, the man who turned up from Australia to establish his right to a disputed estate. Which criterion has priority in deciding whether he is the same person who left England many years before? There is his bodily continuity and the criteria for deciding that; and there is his continuity of 'psyche' with the public and private displays of what one might reasonably call mental aspects of his being, for example, his personality, avowed knowledge, demonstrated skill; and his public claims to a private sense of identity, his claims to remember his alleged past life. The major problem of the balance between bodily and mental criteria arises through the difficulty of deciding, in particular cases, which should have priority (Williams, 1973).

By inventing hard cases, philosophers have tested the force of these criteria to try to disentangle their relationships since they are not always clearly distinguished in practice. The first question to be addressed is whether bodily continuity is a necessary condition for personal identity. That is, if one were able to establish similarity of personality and good agreement as to what an individual purported to remember, would this require us to say that two apparently bodily distinct individuals were really (and perhaps necessarily) one and the same person? By considering fantastic examples philosophers are able to put pressure on these distinctions to see under what conditions they break down. These examples serve as tests to disclose unconsidered aspects of the use of taken for granted distinctions in ordinary unproblematic contexts. Two kinds of examples are usually offered.

Case One. The case of the Emperor and the Peasant exemplifies a typical philosopher's test example. The two people have distinctive bodies—on the one hand plump, well-nourished, and on the other, gnarled and worn by toil. Each has distinctive memories, and radically different personalities. They fall asleep in some contrived situation. When they awake, the man who remembers himself to be a peasant soon discovers he is experiencing the world from the bodily envelope of the emperor and vice versa. Now these individuals are clearly located differently in space at the same time. What are we to say about them? Are they or are they not radically changed? Is the emperor, in the peasant's body and vice versa, or has the emperor had a radical change of personality and beliefs about himself? Suppose the personalities of these two individuals remained associated with their bodies as before, i.e. the emperor's body behaved imperiously and spoke with an authoritative tone of voice, and the peasant's body showed in his cracked tones a suitable deference to authority. However, we are to assume that their memories of their previous lives are radically different. The emperor, the imperious person, remembers being a peasant, and the bucolic individual remembers being an emperor. We now might be inclined to say, not that they had exchanged bodies, but that the peasant now remembers the emperor's past life, and the emperor remembers that of the peasant. We could express this by saying 'He, the peasant by bodily criteria, thinks he is the emperor.'

Case Two. There are people who claim to be the reincarnations of famous historical persons. We have to ask in a spirit of muted scepticism just what is involved in such a claim, and just how strong are our criteria in these cases. We might suppose that all continuous spatio-temporal links have been broken or are unknown and that we are required to adjudicate on whether two individuals whose existence is widely separated in space and time, are the same, that is numerically identical. Here, our grounds can only be personal memory avowals. We might examine the case for numerical identity presented by a Mr. John Smith who exhibits the Napoleonic personality and can tell us in a way that satisfies even the most knowledgeable historian of his memories of the campaigns of the great emperor. Philosophical argument has been brought to demonstrate that these mentalistic criteria, without a bodily proof of continuity, are not enough. The argument runs as follows: if Mr. John Smith could satisfy these requirements there is, it seems, nothing logically impossible about Mr. Bill Brown satisfying them as well. Now what do we have—two Napoleons? Or would we be more inclined to say 'Two individuals purporting to be Napoleon'? It seems clear that there is nothing in our conceptual system which obliges us to say the former.

The upshot of all this is a clear indication that bodily continuity plays a primary role when the cases become difficult. But is it a sufficient condition for personal identity?

To examine the possibility that numerical identity of the body is a sufficient condition for the personal identity of a human being, we shall again examine some hard cases on the borders of real possibility. The case of Miss Beauchamp provides us with a real example (Prince, 1905). She exhibited radically distinct patterns of behaviour with seemingly very different personalities, abrasive and argumentative, soft and agreeable, and so on. To make the matter more interesting, there was good evidence that she was not able to remember the activities and thoughts she had had when she was behaving in some but not all of these distinctive ways. One might begin to feel that both the personality and the memory criteria point towards different persons even though there could be no doubt about the numerical identity of Miss Beauchamp's body. The question for the philosopher to examine, prior to any therapeutic work by psychologists, is to ask whether under these circumstances we would be conceptually obliged to treat Miss Beauchamp as a collection of different persons. Should the differences in behaviour, memory, and so on, be used to individuate several personalities of the one person, or *be allocated to* several persons, conceived as distinctive beings? In the former case, we would have an extension of our ordinary working conception. We could say that the same person has very distinctive personalities, and we would save bodily identity as a sufficient condition for unity of personhood. We could say, though Miss Beauchamp is the same person, her range of personalities is more fully differentiated than those of ordinary 'folk'. One reason for adopting this alternative is the well established fact that even ordinary folk have very distinctive ways of presenting themselves to different people under different circumstances and, indeed, there is some evidence (Helling, 1977) that memory is distributed differentially with respect to each particular personality presentation, though not in the radically discontinuous way that it was with Miss Beauchamp.

It now seems we are in a position to summarize the criteria by means of which we decide questions of identity for other people. The hard cases demonstrate that the conceptual system with which we operate does give priority to continuity of bodily identity and the criteria of physical appearance based upon it. Though we are prepared to distinguish very different kinds of behaviour, and even different clusters of memories as kinds of unities, nevertheless the comfortable thing seems to be to assign these to entities (such as personalities, roles, etc) which are subordinate to or dependent upon persons rather than competitors with them. So, each individual could be thought to have a more or less radically distinguished set of personalities which would be presented differentially for different occasions.

3. THE SENSE OF IDENTITY

To explore the sense we have of our own identity in any disciplined fashion, one must avoid vague discussions of what it feels like to be 'myself'. We can begin to follow an alternative route by exploring the idea of a criterion of personal identity—a criterion I might be imagined to employ to decide about myself. What can be made of the questions 'Who am I?' and statements like 'I'm not myself today'? Does the former represent a genuine puzzle and is the latter the expression of a discovery about personal identity? To answer this, one must ask what conditions have to be met for there to be a criterion for an entity to be judged to be this or that kind of thing (Shoemaker, 1963). Clearly, one important condition must be that we admit the possibility of the criterion not being met and candidates being rejected. In attempting to answer the question 'Who am I?', could I make the discovery that I am not, after all, myself? Could I, for example, find out I was someone else? It is intuitively obvious, I think, that these considerations are nonsensical. They are nonsensical because, to query one's own personal, as contrasted with one's social identity, undermines one of the very presuppositions that are required for first-person utterances to make sense, namely that they are the utterances of an individual. When I ask 'Who am I?', the most I could mean would be 'Which of various possible social identities, publicly identified, is legitimately or properly mine?'.

Amnesia is not a loss of the sense of identity, but rather involves the inaccessibility of various items of knowledge about my public and social being, my past history. Similarly, the question implied in the statement 'I am not myself today' can only mean that I do not feel the same as I did yesterday, which presupposes a conserved sense of identity. Since, then, I cannot doubt that I am the author, as it were, of my own speech, the very idea of a criterion for my sense of my own identity, is empty.

Philosophers have made this point in various ways. Butler (1900) for example, argues that memory cannot be the basis of a sense of identity since the very notion of memory presupposes that identity. For instance, it is empty to ask whether these memories I am remembering are mine or whether they are perhaps recollections of someone else's experience. Whichever they are, they must be my experiences since I am experiencing them. At best, I can be amazed that my imaginings are like your rememberings, so alike as to be qualitatively identical with your recollections in so far as we can make comparisons. But even in that case, my discovery that you and I have identical recollections of a great many events, is no ground whatever for the hypothesis that I am you.

What, then, are the origins of this strong sense of identity? Ideally, one would wish to show that though the sense of identity is conceptually and logically distinct from the fact of personal identity, nevertheless the former, in the course of human development, derives from the latter. In the absence of adequate empirical studies of this matter the most one can do is to point out the relevant features of the notion of identity, brought out by philosophical analysis, features that could serve as the basis of hypotheses to be explored by developmental psychologists.

The arguments of philosophers such as Hampshire (1959) concerning the role of bodily identity in personhood lead, as I have pointed out, to the idea that a person experiences the world from a particular here and now—that is, has a point of view—which is coordinated in the spatio-temporal system with their point of action. This doctrine derives from the necessary conditions for the referential uses of words. If I am to be able to refer to something, point to it, in the world, I must know from where I am pointing as well as to what. That is, I must anchor my frame of reference to the here and now. Ordinarily, this is done through the indexical presuppositions of the uses of the word 'I', presuppositions which embody the very idea that I am here and speaking now. One might wish to argue that having acquired a language and in so doing grasped the indexicality of one's use of referential expressions, a human being is in possession of the concept of numerical identity in space and time, since experience soon provides that person with the idea of a trajectory through a spatio-temporal system which is the locus of their coordinated points of view and points of action.

But in order for this happy coincidence to have been achieved, the actor must be in possession of the system of personal pronouns and know how to use them. The indexicality of 'I' depends, it might be argued, upon the grasp of the simple referential function of 'you'. Since 'myself' is not a thing I could discover it seems I cannot first experience myself and then attach the personal pronoun 'I' to that experience. I must be learning the pronoun system as a whole through the ways in which and the means by which I am treated as a person by others. So that by being treated as 'you', or as a member of 'we', I am now in a position to add 'I' to my vocabulary, to show where, in the array of persons, speaking, thinking, feeling, promising and so on, is happening. In order to be addressed as 'you', I must be being perceived as a definite embodied person, that is as a distinct human but material individual by others. This unity of pronoun system might be one of the things that is meant by the social construction of the self. But it depends upon the recognizable bodily identity that I have even as an infant.

I am also treated by other people as having a distinct point of view and being the locus of exercises of agency. So that these very conditions of bodily identity, identified by Hampshire and others as necessary conditions for having the idea of myself, as a person, are also, it seems, to be taken as presumptions that are embedded in all kinds of social practices. For example, the idea that a person has a distinct point of action is embedded in such practices as moral praise and blame. That kind of talk makes sense only upon the presupposition that one has a point of action through which one's intentions and so on can be realized.

So the acquisition of the idea of personal identity for oneself through which one develops a sense of identity is, at least in part, a consequence of social practices which derive from the fact of identity as it is conceived in a culture. Our first preliminary conclusion, then, must be that a human being learns that he or she is a person from others, and in discovering a sphere of action the source of which is treated by others as the very person they identify as having spatio-temporal identity. Thus, a human being learns that he or she is a person not by the empirical disclosure of an experiential fact. Personal identity is symbolic of social practices not of empirical experiences. It has the status of a theory.

However, there is a great deal more to the sense of personal identity than the realization that one has a point of view and can act upon the world at certain places. We must now turn to what I shall call transcendental conditions. These require certain features of personhood as necessary conditions for the possibility of certain kinds of human activities. In the first section, we have been looking at the origins of the sense of identity in social practices, in contrast to individual experiences. In this section, we shall look at the origins of other features of the notion of selfhood and personal identity in private and personal matters rather than in public and social interactions. Philosophers have insisted, and rightly, since the days of David Hume, that in an important sense the self is not experienced. As Hume (1739) pointed out, 'I never can catch *myself* at any time without a perception, and never can observe anything but the perception' (Book I, Part IV, Section IV).

The first step towards identifying transcendental features of self-hood involved in the sense of identity, is to notice that the considerations advanced above and the analysis based upon them, depend upon the assumption of the existence of two kinds of unities.

There is a unity of the realm of consciousness in that, for instance, the experiences I have as a being, spatio-temporally and socially located, and acting where I am, are coordinated in one realm of experience. Consciousness is not divided, and hence does not have to be combined. But this is not to say that that of which I am conscious is not ordered. Clearly, there is an indefinite potential hierarchy of awarenesses which is given by the possibility of reflexive consciousness. Thus, I can become aware of an orange, pay attention to it, and perhaps, if suitably prompted, be aware to my attending it, and so on. One of the commonplace techniques of dealing with pain is to attend, not so much to the pain, but to the relation in which I, as experiencer, stand to that pain.

This leads to a second kind of unity. The hierarchy of experience is parallelled for human beings by a hierarchy of action. I can act upon the things in the world, for instance tennis balls, and I can act upon my actions upon the things in the world, for instance I can improve my forehand stroke. It would not be unreasonable to say that the hierarchies of awareness and of action involve a regress of the very same self; that the centre of consciousness and the source of action are one self. I act according to a rule; I adopt the rule according to some principle; I accept a principle according to some theory, and so on. It would not be unreasonable to argue that it is the very same 'I' who is aware of the peeling of an orange, who is aware of the awareness of peeling an orange, and so on.

It is now clear, I hope, from whence comes the need for a transcendental hypothesis. These coordinated unified hierarchies are unified via the self which is presupposed in them. Each time that an individual is able to make a start up the hierarchy of action and hopes, naively, to experience the self which makes that step, and which is, as it were, the origin of the sphere of experience, that self must remove itself from the realm of experience. The sense I have of myself, then, must include the very complex idea of something not experienced but presupposed as a necessary condition for the form that experience takes; in particular, its unified and hierarchical form. The fine structure of this kind of hierarchy has been perceptively explored by Langford (1978). From the point of view of the philosophy of science, 'the self' is a theoretical concept, and the sense of self derives from the way we experience our experiences as unified, but is not reducible to it.

4. THE ORIGINS OF SOCIAL IDENTITY

Having developed in detail the general theory of personal identity, I turn now to some particular applications of the conceptual system I have developed. The first point to notice is the parallel between the philosophical distinction of numerical from qualitative identity, and the social psychological distinction between personal and social identity. Personal identity corresponds to numerical identity and social identity is a form of qualitative identity.

One's social identity is, roughly speaking, the set of social categories to which one belongs. This notion defines only qualitative identity because there is nothing in principle that prevents another human being occupying a similar locus in the social order as one occupies oneself. The constituents of social identity can be analytically reduced. For my purpose, I wish to concentrate on only two possible constituents, namely role—that is the typical actions, self-representations and so on, required of persons occupying a particular nexus in the social order, and secondly, a more generic constituent, which I shall call, for want of a better term, human category. The distinction between child and adult, male and female, black and white, and so on I shall call one of category, while that between bank manager and priest I shall call 'role'. It is obvious that role is a culturally relative notion. Those social identities in which role plays a conspicuous part are clearly culturally and historically conditioned. One might be tempted, however, to conclude that the apparent ubiquity of the distinctions between child and adult, male and female, old and young, provide us with a universal system of social identity which we would expect to find exemplified in any form of human association. But to suppose that would be to betray the limitations of one's historical and anthropological reading. For instance, even so apparently obvious a pair of social identities as that of child and adult has been demonstrated by recent historical research to be relatively modern. In the seventeenth century, for instance, from the point of view of social identity, the distinction was not made, so that children were treated as if they differed from adults, only in degree. From the point of view of social identity they were brought under the same categories. They were judged on the same moral principles, they had the same legal responsibilities, could inherit titles, and even in some cases contract marriages. The cultural relativity of social identity makes a certain kind of identity project possible.

If social identities are culture relative, then they must be malleable. We can unlearn what we once learned and set about learning something else. I shall return to this point.

Personal identity, too, is a psychologically and sociologically complex notion. I shall distinguish between those constituents of an individual's personal identity which are essentially social, and those which are essentially individual or personal. The social constituents of personal identity include the physical features which differentiate one human being from all others. These features enable other people to recognize someone at a glance. But the individuation of people goes further, in that they are conceived of not only as physically distinct but also as distinct in character. Indeed, some people may have such striking personalities that they may come to acquire the soubriquet, a character. All this has to do with the activity Goffman (1969) has called 'impression management', that is the way we display our personal attributes for other human beings in the hope of their forming such an opinion of our character as we wish to project. So necessarily, that aspect of personal identity which we call 'character' is socially based since it exists in the impressions others have formed of us. Closely related to this is the reciprocal activity where the social group within which we have our being treats us in distinctive ways for particular social purposes creating a character for us. For instance, in the study of nicknames (Morgan, O'Neil and Harré, 1979) we have been able to demonstrate that individuals are singled out, and indeed acquire a measure of personal identity in a social group, by virtue of possessing in some marked way a stigmatized attribute such as, for example, excessive height or extreme short-sightedness. Naming practices that identify individuals by virtue of the social stigmatization of certain of their personal attributes ('Lofty', 'Stinker', etc.) not only draw attention to existing flaws but often serve to encourage their more florid manifestation.

But personal identity must have individual constituents. The general argument of Parts 1 and 2, demonstrated that the sense of personal identity depends upon a socially enforced theory of self by which a human being conceives a continuous coordination of point of view and point of action within the general spatio-temporal system of material beings including other people. A person is at the 'focus' of only one field of consciousness. Similarly, the association of exercises of agency with a point of action introduces a second transcendental unity, namely that of self as agent. I have argued that this is universally but contingently associated with the hierarchy of consciousness in normal persons. These constituents, as the paired hypothetical entities of a theoretical scheme, organize our experiences in such a way as to provide us with a moment-by-moment sense of identity. In order for that sense to unify our experiences in time, there must be an autobiographical system of beliefs to which one refers in identifying the present moment of one's life as part of a life trajectory. The indexicality of self-references is both to here and to now, so creating a sense of temporal location from which one refers in planning the future, recollecting the past, and so on. Both agency and unity of consciousness are transcendental conditions. They are theoretical concepts by which we organize our acting upon things in the world and upon ourselves, as well as how we are aware of the world and of ourselves. As inexperienceable, theoretical entities they are merely formal attributes of personal identity. In consequence, I conclude that the autobiographical belief system of a person constitutes the central core of the psychologically researchable features of personal identity. I would go so far as to argue that a good many of our projects are decided upon with respect to the contributions they are likely to make to our beliefs about ourselves—that is to our autobiographies—and if all goes well, to the biographical sketches other people are building up about us.

Finally, one should notice that for most people most of the time, both bases of identity are given and relatively stable. For instance, every sane person has an individual sense of personal identity. One knows who one is, that is has a well-ordered if incomplete understanding of the social and individual constituents of the sense of identity that I have described above. Pathological conditions may, of course, involve the loss or weakening of some of these constituents. Amnesia may abrogate autobiography. Akrasia may paralyse agency. Social incompetence may prevent the formation of a desirable character in the eyes of others, and so on and so on. In relatively stable social conditions most people have their social identity fixed for them. They know who they are socially.

A person *knows* that he is a bank manager, that she is a Prime Minister, that is knows their identity as role-holders. Most people are fairly clear as to their human category. Most people know whether they are children or adults, men or women, which is *not* the same as knowing whether one is male or female (Morris, 1974). Once again, we can identify the boundaries of such social identity in pathological cases. There are those who experience role conflict trying to fulfil contradictory social demands. There are those in the adolescent years, when they are neither child nor adult, who suffer identity crises. As we have become increasingly aware in recent times, there are those who are, in some way or other, uncertain about their location with respect to the boundaries of gender, ethnicity, and so on. In Florida, any day of the week, one can observe with astonishment very large numbers of people who have forgotten that they are actually old.

Now all of this suggests that social identity is constructed. As I remarked before, anything which is constructed by processes which are normally unattended can become the object of conscious human enterprise. Identities can be made. This leads to the idea of there being identity projects. My attention was first drawn to the possibility of thinking of certain social activities as the attempt to realize identity projects by J.-P. de Waele, whose development of the technique of assisted autobiography has been an important development in the empirical study of identity (De Waele and Harré, 1976).

Under what conditions is an identity project called for? I propose to simplify the possibilities by concentrating upon two obvious cases, though of course there may be others. Given that we have distinguished personal and social identity, and assuming that a human being may have a sense of both, it is clear that there are two major ways in which a human being's identities can come unstuck, so to speak.

(a) The personal sense of identity may not be matched by adequate social constituents of personal identity. So, for example, the view that one may have of oneself, for example the conception one may have of one's life-course, may not be matched by the beliefs others have about one's history. Consequently, one's projects may not be matched by what other people take to be one's prospects. In these circumstances an individual can undertake an expressive project to remedy this. For example, he may set about the management of a moral career (Goffman, 1968a).

(b) On the other hand, in conditions of social disorder, one's normally unattended social identity may be felt to be in question. For example, one may feel that one's social identity is weak, or perhaps a public acknowledgement of one's existing social identity may be dangerous. This will be particularly so for an individual who is, so to speak, on an identity boundary. Again, I think in principle at least, one can see how an individual might make a deliberate effort to display the distinguishing marks of an approved social identity. When these marks are mainly symbolic one could call this undertaking an 'expressive' project. I think these kinds of cases are actually rather rare. But when they do occur, the tension between social and individual constituents of identity provides just the conditions for the way of thinking that Tajfel (1978) has called 'social comparison'. This is a piece of cognitive machinery which Tajfel and his co-workers have investigated in relatively unstructured social conditions. They have demonstrated that most people are competent in making social comparisons; that is, in comparing their own conceived social identity with what they perceive to be that of others. It should be noticed that this is an essentially individualistic theory of social identity since it is individuals who make social comparisons, though a group may each make them similarly.

The important social-psychological question, if we restrict our conception of psychology to these relatively sophisticated individual processes, is 'When does a person use this way of thinking, and for what purpose and what project?'. I do not wish to dispute that that cognitive machinery may sometimes be used for social identity projects. Indeed, I think I can delineate the general conditions under which that occurs. However, I believe it is a matter of fact that personal identity projects will tend to be dominant for most people most of the time. For most people, social identities are provided and need not be constructed. The difficulty for most shop stewards, the difficulty for most rugby forwards, the difficulty for most women wrestlers, the difficulty for most violinists, and so on, is to stand out as an individual, while maintaining their claim to be a member of the social category or to retain the right to a role performance, which gives them social being at all. *A fortiori* cognitive processes of social comparisons can play no role at all in the living out of personal identity projects.

The relation between individual cognitive processes and public displays of the marks of identity is more complicated than the above discussion suggests. If one divides the world of a human being roughly into two regions—the public and the private domain—then this suggests the possibility of social certainty and competence being displayed in public identity demonstrations that is actually coupled with considerably private social unease. There is plenty of clinical evidence to suggest that this condition is not rare. On the other hand, we are familiar, I believe, with a style of display in which public diffidence and lack of confidence is coupled with private certainty and perhaps even arrogance. A beautiful instance is reported by Jacques Soustelle (1962) on the social life of the Aztecs, where this combination was highly favoured. And there are, of course, the simpler cases of those who appear confident in public and are confident in their thoughts and private moments too, and there are those whose public uncertainty is just a reflection of their private doubts. The next step will be to look a little more closely at how an identity project can actually be undertaken.

So much for identity troubles and predicaments. The positive site of this—the formulation and achievement of identity projects—will occupy us below.

5. IDENTITY PROJECTS

The considerations so far advanced suggest that there may be disparities between private beliefs and public representations and, more poignant still—publicly displayed beliefs about oneself and private aspirations. These disparities suggest the possibility of projects in the realization of which such disparities might be remedied and resolved. I have emphasized the fundamental psychological distinction rooted in a deep philosophical dichotomy between personal identity and social identity, between the individuality one has as a numerically identifiable being and the attributes one shares with the others that make up some relevant reference class.

What, then, might be the rough outline of a theory of social identity projects? The first step would be to identify people in a predicament which would define the range of possibility for efforts of various kinds to modify one's identity displays and so the perception of one's social identity by others. The sociological category of 'the marginal' seems exactly suited to this. I take it that marginal people are those who do not share, but might aspire to share, a certain social identity. Typically, amongst such people would be immigrants, those who are moving from one kind of social world to another—for example, the socially mobile—children on the way to adulthood and so on. It is clear that these people are in the position to experience the kind of disparity in terms of which I defined identity projects above. They are able to realize what it would be like to have the attributes of the group to which they are nearest and at the same time to have it borne in upon them in various ways that they do not possess them.*

It is clear, then, in what a social identity project might consist. It would involve efforts to acquire the attributes of an existing social identity, and I shall look into what these efforts might be in a moment. One necessary condition must be noticed. In order for there to be the possibility of an identity project of this sort, one has to know what the attributes of the desired social identity might be and furthermore, one has to be right about them. The social world is full of people who are, or have been, aspiring to social identities which do not exist, either because they have never been or because they have recently ceased to be. Presuming, then, that a person realizes what social attributes he or she must acquire, the next step is to convince others that one has these attributes and that one has them as of right, whatever that right might be. For example, it may be necessary to perform in such a way that others take one's social attributes to have been inherited, and so on. Again the Tajfel notion of social comparison might properly identify a cognitive condition necessary for the accomplishment of such a project; though such a process, presuming individualistic comparisons between persons cannot be relevant to projects involving fancied or extinct social identities.

Efforts of this sort can be separated into two different categories:

(i) There are actual role performances by which the attributes that one

* This is a very heavily researched area—albeit most of the work has been individualistic *and* statistical.

wishes to have ascribed to oneself are displayed in the appropriate circumstances and with the right degree of verisimilitude. These might consist of such attributes as correct speech, proper manners, impeccable dress, appropriate job, and so on and so on. Veblen (1899) has demonstrated that this feature of social identity projects is ubiquitous to western society and has provided a powerful dynamic for the strange gyrations of fashion. In his studies of hypercorrection Labov (1966) has examined the dynamics of identity presentation in speech.

(ii) But the Veblen-like process of social emulation (and the reasoning involved could fit Tajfel's 'social comparison' theory) which drives the persons in Western society occupying, as of right, identities to which others aspire, to more extravagant means of representing their differences, is only one aspect of an identity problem. As I pointed out above, it is necessary to establish that one has the attributes as of right. In general, rights in the social world are established by the existence of appropriate biographies, i.e. beliefs about a person's previous life held by others. So, part of an identity project involves a construction directly, or by implication, of an appropriate biography or autobiography.* Indeed, such projects involve quite radical changes in presentational features such as, for example, changing one's name, e.g. adding 'de' or 'von'. They must also require successful concealment of one's real biography (Goffman, 1968).

So far, I have pointed to the outlines of a theory of social identity projects in which an individual strives for social identities real or mythical. But the title of this work suggests that social identity projects might take another form. There might very well be cases where an individual's problem is to retain a given social identity against various destructive influences. So far as I can see by *a priori* reflection on the matter, the psychological structure of the reasoning involved in managing these projects which I have suggested in the previous paragraph, would be identical to that required for positive social identity projects. But, whereas in the former the actor can presume a shared knowledge of the matters of the identity aspired to, in the latter, an actor's problem would be to secure that others (who might conceivably doubt if there is or ought to be such an identity) came to accept that such an identity existed. One would also need to make sure that the moves appropriate to the public display of that identity were widely enough known for one to be able to be seen to have achieved it. It seems theoretically possible that the actual efforts which a real person might undertake would turn out

* Cf. the Australian cousin searching the parish registers for impeccable British antecedents. Here, if there is social comparison it is with a mythical social identity type.

to be the exact complement of the demands of the positive identity project. It may be that a person is seen by others to have certain attributes and is believed to have a certain biography. The problem for that person might be to create in others the impression that these attributes and this biography is not some idiosyncratic failure to achieve the attributes and biography of some worthy social identity, but is already the achievement of a mode of social being which has been forgotten, overlooked, not understood, etc., by the others. In short, it will be to make public the existence of a social identity corresponding to the personal attributes which are displayed and known.*

These remarks provide a theoretical background for studies such as Weinreich's. They are an attempt to lay out the various aspects of social identity projects, aspects which derive from a conceptual analysis of the notion and commonsense understanding of its application. Like any theory, they stand in need of empirical investigation, justification and test. Further reflection suggests that the way in which the cluster of hypotheses above ought to be tested, would be by some form of ethogenic method. A prior social analysis would be checked against the beliefs of the various folk involved, access to which would be obtained through an analysis of their accounts. Further elaboration of accounts could be obtained through the use of the methods of George Kelly (Bannister and Fransella, 1971). These methods would be appropriate for this part of identity investigations because what we are in search of is the systems of beliefs, knowledge, etc., which are the necessary conditions for the success of the reasoning required of an actor in the production of the action in which the realization of his or her project consists.

Ordinary action-theory of the type developed by Von Cranach (Von Cranach and Harré, 1982) and others should be an adequate basis for empirical studies of the reasoning involved. According to action-theory the activities by which people go about realizing their social knowledge and beliefs are conceived of as controlled by reasoning which can be represented by hierarchical means-end structures. An end or goal could be represented in an intention and the means of realizing it in a rule. The means-end structures, which make up the intentional aspects of an actor's psychology, could be very complex. It would be necessary to use account analysis to investigate the appropriate systems of beliefs and interpretations to provide the decodings necessary to understand the meanings of a particular public performance by the actor engaged in a project. Unexamined common sense could lead

* Peter Weinreich's (1982) study of Muslim Youths in British Schools; also Lyman (1970) on Japanese–Americans of the first post-immigrant generation (*nisei*).

one widely astray unless one already shared the criteria for the social identity in question.*

Personal identity projects, on the other hand, depend upon an individual being well established in a role position or in some more general social category. By well established, I mean that both the actor and the other persons who constitute his or her social environment are agreed on all hands that this person has the social identity manifested in public performance as of right. We would be dealing here with centrally located people such as certified office holders, arbiters of social propriety as in Labov's study of the powerful women who determine what is and what is not upwardly mobile speech in Philadelphia, well-defined role-holders such as bank managers, policemen, members of the picket line, males who believe they are men and so on. The identity problem for such centrally located people is the obverse of that for the marginal, namely, how are they going to be seen to be both worthy exemplars of the social identity they rightly claim *and* individual persons. There is a second kind of threat to identity which was perhaps not envisaged in the original formulation of that interesting notion by the organizers of this joint work. There are those who are so well integrated in the social order, whose public performances are such perfect manifestations of what is required of them, whose biographies are impeccable to the last degree, that their problem is to resist dissolution into no more than the cypher at the centre of the role. What is threatened in these cases is personal identity.

Again, there are two forms of action that are necessary to create personal identity in the midst of a tight-knit social order.

(i) The role performances, the demonstrations of impeccable claims, must somehow be put on in such a way that they are given what Martin Hollis (1977) preceptively called 'the stamp' of one's uniqueness. As one king succeeds another, how are we to notice the difference between them? A good beginning can be made with the help of physical peculiarities. Successive presidents look different from one another, have different names, but that is only the beginning. There must be some way, and it is very apparent in utterances of such persons, that a presidency is to be marked by a particular style of doing prescribed presidential actions. Just as when a new committee takes over the management of the local jumble sale, the new role-holders try to introduce some differences which mark this year as theirs.

* At most 'social comparison', if it occurs in the real world, could yield either the realization that one is stigmatized and/or knowledge of the public requirements of other social identities (and perhaps some of the private-collective as with those forms of social comparison that have been explored by Goffman (1966)).

Though this point has been made now for some considerable time, and I suppose goes back to remarks by Goffman (1969), very little empirical study, so far as I know, has been devoted to the way in which marks of personal identity are imposed upon standardized role performances. Partly, I suppose, this is because the interest of social psychologists in recent years has been focused on the positive ways in which social identities are generated, i.e. in what sort of role performances are required for the marginals to acquire relevant identities, rather than ways in which, given those role performances, they can be modulated in such a way that a distinct person emerges from them. Could this be because many social psychologists are themselves marginal people with dubious biographies?

(ii) And, of course, complementary to the activities of the holder in attempting to generate a personal identity, there is the interpretative procedure by which the others are able to see him as a distinct person. Such a person has to convince the others that he has the special attributes which his ways of performing lay claim to. And, of course, many of these attributes will be invisible, such as a claim to ancestral or genealogical worth, special kinds of private thoughts and feelings, etc. And, indeed, those claims are themselves double-edged, since a kind of claim may be initiated by someone who wishes to mark his social identity with a personal stamp and is so successful that shortly it generates a new social image. For instance, in the late Victorian era it was perhaps part of the way in which someone engendered a personal identity to display his ''umble' origins as a self-made man, a tycoon risen from the people. But notoriously, that claim very quickly became standardized, and indeed there are apocryphal cases of persons with impeccable middle-class antecedents faking up a working-class background in order to have the right social identity, e.g. some British Labour politicians.

Just as the more interesting cases of social identity projects have not been carefully studied, so I believe little has been done to look at the way in which personal identity projects may be realized. Again, an ethogenic approach seems appropriate since one must be dealing with the interplay between the personal and social distribution of knowledge and belief, accessible through accounts, and the actual performances in terms of which this knowledge is realized. The reasoning by which these performances are controlled should be accessible through the study of means-end hierarchies. Little has yet been done to investigate either aspect of personal identity projects.

One further point needs to be made. I have argued that the appropriate methodology should involve the analysis of accounts in terms of which performances are to be interpreted, using the interpretations of actors and inter-actors. So, in the above theoretical remarks, I have striven to emphasize that these projects, weather of social identity or of personal identity, necessarily require social display because they involve the achievement of social convictions. I have taken it for granted that the achievement of human beings engaged in these exercises are those who have a private sense of personal identity and that is not at issue. In short, this conceptual scheme and the suggested empirical projects which go with it, depend upon the assumption that the individuals with which we are concerned are sane. There are cases, of course, where the disparities between aspiration and achievement are so great that what becomes problematic is indeed the private sense of personal identity and this is a matter for the psychiatric psychologist to investigate.

A further and deeper conceptual issue is implicit in much writing on identity. It has to do with the nature of social groups. A person can be located in a group in two quite different ways. In what I shall call 'locating in a taxonomic group' a person is seen to exemplify a type, a type that defines the group. But taxonomic groups have no internal structure. They are usually purely logical objects. But people can be located in structured groups with a coherent internal order created by the maintenance of certain social relations. Defining a person's social identity by role, for instance, serves to locate someone in a structured group. But the members of a structured group need exemplify no common type. The German wartime occupation and government of Poland created a structured collective but the governors and the governed exemplified no common social type.

Structured groups and taxonomic groups involve quite different identity projects and consequently radically different modes of reasoning are required to carry them out. In a structural group, one would expect to find stable institutions, rituals of role assignment, and rites of passage by which identity transformations are brought about. Typically one would expect an aristocratic or traditional tribal society to be a structural group. In our society, groups of that sort are found in such places as goffmanesque Asylums (Goffman, 1968).

A taxonomic group is typical of middle-class 'models' of society. The free creation of a social identity as a personal project is possible. This is an individualistic social formation, and social comparison involves comparison with categorial others. Garfinkel's 'Agnes' represents the ultimate in personal reconstruction in a taxonomically grouped society. By publicly displaying the marks appropriate to and indicative of a social category, one acquires this identity. But dressing, talking, and even thinking like the younger son of a chief does not make one into one.

The application of expressions like 'group cognition', 'group identity', 'group power' (c.f. Breakwell this volume) is systematically ambiguous having a quite different sense in taxonomic and structural groups. In general, our middle-class bourgeois orientation leads us to read *all* these notions taxonomically, i.e. individualistically. But freeing ourselves from our moral ethnocentricity can open our eyes to the essential collectivity of our lives, since I believe that even in modern industrial societies structural groups predominate over taxonomic.

REFERENCES

Bannister, G., and Fransella, F. (1971). *A Manual for Repertory Grid Technique*. London, Academic Press.

Butler, J. (1900). Of personal identity. In: Bernard, J. H. (ed.) *The Works of Bishop Butler*, London, Volume II.

De Waele, J.-P., and Harré, R. (1976). The personality of individuals. In: Harré, R. (ed.) *Personality*. Blackwell, Oxford.

Goffman, E. (1968a). *Stigma*. Harmondsworth, Penguin Books.

Goffman, E. (1968b). *Asylums*. Harmondsworth, Penguin Books.

Goffman, E. (1969). *The Presentation of Self in Everyday Life*. Allen Lane, London, The Penguin Press.

Hampshire, S. (1965). *Thought and Action*. London, Chatto and Windus.

Helling, I. (1976). Autobiography as self-presentation. In: Harré, R. (ed.) *Life Sentences*. London, Wiley.

Hollis, M. (1977). *Models of Man*. Cambridge, Cambridge University Press.

Hume, D. (1739). *A Treatise of Human Nature*. Macnabb, D.G.C. (ed.) (1962) London, Fontana-Collins.

Labov, W. (1966). The effect of social mobility on linguistic behavior, *Social Inquiry*, **36**, 186–203.

Langford, G. (1978). 'Persons as necessarily social', *J. for the Theory of Social Behaviour*, **8**, 313–332.

Lyman, S. M. (1970). *The Asian in the West*. Western Studies Center, University of Nevada, Reno.

Morgan, J., O'Neill, C. and Harré, R. (1979). *Nicknames*. London, Routledge & Kegan-Paul.

Morris, J. (1974). *Conundrums*. London, Faber and Faber.

Prince, M. (1905). *The Dissociation of Personality*. London, Kegan-Paul, Truscott & Shrubner.

Shoemaker, S. (1963). *Self-knowledge and Self-identity*. New York, Cornell University Press, Ithaca.

Soustelle, J. (1962). *The Daily Life of the Aztecs*. (Trans. O'Brien, P.) New York, The Macmillan Company.

Strawson, P. F. (1959). *Individuals*. London, Methuen.

Tajfel, H. (1978). *Differentiation Between Social Groups*. London, Academic Press.

Veblen, T. (1899). *The Theory of the Leisure Class*. New York, The Macmillan Company.

Weinreich, P. (1982). Identity developments. *See* this volume.

Williams, B. A. O. (1973). *Problems of the Self*, Cambridge, Cambridge Univ. Press.

von Cranach, M. and Harré, R. (1982). *The Analysis of Action: Recent Theoretical and Empirical Advances*. Cambridge, Cambridge Univ. Press.

Threatened Identities
Edited by G. Breakwell

Breakdown of Personal Relationships and the Threat to Personal Identity

STEVE DUCK AND MARTIN LEA

We have set ourselves an apparently simple question (namely, 'why does it matter to people if their significant relationships break down?') and we will answer the question—which turns out to be quite complex—in terms of the threat to identity which is consequent upon such upset. Such a viewpoint retains theoretical parsimony, since it allows us to explain the development *and* decline of relationships in terms of satisfaction or dissatisfaction of the same aims and goal points. It also allows us to indicate the sorts of reasons why relationship breakdown has consequences that can reach as far as complete psychological breakdown or death. In adopting this stance we wish to reject clearly and unequivocally the implication of much research into interpersonal attraction; namely, that personal relationships are formed only from affective roots and that the disruption or breakdown of relationships is merely an affective disturbance. We take the view that relationships are forged from a complex interaction of affective, cognitive, social and ritual behavioural forces, the effects of which are only beginning to be fully understood. Likewise we reject the view of Altman and Taylor (1973) that the process of breaking a relationship is comparable to the reverse of its formation ('like a film shown in reverse' is their elegant but incorrect analogy). Furthermore, in adopting these views we shall attempt to use a distinct terminology, sadly lacking hitherto. We shall adopt the following terms from Duck (1981): *breakdown* of relationships will refer to the (perhaps unintentional) disruption or disturbance of the conduct of a relationship; *decline* of relationships will refer to the diminishing of intimacy or liking for a partner or for the nature or form of the relationship; *dissolution* will refer to the permanent dismemberment of the relationship through negotiation or through unilateral withdrawal.

Breakdown and dissolution of relationships have been given far less attention than they deserve and far less attention even than growth and development of personal relationships have received—and that's saying something. Simple assumptions and naive theoretical propositions have been all that there are to explore (see, e.g. Levinger, 1979). Only recently have several authors begun to turn their attention to this subject (e.g. Graziano and Mather-Musser, 1982; McCall, 1982; Miller and Parks, 1982) and naive beliefs about the reversibility of intimacy growth have been overthrown (Johnson, 1982). Also questioned have been shallow assumptions that relationship dissolution is simply an epiphenomenon or simply a decline in affective states (Duck, 1981; Graziano and Mather-Musser, 1982; La Gaipa, 1982).

Growing relationships grow in more than intimacy and declining ones decline likewise. Relationships do not merely grow from mutual attraction, they have to be made to work; and when the affection dies, so too the workings change. As a relationship grows, so it develops its own properties and as it dies so, too, it develops characteristics of its own which may upset or stifle its participants. Many features of developing relationships are not properties of individuals and do not have simple effects upon individuals: so, too, a breaking relationship alters itself as well as the people in it. For instance, researchers (in particular Hinde, 1979; 1981) have clarified the 'emergent properties' of relationships—properties which are essential to a relationship's future, but are not strictly speaking present in the partners individually. They are properties which influence the partner only when the two of them enter a relationship. We do not, however, here make the simplistic point made by Levinger (1974) that some things about a partner—deep things—take *time* to emerge; we follow Hinde's (1981) more insightful view that relationships create, demonstrate and are influenced by properties which emerge from the relationship of the two partners. Thus 'similarity' is not strictly a property of either partner individually but something which can emerge only as the two partners come together and which they may not both be fully aware of or attach equal significance to. Its importance lies in the perceptions that partners have about it, or the uses to which it is put by them. 'Intimacy' is another emergent property of a relationship, yet one which describes not only partners' behaviour but also the quality of a relationship. Intriguingly, workers in personal relationship research have never defined intimacy satisfactorily and have not attempted to map out intimacy growth in any except the vaguest statements about linear increases in affect—whatever that means. It seems probable that relationship decline therefore would be understood by such theorists simply in terms of decline in affect, then, although the important question in this context is the extent to which it is sensible to treat decline of relationships as the mere opposite of relationship development (Duck, 1981). A third emergent property of a relationship is its public identity and the way in which it is presented to, or managed in, the world. Thus clandestine affairs may be as intimate and as much based on similarity as a marriage—but clearly they are different in non-negligible ways, too.

Such points assume a greater significance than a mere critique of existing work on attraction once one begins to try and explain the psychological significance of relationship decline. To judge from the consequences, relationship dissolution is clearly not an epiphenomenon nor *simply* a decline in affective states. Increased anxiety and depression and their behavioural correlates are familiar enough consequences that suggest that relationships act as a vehicle for the fulfilment of some deep human need, so too does the incidence of suicide prompted by the breakdown of a significant personal relationship. Less well known, perhaps, are other severe disturbances to physical health that can arise from relationship breakdown, such as increased risk of coronary occlusion (Rahe, *et al.*, 1964) or certain infections (Lynch, 1977) or, to take one example from the more recent literature, that arise by an indirect causal path: a greater delay in approaching a health professional for diagnosis of cancer symptoms (Worden and Weisman, 1980). Research into such effects on physical health of relationship breakdown is only in its infancy, but we shall return to it later on in this chapter.

We must conclude from this, that such disruption has its effects because of the complexity of items that it influences, and we will spend the rest of this chapter identifying the effects of the central feature of this complexity: identity.

Readers can find elsewhere a discussion of some of the logical and topographical issues that are involved in mapping out the probable consequences of loss of particular sorts of relationships (Duck, 1980; 1981; 1982), but one can immediately see that destruction of *social* identity (e.g. through divorce) may be one of the threats posed by relationship collapse. In various ways that are interesting to psychologists, the establishment of a personal relationship with other persons can have essentially social consequences. Thus marriage may be based on love (i.e. is a personal relationship) but carries implications for social status and is a legal contract with social norms and expectancies as well as personal ones. In some important senses, certain types of relationships establish a social identity for individuals and their decline has social as well as personal implications. We will comment briefly on these later, since we take the view that the social identity implications follow from the personal ones rather than vice versa, and that the personal ones can be seen more generally across a wider range of relationships. However, we need to make clear here that we are not intending to consider more mundane or practical aspects of relationship breakdown, such as the loss of income, of shared possessions or of status that can be consequences of particular sorts of relationship dissolution (e.g. divorce or the ending of a cohabital arrangement). Many such consequences pose a threat to social identity and are often associated with a large stigma that further threatens the victim. However, we are primarily concerned with the 'psychological loss', the loss of psychological support, which is a direct consequence of relationship dissolution. In order to develop this concept we shall now explore the ways in which the formation of relationships may serve the function of establishing, maintaining and supporting persons' identity. Although we draw on Weiss's (1973) list of functions for relationships, we use the term 'support' more widely. Weiss distinguished five probable functions: (1) emotional integration; (2) social integration; (3) opportunity for nurturance; (4) reassurance of worth; (5) assistance. Other people, according to Weiss (1973), provide us with any or all of these five types of support. Whilst recognizing the value of such a distinction, we use the term 'support' to mean, over and above these five, the validation of a person's attitudes or personality. The sense in which we mean this will become apparent later. We now review the history of attraction research very sketchily in the special light of the criticisms above and of this latter general aim of the paper.

A. IDENTITY THROUGH RELATIONSHIPS

Far from finding ways in which relationships establish a person's identity, early research on interpersonal attraction explored the outward or apparent features of individuals that would render them generally attractive to most others. Thus, Perrin (1921) detailed the physical and behavioural features of people which made them generally likeable, whilst Thomas and Young (1938) explored the personal characteristics which were generally liked and disliked. It would be absurd and implausible to claim that all the research at a given time was 'all of a piece', but as a generalization, one can claim that little attention was given in such research to the question of *why* such things as physical attractiveness were liked and conceitedness disliked. Several possible reasons can be proposed: people with such characteristics may have been likeable or dislikeable in the judges' previous experience; people with such characteristics may be represented in the cultural norms as ideal or nonideal (circular argument!); people with such characteristics may be pleasant or unpleasant to interact with; people with such characteristics may be either accepting or threatening; or the characteristics themselves may be merely tips of an iceberg of other acceptable or unacceptable characteristics; or, very probably, a combination of these reasons act as the causal force, with the latter component being strongest. In the case of physical attractiveness, there is now a body of work (Berscheid and Walster, 1974) to suggest that observers do attribute positive *personality* characteristics to physically attractive others and that it is this set of attributions that is the mediating and significant influence on the ratings of liking or attraction. An important extension of such an argument is to propose that the personality characteristics of others are the truly important feature of them, as far as relationships are concerned, and that physical features merely represent short cuts to their comprehension—albeit unsafe and unreliable ones (Duck, 1973; 1977). In this view, features of other people are significant to the extent that they inform us, or can be used to inform us, about personality—a point with several implications for the present case.

As a development of early work, social psychologists soon turned to exploring the influence of personality and attitudinal characteristics on relationships, but for reasons other than those above. A literature was rapidly accumulated to support the general statement that, with all sorts of reservations and special instances, it was, by and large, true that individuals preferred others who were similar to themselves in personality and attitude. The sorts of 'reservations and special instances' were mostly concerned with the types of relationship explored, the findings for, say, courting couples being different in degree from the findings for, say, newly acquainted friends. There are other points to be made in this connection later, concerning the uniqueness or the difficulty of finding certain sorts of similarity to other persons. However, the point was always missed, in this confusing literature, that there can be different types of similarity between two people; even that people can be *both* similar *and* different depending on what the experimenter chooses to measure (Duck, 1977). The importance of this point is only realized once the additional point is made that different things are important to people at different times in the development of a relationship. Accordingly, they may seek different sorts of similarity to a partner at different points in their relationship's growth. Such a view can be made the basis for an explanation of relationship growth (Duck, 1977) and for taxonomizing different parts of the growth of friendship (Lea, 1979). However, it depends also on the provision of a functional explanation for the influence of similarity upon attractiveness.

In the early days of the research, such functional explanations were not offered very frequently and the reader was usually left to work out *why* people should seek similarity. Explanations were most often offered in terms of preference for balance and consistency—but reasons for this preference were not always given. Essentially, the proposal was that individuals preferred harmony, concord, balance, freedom from tension, internal consistency and cognitive consonance between different parts of their system of thought. To encounter instances of similarity to oneself was to encounter such harmony and tension reduction, whilst instances of dissimilarity raised tension, caused internal discord and cried out for the effort of resolution. The explanation fell upon the individual cognitive system of each partner, therefore, and was not a truly social explanation for attraction, nor even a very satisfactory individual one.

Even those alternative explanations which explained the attractiveness of similarity in terms of easiness of communication were unable to advance our thinking much further. To assert that we seek similar others merely because they are easier to talk to, is to take no account of the arguments and discussions which characterize most friendships, the stimulation that they can provide and the challenges that they offer us. Nor does it truly explain why similarity is attractive. If we truly seek an easy life, then the superficial and easily obtained similarities of superficial discussion should be more important to us than those obtained with difficulty. There must be more to it than these consistency and communication models suggest.

When Byrne began publishing his series of studies into the effects of attitude similarity and attraction in 1961, he also began to develop the view that attitudinal similarity was attractive because of its association with positive affect. Through classical conditioning, an individual—who happened to value attitudinal similarity—came to associate the positive feelings generated by attitudinal similarity with the source of the similarity (i.e. the other person). In 1974, Clore and Byrne argued that the happenstance of the affective value of attitudinal similarity came from an individual's need for effectance. That is, Clore and Byrne (1974) proposed that individuals have a genetically programmed need to feel and be competent at dealing with the world; that attitudes constituted one way of representing the world to oneself in ways which could be good and effective or bad and ineffective; and that instances of attitudinal similarity supplied by another person serve to validate or support such representations. Thus, Clore and Byrne argued, attitudinal similarity was attractive because it demonstrated the individual's probable competence and hence subserved the need for effectance. The search for and consequences of attitudinal similarity thus assume a *functional* significance for the individual and the causes of attraction then become something more than mere baubles which attract inconsequentially through glitter.

Of course, it cannot be that simple and it is not. It would be absurd to argue that attitudinal similarity is attractive under any circumstances, from any source, on *any* attitude irrespective of its importance to the person, and independent of the lifesome process or context. Nobody does argue that, except a few voluble straw men in books written by critics of attraction research. It is clearly recognized, by attitude-attraction researchers anyway, that the impact of attitudinal similarity will be modified, reduced or even exaggerated by a number of factors (see Byrne, 1971; Clore, 1977; Duck, 1977). Not only this, but the attractiveness of an individual was never stated by Byrne to depend solely on attitudinal characteristics and the work on social exchange in relationships, on equity, on relationship management, on information exchange, social penetration and many other things combines to emphasize the fact that, at best, many sorts of cognitive activity coexist with many sorts of social, ritual and management processes in the dynamics that surround forming relationships.

However, the *principle* of Byrne's work is important. The point is that attractive cues—cognitive contours in this case—are attractive not in themselves but because, as they emerge in a relationship's processes and interweave with those of the partner, they begin to signify things about the partner which have not yet been seen. Further, they show the sort of relationship that will develop, and, we would argue, most importantly, not only the amount of support that the relationship could provide for the individual's identity but also the form that this might take. Thus, to take up an earlier point, it can be argued that one reason (and there are many others) why physically attractive others are attractive is that their physical attributes imply a particular personality structure which is generally supportive—or at least is not threatening—to many people. As such, however, physical attractiveness retains its significance for relationship development for only a short time, and loses its power as the partner reveals his or her personality structure to be what it is.

This argument (that early attractive cues serve an essentially predictive function to later personality and identity support) forms a useful basis from which a functional explanation for many of the features of relationship development can be advanced in terms of identity support. This, in turn, permits an analysis of relationship breakdown and dissolution in terms of identity threat. For this reason, then, before proceeding to such an analysis we shall devote the next section to a consideration of relationship development which focusses on the emergence of similarities therein, and we shall be paying particular attention to the timing of their emergence in explaining their significance for relationship development.

B. IDENTITY SUPPORT THROUGH RELATIONSHIP DEVELOPMENT

Weiss' (1973; 1975) attempts to classify different relationship functions give some indication of the difficulties that arise when we try to describe the range of support that relationships can provide. However, we begin this section by singling out the sort of psychological supports that similarity could provide, and then considering the types of similarities most likely to provide them.

Byrne (1971) established for us the basic concept of consensual validation which has become widely accepted as a major reason behind the attraction of attitude similarity. 'Consensual validation' refers to the individual's belief that similarity of attitudes or other cognitive features means that those attitudes and opinions which he or she shares with his or her partner are essentially correct (that is, are ratified, supported or validated by the agreement or consensus provided by the partner). An extension of this basic concept is that it indicates effectiveness in dealing with the world (as we have already mentioned) or, in a similar vein, but from a different perspective, that a certain construction of the world has predictive validity (Duck, 1973). However, we recognize that such support does not imply mere sterile reinforcement of the existing personality structure and hence provide only incentive for it to remain as it is. Support can lead to elaboration of the personality by providing a secure psychological base from which to make exploratory endeavours and by encouraging and supporting the person to meet new challenges. Analogous to this is the concept of stimulation value (Wright and Crawford, 1971) that similarity may provide, for example, by promoting a deeper discussion of issues upon which there is some basic agreement or common interest. These authors also suggest that partners may encourage one another to take on new interests, or may suggest new activities based upon pre-existing similarities. If these interests or activities are associated with a person's identity then similarity to one's partner on these things in turn becomes a powerful indication of probable acceptance and support for one's identity.

We wish, however, to underline the fact that we are arguing that similarity and support must not be treated as equivalent concepts, as they have loosely been treated in the past. Rather, similarity is just one form that support may take and the amount of identity support that can be derived from similarity depends on a number of key contextual factors, some of them pre-existing the relationship, some of them emerging as the relationship begins and some of them assuming importance only at later stages in the relationship's development.

The first factor that affects the amount of support derivable from similarity is the extent to which it lies in an area which forms a significant component of an individual's self concept or identity. Thus similarity on important attitudes, dominant values or key constructs is especially important when found (Byrne and Rhamey, 1965; Byrne and Nelson, 1965; Clore, 1977). A second related modifier of the attitude-similarity/attraction relationship was shown by Byrne, Nelson and Reeves (1966) to be the verifiability of the attitude statement. Attraction is greater towards other persons who are similar in attitudes whose truth is more difficult to verify objectively. We would want to extend this point to cover similarity in areas other than attitudes, for instance personal constructs.

A third modifier of the influence of similarity comes from a social, rather than a cognitive source. The impact of a given relationship on personal identity should, of course, be seen in the context of the system or network of relationships in which it occurs—a particularly important point when it comes to explaining the significance of the breakdown or dissolution of a given relationship, and itself a point that has been universally underemphasized in previous work on relationship breakdown. For instance, social exchange theorists (e.g. Thibaut and Kelley, 1959) have realized that an individual's social network exerts an influence over the development of each relationship within it. One such influence which has recently been shown to have a powerful effect on the attractiveness of rewards is the extent to which the rewards exchanged in a relationship may be obtained elsewhere (Kelley, 1979). In deciding whether to invest time and other resources into a particular relationship, an individual may take into account not only the potential supports that he or she feels that the relationship could offer, but also the rewards offered by his or her *other* relationships or potential relationships. In particular, the person has to decide whether the supports available in one relationship are obtainable equally in others or whether they are uniquely attached to that relationship alone, in which case it would be well worth developing and maintaining it.

Thus it does not follow from the above analysis that all of a person's friends will provide similar kinds of support for similar parts of his or her system and, consequently, it does not follow that all of his or her friends will be similar to one another. Indeed a functional explanation would suggest that large amounts of redundancy of support are unnecessary and undesirable. Naturally, some overlap will result from a variety of causes, amongst which are cultural background, social status, class, intellectual level, educational experience and so on but these may be expected to be relatively superficial similarities in most cases—at least so far as the present view of 'personal identity' is concerned. Indeed, the more *difficult* an individual finds it to obtain support of a particular type or for a particular aspect of his or her personality, the more attracted he or she should be to a partner who offers this support. Applied to similarity, then, the uncommonness of different sorts of similarity between an individual and his or her pool of acquaintances determines the areas of similarity, and hence the acquaintances, which he or she finds most attractive (Lea and Duck, in press). Certain similarities, or other supports, may be so difficult to find as to make the relationship which provides them unique and irreplaceable and the breakdown of such a relationship would then be acutely threatening to identity. In contrast, the presence of many of the same similarities between an individual and his or her pool of acquaintances may cause the individual to feel that his or her identity is not sufficiently distinct from theirs and that these sorts of relationship stifle rather than support his or her identity (Jarymowicz and Codol, 1979; Snyder and Fromkin, 1980). In these cases, the individual is likely to withdraw voluntarily from such relationships with no loss or threat to identity incurred.

Of course, this does not mean that the more trivial and easily shared similarities that may emerge in a relationship are without significance or function. We have already mentioned their significance as aids to easy communication, and a second and related advantage may be that they facilitate voluntary interaction. Similarity of activity preference might serve this function for example (Wright and Crawford, 1971). Of course, some activities, such as sports, may require a partner but often this sort of similarity can provide a useful vehicle for the development of a relationship in the early stages without necessarily being a cause for the relationship. However, we believe that the function of these similarities extends beyond merely providing an easy and comfortable situation in which the relationship may take off. Rather, their overriding function is another generally *predictive* one for the individual who is concerned with changing an encounter into a relationship and obtaining support from it. This function they accomplish by signifying the likely outcome in terms of support and threat of further developments in interaction, self-disclosure and intimacy growth and at the same time indicate the relative profitability of the relationship compared with whatever others the individual may have or can realistically expect to form within his or her social network. Thus, for example, the discovery of similarities which because of their common occurrence the individual expected to find in the relationship may enable the individual to decide that his or her partner is 'normal' (or at least not too abnormal) and hence a person whose support would be valued. The point is that an individual's interpretation of similarity as supporting is determined not only by the amount and type of similarity offered, but also by the source of the offer. Thus, high status may make one source of support highly valued while, on the other hand, the same support coming from a stigmatised person may be perceived as more threatening to the individual's identity than supporting (e.g. Novak and Lerner, 1968). Similarities early on in a relationship may be one way of validating the source of support.

However, the importance of the predictive function can best be gauged by considering that the sorts of similarities that have been described above as most ego-supportive—similarities that relate to key areas of identity and for which it is unusual to find support—are precisely the kind of similarities which can only emerge in a relationship through the exchange of personal and intimate information which, if rejected, derided or despised would have a psychologically damaging effect. Thus, the acquainting individual faces the problem in a relationship that, in order to obtain support or acceptance, he or she must first expose himself or herself to threat of rejection. Consequently, anything that can reduce this perceived threat is most attractive at this early stage in the relationship. Leaving aside similarities for the moment, we earlier suggested that certain cues such as physical attractiveness that are readily observable at the start of a relationship may be attractive partly for this reason. There is also some evidence to suggest that the very act of revealing some personal information, particularly self-derogatory or negative personal information can have an uncertainty-reducing effect upon another, and the existence of the so-called rule of reciprocity for self-disclosures in encounters probably means that a failure to respond to an intimate disclosure with one of equal intimacy is interpreted by the original discloser as nonsupportive or threatening.

Nevertheless, similarity is a particularly potent form of information in this respect as the literature on client-therapist similarity in psychotherapy testifies (see e.g. Hlasny and McCarrey, 1980). By rendering the therapist more predictable or familiar to the client, similarity encourages the client to disclose more intimate information about himself or herself leading to an improvement in the effectiveness of the therapy. In the naturally-occurring relationship that we are considering, the process of gradual information exchange that the partners engage in begins with nonintimate information, or information for which there is a high probability of acceptance such as commonly shared similarities, and progresses to more intimate information. This allows the individual to make his or her more intimate and otherwise potentially risky disclosures against a background of reduced vulnerability based upon past similarities and agreements with the partner and the expectation of future ones. This latter is achieved because the relatively trivial similarities discovered early on in a relationship, though not themselves supporting of identity, provide some indication of the extent and types of more fundamental similarities that are present but are as yet unrevealed. A number of small behavioural similarities, for example, together may indicate to the individual the presence of a major underlying similarity between them (say of a major life-value, or fundamental view of the world) whose full emergence and realisation in the relationship would provide fundamental support for his or her identity (Duck, 1977; Lea and Duck, in press).

This present view of relationship emergence, then, argues that the role of similarity extends beyond that of a mere rewarding stimulus and the assurance of a pleasant encounter or easy interaction. Instead its full significance should be understood by considering the process by which the interactants can build their encounters into a relationship which provides them with fundamental supports and stimulations. Exchanging personal information, making predictions and forming expectations about their partner and their future relationship are important components of this process that similarity contributes to in addition to being a direct source of reward. A relationship can fail to develop, irrespective of the rewards it could have provided, simply because one or other individual does not possess sufficient social and cognitive skills for these tasks. However, for a full understanding of which relationships succeed and which break down during the course of their development we must examine, as indeed the partners in the relationship do, the features of each relationship in the context of whatever other relationships the partners may have or could form at that time. In passing, we may note one other research point stemming from this discussion, namely that we need to examine the *causal* connections during relationship development between such emergent properties as different similarities, self-disclosure, trust, voluntary interaction, and ego or self-concept support, rather than treating them simply as competing attractor-variables as has been done in the past.

What does this analysis of relationship development and the functions of similarity in relationship tell us about relationship breakdown and identity threat? To begin with, we have made it clear that relationship development, as well as breakdown, can pose a threat to identity by exposing the two partners to risk and vulnerability and that, as a consequence, the intimate information-exchange necessary to obtain full acceptance and identity support does not occur until a satisfactory prediction of support has been made. In all probability, then, it is only those relationships which are well developed to the point where they provide support, and then break down causing the withdrawal of support, which cause actual psychological damage, and even then perhaps only when one's partner initiates the dissolution. In these terms, the sorts of relationship whose breakdown would be most threatening are those which provide support which is not only important to the individual, but also is difficult to find or replace, and comes from a valued source. Too many similarities shared with too many people, we have observed, may lessen an individual's sense of uniqueness and identity and these relationships may be left in order to preserve identity. As we hope we have made clear, relationship development is a gradual process and it is only fairly long-standing relationships which are ever likely to reach the stage where the support they are seen to provide is irreplaceable.

We have thus emphasized the reasons why similarity may or may not provide support for identity and thus the ways in which its withdrawal may or may not threaten identity. We have not spend time yet on the consequences for identity of withdrawal of support from an irreplaceable other, and we turn to this in the next section. However, before doing so we make one other point that rounds off this discussion of identity support during the growth of relationships.

One would not be surprised to find that there are different extents to which different individuals required or 'used' support in their relationships and there is possibly some evidence to support this. For example, insecure people have been found to be more attracted to strangers who are presented as similar to themselves than are secure people (Goldstein and Rosenfeld, 1969). However, the implications of this finding for real-life relationships are unclear because experiments such as these differ from real-life in at least one important respect: in real life individuals are not presented with a personality profile of the strangers they meet, but are faced with the task of discovering similarities themselves. Given that this task requires complex information-processing and social skills, such as we have been discussing, it is equally plausible that certain individuals with only low levels of skill would be unable to develop and maintain a full and supportive relationship (Dryden, 1981; Trower, 1981). One disturbing possibility that arises from this argument is that some of the people who most desire support for their identity are also people who are least able to establish a stable, supporting relationship. The pattern of repetition of relationship breakdown and withdrawn support that they may then experience would be particularly threatening to identity, possibly compounding their problem.

C. IDENTITY THREAT THROUGH RELATIONSHIP BREAKDOWN

The above discussion focuses on several different features of relationships and on several processes of relationship growth that may be relevant to relationship breakdown. We shall now argue that relationship breakdown acts to threaten identity through these self same processes and features of relationships.

It is necessary at an early stage to make two points that lurk beneath the foregoing analysis. Firstly, relationships take many forms and so also do relationship breakdown and dissolution which may differ in their general causal mix—we are interested in those where personal identity is seriously afflicted or spoiled as a consequence. Secondly, the above discussion actually predicts that some forms of relationship breakdown will function to *preserve* the partners' identities or will be carried out for the reason that the partners believe that their identities are better developed by dissolving the relationship than by continuing it. For instance, plausible causes of such termination of relationship that stem directly from the functional analysis of relationships themselves are dissatisfaction with likely support, or an expectation that growth in support is unlikely. Furthermore, since both partners are conceptualized as having dynamic and developing cognitive structures, it is possible for the development of each to take a different course (although evidence suggests that friends probably become *more* similar through interaction). If such differences arise in fact, then it is possible also for actual support to diminish or decline over a period and hence for the relationship to be terminated by either partner or by mutual consent, for the reason that support in the relationship does not exceed that obtainable elsewhere. In such cases, the dissolution of the relationship is as likely to serve an integrative and supportive function as it is to threaten personal identity and it should be clear that not all decline of relationships is necessarily psychologically detrimental to the persons involved, although it may be a cause of disappointment or unhappiness. Once one begins to consider the possibility of differentiating *types* of relationship and relationship breakdown, however, one begins to ponder a complexity that exceeds the limits of space avilable to the present paper (but see also Duck, 1980; 1981; 1982). Suffice it to say that it is possible to consider relationship breakdown not only from the point of view of a taxonomy of causes for decline but also by describing the special effects of each on the *experience* of collapse and on the psychological changes that are consequent upon it. Here it will be possible merely to draw broad distinctions between quick, unexpected termination and termination that emerges through a slow decline of some key features of the relationship. It is also necessary to distinguish those relationships that dissolve by reason of the intentional acts of the person who is studied, and those that are ended inadvertently, or worse, through the sole agency of his or her partner. Such differences seem primary influences on the nature of the experience of breakdown and its consequences to the person and person's self-concept or identity.

Even so, it important to note that 'breakdown of a relationship' is a simple category term that runs a serious risk of misleading researchers (as it has done in the past) into imagining that it is adequately accounted for in terms of a simple decline in intimacy. It may indeed be the case—it is a researchable question—that forming relationships decline in intimacy much as they increase in it. Altman and Taylor (1973) speculated that relationship decline was rather like a film shown in reverse. However, the analogy cannot be useful for *established* relationships, even if it were valuable as a guide to understanding the unpicking of early acquaintance. Established relationships grow in intimacy—and many other things—but, in doing so, change their form. The best analogy for the growth of relationship is insectival: just as pterygote insects metamorphose from egg to larva to pupa to adult and change at each stage, sometimes almost unrecognizably, in order to achieve their proper growth, so too do relationships. Those that are established and long lived (hence those that are most important to the person and so interest us most from our present perspective) are precisely those that do not simply go into reverse. They break down by changing form again, not by merely diminishing.

Even so, researchers need to recognize the likely differences between different sorts of breakdown. Disturbance in the conduct of relationships causes distress in ways that Equity Theorists and others have explored but it does not always lead to the dissolution of the relationship—for all sorts of reasons that are just starting to be clarified (Hatfield and Traupmann, 1981). Breakdown may be due to one partner's social incompetence or insensitivity just as much as to incomplete development of the relationship or to partners' inabilities to transmute the relationship into its next stage of intimacy (Trower, 1981). Incompetent negotiation of required roles in the relationship can account for breakdown (La Gaipa, 1982), as can the arrival of attractive alternative partners. However, Kelvin's (1977) work indicates the naivety of assuming that attractiveness resides in the attracter: he shows that attraction is accounted for by the person who is attracted. Similarly, to argue that a relationship breaks down because of the arrival of a rival is to assume that the rival is *inevitably* attractive. In reality, of course, the attracted person has to *allow* the rival to become a rival, has to choose to show an interest and open up the possibility of a relationship, has (implicitly) to decide that the present relationship is unsatisfactory and deserves a competitor.

For all of these reasons, it is important to note that decline in intimacy is a thoroughly unsatisfactory explanation for relationship breakdown. Relationships are formed and maintained by too many different other forces in addition to intimacy and liking alone.

On reflection, it is obvious that a relationship has many features—each of which has a complex kinship to the others and each of which can dissolve in its own way independently of any others (McCall, 1982; Miller and Parks, 1982). It is likely that, just as at the start of a relationship some features have not yet fully developed their final significance (e.g. intimacy of self-disclosure), so in an established relationship some features can decline without serious impact on the relationship (e.g. strict equity of exchange of goods). Equally, the decline of some could be sufficient causes of breakdown (e.g. decline of trust or loyalty); and some may decline only as new features arise to prolong and sustain the relationship in a new form (e.g. strict exchange of goods declines as exchange of love increases). Thus simple measures such as 'intimacy' are unlikely to capture the concerted symphony of a relationship and are probably inadequate to account for the subjective experiences associated with termination of relationships. For instance, a decline in acts of intimacy coupled with increased asseverations of liking could conjoin to create an experience as distressing as the simple decline of liking: it suggests not only that partner is deceiving but also that the relationship is judged to be an unsatisfactory one for the open and honest expression of feeling. For another example, the breakdown of a relationship that is societally recognized as an 'experimental' relationship (e.g. courtship) is likely to create different experiences from one labelled as 'permanent' (i.e. marriage).

Equally, greater threats to identity will be created by relationship breakdown which cannot be attributed externally. For instance, those relationships that end because of promotion and relocation of one partner are likely to cause unhappiness but not damage, as long as both partners accept the same version of the causes. In cases where attributions are internal to the relationship, or (worse) are clearly placed at the door of one partner, then we would expect that the experience of the breakdown will be more disruptive psychologically. In these cases, the implication is that a previously supportive partner, having weighed everything up, decides that the support is not worth it and wishes it to be withdrawn. Such a judgement is a deep threat to the identity of the partner, since it suggests the belief that that person's identity no longer matters to the previously supportive partner. For these reasons the experience of breakdown will be much influenced by the attributions that are made about its origins (Harvey *et al.*, 1982).

As noted above and argued elsewhere more fully (Duck, 1980; 1981; 1982), it is important to distinguish the research on the *experience* of relationship breakdown from the research on the *causes* of relationship breakdown. We will here focus on the former. Given this narrowing of focus, one becomes more interested in the consequences of relationship breakdown as far as the experiencer is concerned. In the above analysis, it follows that the consequences are greater where the function of relationships is most seriously sapped by the breakdown.

The concept of function for relationship and the notion of identity through relationships both do help us to establish in each case a likely set of assumptions that narrow down the analysis of probable threatening consequences. By taking the view that personal relationships have a function and that it is closely connected with identity, one can see that it is an error to classify sorts of breakdown or dissolution merely by means of *external* criteria, since apparently different sorts of ending of relationships are best described in terms of consequences for the individual rather than in terms of apparent external categorical similarity. This can be illustrated by the apparently simple distinction between 'fast' and 'slow' breakdown, since it rapidly becomes clear that the seeming difference between the two is a spurious one—for which the consequences to the person ultimately define the relative impact of the two. For example, whilst it first appears that sudden dissolution is more damaging, this cannot in a given instance be proposed confidently until a number of assumptions are clarified: it is first necessary to state the kind of relationship involved—e.g. friendship, marriage, kinship, courtship—since some are more predictably subject to sudden termination. Assuming that the relationships are the same in kind, then one must assume further that they are of equal significance to the person (a control that has not often been done in the research). In addition, one must presume that the two relationships (one of which breaks up slowly and one fast) have followed roughly comparable developmental courses and provide about the same sort of psychological support for the partners—all of which are large assumptions, but assumptions which are necessary in any explanation of differences in effects of the two.

It can be seen that all of these assumptions, in fact, derive their importance from a fundamental assumption that relationships are there to provide support in some shape or form. Given this, it can be seen that sudden break up of relationships is not itself threatening except in the case where the partner is uniquely supportive of a significant type and quantity of the individual's cognitive system (for which reason the relationship would, *ex hypothesi*, have been a very intimate one), and where the origin of the break is the partner and not the self. In such cases, one would expect serious psychological damage to be done, and, if the literature on marital disruption is reexamined, it seems clear that this is the case. Bloom *et al.* (1978), for example, distinguished three sorts of response to marital disruption, one of which is such a high level of stress that psychological disturbance can result. Lynch (1977) also notes that serious medical consequences follow from what he calls 'loneliness', but what is actually the breakdown and dissolution of an established relationship. Re-examination of both reports reveals that maximal stress and maximal damage occur in precisely the category of relationship collapse noted above (which, in Lynch's case, includes the sudden relationship collapse brought about by the death of one partner).

Slow decline of relationships, on the other hand, can be seen, on this analysis, to be likely to be *less* threatening insofar as it occurs in a way which enables both partners to realign their expectations of support by the other person, or to the extent that it focuses the two persons on the inability of the relationship to support them to an acceptable degree. Whilst the management of a slowly declining relationship is likely to be cumbersome, it is also an intriguing problem for research. However, since relationship breakdown is a largely 'unscripted' piece of behaviour (in Langer's, 1978, sense) it is likely that individuals who are experiencing it become unusually and abnormally liable to focus upon the relationship and its progress. Their attributions about relationship decline are thus likely to be unusually and abnormally misleading to the researchers who explore them. We must not fail to take into account the likely attributional biasses that are caused by the functions which relationships serve and which, as relationships break down, begin to influence the psychodynamics of the individuals involved. It does not follow, therefore, that the slow breakdown of relationships is in any way indicative of the processes that would follow from the fast dissolution of the same relationship.

Yet workers exploring the links between social and physical disorders often overlook this point, presumably, at least, in part because social psychologists have not yet been able to make the inputs necessary for other (medical) workers to address it. For example, Lynch (1977), in discussing such medical consequences of loneliness as increased abuse of alcohol, younger mortality and higher incidence of coronary thromboses, draws few distinctions between the *types* of relationship involved nor the *manner* of their dissolution nor the *extent* of identity support that they provided. Also, Bloom, *et al.* (1978), in reviewing marital distress and its consequent enhancing of stress illnesses, suicide rates, premature death and neurosis, assume that all marriages are of equal intensity, equally supportive, equally intimate and have comparable histories. Yet Huston *et al.* (1981) show convincingly that courtships may be classified into at least four categories distinguished, amongst other things, by the depths and extents of joint activities and sharing that are discovered. Furthermore, Hagestad and Smyer (1982) distinguish several different sorts of divorce and we should not make any simple assumptions about the generalities of the psychological consequences of disturbance in difference sorts or depths of relationships.

Our aim here has indeed been to show that the nature of identity establishment, the context of identity support and the development of identity buffering during relationship growth are all crucially relevant to our interpretation of any effects of relationship dissolution. The central point here can, therefore, be plainly and concisely stated: relationship breakdown *per se* is not necessarily as threatening as some workers have argued. The key factor in the determination of the consequences of relationship breakdown lies jointly in two facts: the extent to which the particular relationship has been established in a manner that supports a key amount of a person's identity; and in the extent to which the breakdown of the relationship consequently threatens to undermine valued support for that identity. Although plenty of work on relationships and illness has shown that disturbances in social support create disturbances in physical health, many incomparable types of relational disturbance have been compared. We must distinguish between those which threaten identity severely and those which do not if we are to unpick the causal tangle between relationship dissolution and physical or psychological collapse.

REFERENCES

Altman, I., and Taylor, D. A. (1973). *Social Penetration: The Development of Interpersonal Relationships.* New York, Holt, Rinehart and Winston, Inc.

Berscheid, E., and Walster, E. H. (1974). A little bit about love. In: T. L. Huston (ed.) *Foundations of Interpersonal Attraction.* New York, Academic Press.

Bloom, B. L., Asher, S. J. and White, S. W. (1978). Marital disruption as a stressor: A review and analysis, *Psychological Bulletin*, **85**, 867–894.

Byrne, D. (1961). Interpersonal attraction and attitude similarity, *Journal of Abnormal and Social Psychology*, **62**, 713–715.

Byrne, D. (1971). *The Attraction Paradigm*. New York, Academic Press.

Byrne, D., and Nelson, D. (1965). Attraction as a linear function of proportion of positive reinforcements, *Journal of Personality and Social Psychology*, **1**, 659–663.

Byrne, D., Nelson, D., and Reeves, K. (1966). The effects of consensual validation and invalidation on attraction as a function of verifiability, *Journal of Experimental Social Psychology*, **2**, 98–107.

Byrne, D., and Rhamey, R. (1965). Magnitude of positive and negative reinforcements as a determinant of attraction, *Journal of Personality and Social Psychology*, **2**, 884–889.

Clore, G. L. (1977). Reinforcement and affect in attraction. In S. W. Duck (ed.) *Theory and Practice in Interpersonal Attraction*. London, Academic Press.

Clore, G. L., and Byrne, D. (1974). A reinforcement-affect model of attraction. In T. L. Huston (ed.) *Foundations of Interpersonal Attraction*. New York, Academic Press.

Dryden, W. (1981). The relationships of depressed persons. In: S. W. Duck and R. Gilmour (eds.) *Personal Relationships 3: Personal Relationships in Disorder*. London, Academic Press.

Duck, S. W. (1973). *Personal Relationships and Personal Constructs: A Study of Friendship Formation*. London, John Wiley & Sons.

Duck, S. W. (1977). *The Study of Acquaintance*. Farnborough, Teakfield (Saxon House: Gower Press).

Duck, S. W. (1980). The personal context: intimate relationships. In: P. Feldman and J. Orford (eds.) *Psychological Problems: The Social Context*. Chichester, Wiley.

Duck, S. W. (1981). Toward a research map for the study of relationship breakdown. In: S. W. Duck and R. Gilmour (eds.) *Personal Relationships 3: Personal Relationships in Disorder*. London, Academic Press.

Duck, S. W. (1982). A topography of relationship dissolution. In: S. W. Duck (ed.) *Personal Relationships 4: Dissolving Personal Relationships*. London, Academic Press.

Goldstein, J. W., and Rosenfeld, H. (1969). Insecurity and preference for persons similar to oneself, *Journal of Personality*, **37**, 253–268.

Graziano, W., and Mather-Musser, L. (1982). Initiation and conduct of relationships and the parting of the ways. In: S. W. Duck (ed.) *Personal Relationships 4: Dissolving Personal Relationships*. London, Academic Press.

Hagestad, G. O., and Smyer, M. A. (1982). Dissolving long term relationships; Patterns of divorcing in middle age. In: S. W. Duck (ed.) *Personal Relationships 4: Dissolving Personal Relationships*. London, Academic Press.

Harvey, H., Weber, A. L., Yarkin, K. L., and Stewart, B. E. (1982). An attributional approach to relationship breakdown and dissolution. In: S. W. Duck (ed.) *Personal Relationships 4: Dissolving Personal Relationships*. London, Academic Press.

Hatfield, E., and Traupmann, J. (1981). Intimate relationships: A perspective from Equity Theory. In: S. W. Duck and R. Gilmour (eds.) *Personal Relationships 1: Studying Personal Relationships*. London, Academic Press.

Hinde, R. A. (1979). *Towards Understanding Relationships*. London, Academic Press.

Hinde, R. A. (1981). The bases of a science of interpersonal relationships. In: S. W. Duck and R. Gilmour (eds.) *Personal Relationships 1: Studying Personal Relationships*. London, Academic Press.

Hlasny, R. G. and McCarrey, M. W. (1980). Similarity of values and warmth effects on clients' trust and perceived therapist's effectiveness, *Psychological Reports*, **46** (3), 1111–1118.

Huston, T. L., Surra, C. A., Fitzgerald, N. M., and Cate, R. M. (1981). From courtship to marriage: mate selection as an interpersonal process. In: S. W. Duck and R. Gilmour (eds.) *Personal Relationships 2: Developing Personal Relationships*. London, Academic Press.

Jarymowicz, M., and Codol, J. P. (1979). Self-others similarity perception: striving for diversity from other people, *Polish Psychological Bulletin*, **10** (1), 41–48.

Johnson, M. (1982). Social and cognitive features of dissolving commitment to relationships. In: S. W. Duck (ed.) *Personal Relationships 4: Dissolving Personal Relationships*. London, Academic Press.

Kelley, H. H. (1979). *Personal Relationships: Their Structures and Processes*. New Jersey, Lawrence Erlbaum Association, Publ.

Kelvin, P. (1977). Predictability, power and vulnerability in interpersonal attraction. In: S. W. Duck (eds.) *Theory and Practice in Interpersonal Attraction*. London and New York, Academic Press.

La Gaipa, J. J. (1982). Rituals of disengagement. In: S. W. Duck (ed.) *Personal Relationships 4: Dissolving Personal Relationships*. London, Academic Press.

Langer, E. (1978). Rethinking the role of thought in social interaction. In: J. Harvey, W. Ickes and R. F. Kidd (eds.) *New Directions in Attribution Research* Vol. 2. New York, Erlbaum.

Lea, M. (1979). Personality similarity in unreciprocated friendships, *British Journal of Social and Clinical Psychology*, **18**, 393–394.

Lea, M., and Duck, S. W. (in press). A model for the role of similarity of values in friendship development, *British Journal of Social Psychology*.

Levinger, G. (1974). A three-level approach to attraction: toward an understanding of pair relatedness. In: T. L. Huston (ed.) *Foundations of Interpersonal Attraction*. New York, Academic Press.

Levinger, G. (1979). A social exchange view on the dissolution of pair relationships. In: R. L. Burgess and T. L. Huston (eds.) *Social Exchange in Developing Relationships*. New York, Academic Press.

Lynch, J. J. (1977). *The Broken Heart: The Medical Consequences of Loneliness*. New York, Basic Books.

McCall, G. (1982). Becoming unrelated: The management of bond dissolution. In: S. W. Duck (ed.) *Personal Relationships 4: Dissolving Personal Relationships*. London, Academic Press.

Miller, G. R., and Parks, M. (1982). Communication in dissolving relationships. In: S. W. Duck (ed.). *Personal Relationships 4: Dissolving Personal Relationships*. London, Academic Press.

Novak, D. W., and Lerner, M. J. (1968). Rejection as a consequence of perceived similarity, *Journal of Personality and Social Psychology*, **9** (2), 147–152.

Perrin, F. A. C. (1921). Physical attractiveness and repulsiveness, *Journal of Experimental Psychology*, **4**, 203–217.

Rahe, R. H., Meyer, M., Smith, M., Kjaer, G., and Holmes, T. H. (1964). Social stress and illness onset, *Journal of Psychosomatic Research*, **8**, 35–44.

Snyder, C. R., and Fromkin, H. L. (1980). *Uniqueness: The Human Pursuit of Difference*. New York, Plenum Press.

Thibaut, J. W., and Kelley, H. H. (1959). *The Social Psychology of Groups*. New York, Wiley.

Thomas, W. F., and Young, P. T. (1938). Liking and disliking persons, *Journal of Social Psychology*, **9**, 168–188.

Trower, P. (1981). Social skill disorder. In: S. W. Duck and R. Gilmour (eds.) *Personal Relationships 3: Personal Relationships in Disorder*. London, Academic Press.

Weiss, R. S. (1973). *Loneliness: The Experience of Emotional and Social Isolation*. Cambridge, Mass., MIT Press.

Weiss, R. S. (1975). *Marital Separation*. New York, Basic Books.

Worden, J. W., and Weisman, A. D. (1980). Psychosocial components of lagtime in cancer diagnosis, *Journal of Psychosomatic Research*, **19**, 69–79.

Wright, P. H. and Crawford, A. C. (1971). Agreement and friendship: A close look and some second thoughts. *Representative Research in Social Psychology*, **2**, 52–70.

Threatened Identities
Edited by G. Breakwell

Negativism and the Sense of Identity

MICHAEL J. APTER

Negativism is generally regarded as a 'negative' characteristic—and tends to be associated with deviance, aggressiveness, immaturity, selfishness and social incompetence. The theme of this chapter, however, is that although negativism may often have undesirable properties, it may also in some circumstances have 'positive' features. Indeed, while negativism may even be pathological on occasion, the human propensity for negativism, it will be argued, is nevertheless essential for healthy psychological development and maturity. The argument will be that the development of a sense of personal identity, and its maintenance in the face of threat, is fundamentally dependent on the capacity to feel, think and act in a negativistic way. After all, it can hardly be by chance that the two most obviously transitional periods of development—that from babyhood to childhood, and that from childhood to adulthood—are both characterized by negativistic behaviour; in both cases the search for a new identity appears to be mediated by defiance of adult authority.

In order to pursue this theme, it will first of all be necessary to discuss the nature of identity, and then to define negativism.

I. THE EXPERIENCE OF IDENTITY

Although the concept of 'identity'—like the related concepts 'self' and 'ego'—is one which has been formulated in a variety of different ways by different writers, it should be obvious that a complete account of the sense of identity would have to refer to at least three component characteristics. These characteristics are a sense of personal *distinctiveness*, a sense of personal *continuity*, and a sense of personal *autonomy*.[1]

A satisfactory discussion of these three characteristics requires a preliminary discrimination between two different levels of experience in relation to identity. The higher level is that of what has been called the 'I' or subject of experience, and the lower level is that of the 'Me' or object of experience. The 'Me' is that part of the phenomenal field which relates to one's self; the 'I' is that which experiences the whole phenomenal field including the 'Me'. This distinction, which was made initially by William James (1890), does present certain philosophical problems; but it would seem to be unavoidable in any discussion of the nature of identity. The distinction was later taken up and modified by G. H. Mead (1934) and others, but in what follows I shall be using the terms in their original sense as defined by James. It is, of course, much more difficult to introspect about the 'I' than the 'Me' because there is always a tendency to objectify the characteristics of the 'I' by turning them into properties of the 'Me'. To give an example: it is quite possible to think of the 'Me' as dying, but almost impossible to think of the 'I' in this way. The concept of personal death is therefore to this extent deflected and distanced from the 'I'. (It is notable, incidentally, that all those ways in which people feel distinctive at the 'Me' level can be described as possessions: one *has* a name, a home, a role to play, membership of a group, a certain status, a washing machine. The 'I' is more difficult to characterize in this way: it is, following the distinction of Erich Fromm, 1978, a form of *being* rather than *having*.)

At the higher level then, that of the 'I', the nature of identity is bound up with the very nature of conscious experience itself. Thus consciousness is essentially personal, which means that it embodies the recognition of a *distinction* between oneself and an external world which contains other consciousnesses. (This distinction, of course, is one which may take time to develop fully, as Piaget, in particular, has emphasized.) Consciousness also provides a feeling of *continuity*; even if there are gaps in this continuity occasioned by sleep or induced in other ways, there is a sense in which consciousness before the gap 'goes together with' consciousness after the gap. In other words, consciousness coheres over time, largely one would suppose through the effects of memory. Thirdly, an integral part of normal conscious experience is the feeling that one is in control of one's own thoughts and, in turn, of one's own actions; in this way consciousness provides a sense of *autonomy*. In all these respects, William James' metaphor of consciousness as a stream is particularly apt: a stream is distinctive from its surroundings and has a clear-cut boundary; it has continuity over its length; and it moves forward autonomously under its own weight and impetus.

At this level, the loss of one or more of these three aspects of the sense of identity is associated with the depersonalization of psychotic breakdown. It is experienced, for example, as an impression that one's boundaries have dissolved to such an extent that other people can 'see into one's soul', or as a feeling that one is lacking in personal cohesiveness and continuity, or as a conviction that one's actions and thoughts are being controlled by some outside force. Laing has argued (see especially Laing, 1959) that the problems of schizophrenia essentially stem from an attempt on the part of the 'I' to withdraw and isolate itself from the 'Me', largely as a matter of self-protection: 'There is still an "I" that cannot find a "Me".' What I am suggesting here, however, is that the problem is even more basic than Laing supposes: it is not so much that the 'I' is distancing itself from the 'Me', and with it from the real world, but rather that the 'I' itself is disintegrating.

The loss of one or more of these three aspects of the sense of identity at the level of the 'I' is also associated with mystical experience, although in this case the experience is typically interpreted as self-transcendence rather than self-loss. Thus some mystics argue that a true understanding of self reveals that it is not fundamentally autonomous (e.g. Ramana Maharshi, Thomas Merton), others that it is not inherently continuous (e.g. Gurdjieff, Krishnamurti), and yet others that it is not essentially distinctive (which is emphasized in the writings of Buddhist mystics). Although these views imply that the self is not in any ultimate sense dependent on the three features listed here, they also imply a recognition that all three aspects of identity *are* characteristic of *normal* everyday experience—which is the point which I am making. (A good introduction to the ideas of the mystics mentioned above is Bancroft, 1978.)

Let us now turn to the 'lower' level, the level of the 'Me'. By 'sense of identity' here one means the sense of selfhood which is derived from the way one sees oneself, from one's self-concept *within* consciousness. A strong and solid sense of identity requires firstly, that the individual sees himself as different from other people, as *distinctive* and indeed unique. Secondly, it requires that he sees himself to be self-consistent, displaying *continuity* in his attitudes, beliefs and actions. Thirdly, it requires that he conceives himself to be *autonomous* in the sense of being in charge of his own life, making his own independent decisions, and not being 'pushed around' by other people or external forces in general. By contrast, a person will lack a strong sense of identity if he sees himself to be anonymous, inconsistent and moulded by the exigencies of the external environment. And he will feel his identity to be threatened if he interprets his situation as one which might lead to the loss of one or more of the three essential components of his sense of identity.

A strong sense of identity, then, stems from having a clear self-concept.[2] It should be evident, however, that a strong sense of identity is not the same as high self-esteem: it is not necessarily related to whether a person *likes* his self-concept or not or whether, in Carl Rogers' terms, the self is congruent with the ideal self (Rogers, 1965). For example, a teenager may prefer to be laughed at rather than ignored, because this makes him feel distinctive. Conversely, as the work on major life-changes shows

(Holmes and Rahe, 1967; Rahe, 1975) great success, and therefore presumably increased self-esteem, can be stressful and have detrimental somatic effects; it is reasonable to suppose that this is due to the threat caused to the individual's sense of continuity. The need for a strong sense of identity is therefore different from, and in some respects more basic than, the need for a positive self concept. If the individual strives for the former, even at the expense of the latter, it is because in this way, and to this extent, his life is given meaning. A weak or threatened identity at the level of the 'Me' may be less serious than at the level of the 'I', where it is associated with psychosis; but it is still likely to generate, or be bound up with, problems of a neurotic type.

There are many ways in which people can enhance and help to maintain their sense of identity at the 'Me' level, especially in relation to distinctiveness. They can define themselves, among other things, in terms of their names and other aspects of what Erikson calls 'paper identity' (age, marital status, etc.), their various roles in life (past, present and future intended), their abilities and skills, the things which they create through their work (a process of self-definition which Marx saw as pathological and referred to as 'alienation'), and their possessions and territorial rights. But one of the most salient forms of self-definition in most people derives from the membership of groups, both primary and secondary groups. (It is to this aspect of identity that Tajfel and his colleagues have particularly addressed themselves viz., other chapters in this volume.) Extending the 'I' and 'Me' terminology, belonging to a group could be said to provide a way of giving meaning to 'Me' in terms of 'Us'. Each individual partakes of a number of 'Us's which together contribute significantly to this understanding of 'Me'.

Joining a group is a seemingly paradoxical way of increasing one's sense of identity, since it necessitates a temporary loss of continuity in one's self-concept and a permanent loss of distinctiveness in relation to other members of the group; furthermore, since one must, in some measure, be controlled by the group, there must be some concomitant feeling of a loss of autonomy as well. Nevertheless, the net result of the set of transactions involved in joining the group is likely to be an enhanced sense of identity, provided that the group itself has a strong sense of identity—i.e. provided that it is clearly distinctive from other groups, retains its own special character over time, and is in control of its own activities. Under these conditions the individual who becomes a member of the group can, through identifying with the group, introject these qualities and, to the extent to which the qualities are clear cut and 'visible', gain a more definite sense of personal identity. In societies like our own in which a sense of identity is difficult to establish, one would expect cults and mass movements to proliferate, for this very reason (Klapp, 1969). Again it must be emphasized that the sense of identity which may derive from group membership is different from, and not necessarily related to, any increased self-esteem which might accrue from membership. Indeed, it is possible that someone may join a group to help him in his fundamental search for a sense of identity *at the expense of* a diminished self-esteem.

II. THE FUNCTION OF NEGATIVISM IN RELATION TO IDENTITY

This concept of identity is essentially phenomenological, and negativism will be defined here phenomenologically as well. By 'negativism' will be meant the state of mind which one is in when one feels a desire, or a compulsion, to act *against* the requirements or pressures from some external source. This may mean refusing to do what others wish or even doing the opposite of what is required or expected in a given situation. It is a state of mind with which everyone must be reasonably familiar—in an exaggerated form it is the feeling of 'digging one's heels in', or 'being bloody-minded', or even 'looking for trouble' No doubt, though, some people experience this state more frequently, or more strongly, than others.

If an individual is not in a *negativistic* state of mind at a given time, he may be said to be in a *conformist* state, these two states then being opposite ways which the individual has available to him of interpreting his own actions. Often the same action can in principle be interpreted by him in either way, since negativism to one set of requirements usually implies conformity to some other set from another source; to this extent the interpretation which the individual makes of his action is relatively independent of the action itself. Hence, the significance of defining negativism phenomenologically rather than behaviourally, since an objective description of the action does not, and cannot in itself, unequivocally indicate which of these opposite states of mind the performer of the action is in. To put all this in terms of a concrete example, if a teenager belongs to a gang which is committing some defiant and deviant act, he can see his actions within the gang, at the time in question, either as conforming to the requirements of the gang or as negativistic to the requirements of adult society.

Although in such cases, one interpretation logically implies the other, and so both could logically be held at the same time, nevertheless *phenomenologically* there is a tendency for one interpretation to prevail, the other interpretation being relegated to the periphery of awareness. That is to say, one source of requirements will be more salient to the individual than the other; it will be as it were, part of the 'figure' of his or her phenomenal field, and the other will be part of the 'ground', at a given moment. If the 'figure' is the part of the phenomenal field which involves negativism, the individual may be said to be negativistic at the moment in question; if it is the part which involves conformity, the individual may be said to be conformist at that moment.

It follows from what has been said that a person is always in one or another of these mutually-exclusive phenomenological states, that he is interpreting his actions in one way or its opposite at all times. It is possible at any time, however, that he will experience a reversal from one interpretation to the other, i.e. that the source of requirements at the focus of the phenomenal field will 'swop over' with that at the periphery. Indeed, these 'figure-ground' reversals may even take place in the course of a single ongoing action.[3] The way in which the individual is interpreting his own actions at a given moment will, therefore, not necessarily be evident to an external observer, and often behaviour which is judged from the outside to be negativistic (e.g. an act of teenage vandalism) will not in fact be negativistic in the phenomenological sense defined, at the moment in question. However, if someone is carrying out some act which is conventionally labelled as deviant, then it is reasonable to suppose that there may at least be periods during the performance of this act when he will recognize and be centrally aware of this conventional labelling and therefore be in a negativistic state.

The negativistic state of mind may be induced by a number of different circumstances, and may have a number of different psychological functions. These are discussed more fully in Apter (1982). But none of these functions can be more basic than that of helping a person to gain his sense of identity, and to maintain it in the face of threats of various kinds.

Knowing what something is, means knowing what it is *not*. Saying that something is big is meaningless, unless one also knows what it would mean to say that it was small: the concepts big and small are mutually interdependent. In a more complicated way, knowing that something is a banana means not only knowing that it is a fruit, but also knowing what type of fruit it is *not*. This idea that opposition and contrast are essential for meaning, goes back at least as far as Hegel in modern philosophy; and it is the key notion in contemporary Structuralism in the social sciences. In terms of 'Me', to know who one is also implies knowing who one is not. One's sense of *distinctiveness* therefore can be gained and sustained by doing everything possible to demonstrate to oneself what one is not. To be a socialist means in an obvious way not to be a conservative, and the feeling of being a socialist at least in part depends on contrast with, and opposition to, conservatism. In other words, we understand what we are to some extent in terms of our rejections, be they rejections of parents, school, political party, religious belief, or whatever. Knowing oneself is saying 'No' to what one is not; in this sense, as Lowen (1975) has put it, knowing is 'No-ing'. In short, cognitive contrast in relation to the 'Me' is enhanced through antagonism.

Similarly, one's sense of *continuity* at the level of the 'Me' can be maintained by opposing all forces for change, especially in relation to aspects of the self which are seen as being particularly distinctive. One can feel secure in one's sense of continuity by demonstrating to oneself an ability to identify and oppose potential sources of change. And the clearest way to demonstrate to oneself that one is *autonomous* is by doing things which there is external pressure not to do (or conversely by not doing things which there is external pressure to do). What better way could there be to produce a feeling of autonomy? In particular, if some external source is seen as limiting one's freedom, one reacts in a way which is designed to regain this freedom and which has been characterized by Brehm (1966) as 'reactance'.

It might seem that the point being made here is an entirely trivial one. Any force which is felt to be threatening will be expected to induce a desire to act against that force. This would be true of any kind of threat, be it, for example, a threat of physical injury, or of loss of property, or of loss of honour. Negativism, as defined here, is typically part of the reaction to threat of any kind. The point which I am making, however, is much stronger than this. It is that the negativistic state *can* come first, and then prompt the search for some requirement or pressure to act against. When this happens the negativism is initially 'free-floating', but comes to be attached to some salient pressure. Sometimes this may involve no more than a reinterpretation of an intended or ongoing action, but at other times it may involve searching out or even provoking an external pressure, or 'threat', which can then act as a focus for negativism in the phenomenal field. Either way, in order to gain and maintain a sense of identity, the individual must *search out* or provoke forces to be negativistic against. These forces may not in any obvious way be inherently threatening—they may simply be defined as threatening, and made salient as such in the phenomenal field, and they may be chosen in an entirely arbitrary or opportunistic way; or else forces which, at least to an outside observer, *are* more obviously threatening, may be deliberately brought into action. In all these cases, the real threat is not what it appears to be, but is rather the underlying threat to the individual's sense of identity at the level of the 'Me'—the supposed threats being no more than tools which the individual uses to help him to establish or re-establish his feeling of identity.

The term 'negativism' is used most frequently in the psychological literature in relation to the behaviour of children aged about two. Indeed, the period between roughly one-and-a-half and three-and-a-half has been depicted as the 'negativistic period'—a term which seems to have come into general use in the nineteen-twenties and nineteen-thirties (Reynolds, 1928; Bridges, 1931). The phenomenon attracted attention originally, however, in the context of psychological testing, when it became apparent that it was particularly difficult to test children at this age (e.g. Binet and

Simon, 1905). Although one should not automatically assume that behaviour which is judged from the outside to be negativistic is necessarily associated with the negativistic mental state, it would seem to be reasonable to suppose that there is generally such an association in this case, since the negativistic behaviour of these children tends to occur in a rather arbitrary way and to be easily displaced from one source of authority to another.

At the age of two, the child has already become physically capable of some degree of independence from its parents, and the negativistic period can be seen as a period in which the child attempts to match this physical independence with psychological independence. For example, the child can now walk without help but must test out its ability to decide when to walk and how to walk and where to walk: the child must come to realize fully that he or she has a will which is autonomous and distinct from that of others and that it is possible to choose goals and pursue them in a consistent way over time despite outside interference. Negativistic behaviour allows children to demonstrate to themselves that they are to some degree a 'law unto themselves': if it is possible to say 'No' to someone, and resist that other person's pressures, then one must be independent of that person and in control of one's own actions. (It is also possible to use negativism to 'test the limits' of one's own sphere of autonomy and to discover the rules which are being applied by others, while becoming aware that in the last analysis it is always possible to break these rules.) It could, of course, be said that from birth onwards the child is innately self-willed and self-centred; but the point about the period of negativism is that it is through negativism that the child comes to develop an *awareness* of his or her self-will—as well as an awareness of his or her personal distinctiveness and continuity. In this way, negativism plays an essential role in the child's development of a strong sense of identity. This kind of function of negativism is in fact one of the major themes in the writings of Henri Wallon, a major French child psychologist whose work has been strangely neglected by English-speaking psychologists (see especially Wallon, 1959, 1963, 1976).

Adolescence, or, as some would have it, 'second adolescence' (e.g. Dodson, 1971) is a second major step in the development of an adult identity. This step is also characterised by negativism, in the form of 'defiance' and 'rebelliousness'. Although negativism may have a number of functions at this age (see discussion in Apter and Smith, 1976) the basic function would appear to be the same as that at the earlier 'negativistic period', i.e. to help the developing individual to acquire a more mature sense of identity. However, at this 'metaphysical age' (as Piaget has called it) the sense of identity is related to more abstract considerations than it was at the earlier age. The aim of the negativism now is to help the individual to feel distinctive in terms of 'where he or she stands' in relation to a variety of issues; the sense of continuity which he or she is attempting to establish now relates to an overall perspective, in other words to attitudes, beliefs, values and opinions; and by sense of autonomy at this level is meant the individual's awareness that it is possible to make up one's own mind about things rather than conforming to external pressures. Particular behaviours follow from all of this, but the sense of identity relates at this age more to the underlying personal conceptual systems which the adolescent is attempting to construct than to particular pieces of behaviour which he or she may choose to perform. This considerable task of construction is precipitated by change of various kinds including the advent of sexual maturity, the achievement of abstract thinking abilities, and new social expectations. Erikson's well known characterization of this period as one of 'identity crisis' captures well the urgency of identity formation in the face of these changes.[4]

There is one other transitional developmental period which is characterised by negativism. This occurs late in life and is experienced by those who live long enough to lose such physical powers as are necessary to support independence. The direction of developmental change at this stage is therefore in an obvious sense opposite to that of the childhood and adolescent periods which have been discussed, and the function of negativism at this late stage is to fight rather than aid the natural process of change.

As the proprietor of an old people's home, I am in daily contact with people whose sphere of autonomy has become severely restricted. It is not surprising that many of them are frequently negativistic, since this helps them to shore up their failing sense of independence and to hold at bay for a while some of those forces which threaten to annihilate their feelings of selfhood. These forces include not only the loss of autonomy in some degree, but also the threat to continuity caused by their radical change in circumstances (and in some cases a failing memory), and the threat to distinctiveness inherent in any type of institutionalization. Typical of such negativistic actions are the refusal to take tablets which are normally accepted without demur or even demanded, deliberately sitting in someone else's chair and refusing to be budged, and obstinately holding on to newspapers or books that others want to read. In such cases, there is no obvious extrinsic or rational reason for the sudden and temporary cussedness and one must assume that it is not a reaction to the ostensible situation but rather an attempt to deal with the threat of identity loss. Reaction to negativism by people who look after the elderly in institutions should ideally be enough to validate the negative meaning which the actions are intended to have, but not enough to frustrate the expression of the underlying negativistic feelings. After all, the cantankerous and 'difficult' old person may well, in these terms, be far more psychologically healthy than the placid 'vegetable'.

As noted earlier, one way of gaining a sense of identity is to join a clearly-defined group, deriving a sense of 'Me' from a sense of 'Us'. When someone joins a group it might be expected that, in the context of the group, negativism would no longer be needed, since the group itself should provide the necessary impression of continuity, distinctiveness and autonomy. Negativism may still be needed, however, but now on behalf of the group, in order to help to maintain the *group's* identity against threat. That is, all the members of a group may need to behave in an overtly negativistic way against outside forces in order to demonstrate clearly to each other that the group which they compose is distinct from those forces, undeviating in its aims and principles, and fully autonomous despite outside pressure. Such 'group-negativism' may also be needed in order to prevent the negativism of group members being expressed against the group itself: a viable group is therefore able to transfer residual negativism in its members into negativism in the service of the group. Often external sources of pressure will be identified or even created in order to achieve this end.[5] Encouraging this 'turning outwards' of negativism in this way is, of course, a strategy which has been used by dictators throughout history.

An extreme example of the way in which people 'gain identity in losing their identity' in social groups, occurs in time of war. A soldier, after all, loses his autonomy and distinctiveness in a particularly obvious way in becoming part of an effective combat unit, and the experience of fighting represents a major discontinuity in experience. However, the groups that the soldier feels part of (his unit, the army as a whole, his nation) gain in distinctiveness in his eyes through their confrontation with the enemy, and their autonomy and continuity are enhanced through their expression of negativism in overt and protracted hostilities. If the soldier can identify with the group, then a strong sense of identity is assured. On the other hand, if the soldier cannot for some reason do so, then he will need to fall back on individual negativism in order to regain a sense of personal identity. Events in the First World War clearly illustrate this eventuality. Many soldiers reported hating their superiors more than the enemy and this was found frequently as a symptom in war neurosis. The possibilities for expressing negativism against one's officers in particular and one's own side in general were limited by *force majeure*, but the deliberate breaking of rules and fraternisation with the enemy were less uncommon than is generally supposed. Failing any other outlet, negativism against the self was always possible, and indifference to danger may often have been a form of such displaced negativism. It is also significant that in the year following the termination of hostilities, rebelliousness among the troops before demobilization was widespread among the victors as well as the vanquished. (Historical evidence for all these assertions about the behaviour and experience of soldiers during and immediately after the First World War will be found in Leed, 1979. In particular, Leed discusses extensively the threat of loss of autonomy and continuity experienced by these soldiers).

It will have been noticed that the identity-enhancing function of negativism which I have been describing relates to the 'Me' rather than to the 'I'. In fact, negativism *cannot* be used successfully for this purpose at the 'I' level. If one feels that one's conscious experience is not distinct, but is shared with others, then one cannot act against others as distinct from oneself. If one is not aware of one's consciousness as a continuous whole over time, then the 'I' which decides to act negatively against some outside force may not be the same 'I' as that which perceives the action and its results. And if one feels that everything which one thinks and does is dictated from outside, then acting negatively will not help to establish that one is autonomous, but simply constitute one more impulse and action imposed from without.

This does not mean that the strategy of negativism is never used in the *attempt* to maintain a sense of identity by those undergoing psychotic breakdown. On the contrary, negativistic behaviour of different kinds is observed frequently in different types of psychosis (Bleuler even wrote a monograph on the subject in 1912), and it is not unlikely that this stems from the negativistic state as defined here. But if this is so, then for the reasons just given, the strategy cannot work; and if it is used it may therefore be used with increasing desperation.

III. THE PSYCHOPATHOLOGY OF NEGATIVISM

Far from being an aberration, then, negativism can be seen to play an essential and constructive role in normal psychological development and in the maintenance of adult mental health. Under certain circumstances, however, negativism *can* have detrimental effects; so that this state of mind, which in its origins contributes to the individual's psychological adjustment, can also play a part in the generation of certain types of maladjustment. Let us consider some ways in which this can occur.

(a) Continuity versus distinctiveness

The need to maintain and even enhance one's sense of distinctiveness can come into conflict with the need to maintain a sense of continuity, since increasing one's personal distinctiveness may require *change* in one's self-concept. For example, to accentuate his feeling of distinctiveness a person may join a new group—a religious sect, or a political party, let us say—but joining the group also changes his self-concept, and to this degree threatens his sense of continuity. There is therefore always an inherent potential for conflict between the need for continuity—which is essentially 'reactionary'—and the need for distinctiveness, which tends to be 'progressive'.

One way in which this conflict may manifest itself is through the individual expressing the negativism which arises in the service of continuity, against forces which would help him to improve and develop his sense of distinctiveness. Thus, the individual may act against those who are putting pressure on him to join some group, even though being a member of the group would add a new dimension of distinctiveness to his self-concept. Indeed, if the need for continuity is strong enough, the individual's whole psychological growth may be inhibited and his self-concept may as a result remain relatively impoverished. Furthermore, he may even act negatively against forces helping him to succeed in relation to some goal or another, because success might require a change in his self-concept—he may prefer a strong self-concept, based on the acceptance of always being a failure, to a weaker self-concept in which there is some failure and some success. The so-called 'negative therapeutic reaction' in the face of the 'threat' of therapy succeeding may be brought about in exactly this way.

Alternatively, if there is an overriding need for distinctiveness, there may be negativism against any forces which are construed as working in favour of continuity—in this case the individual may need to be continually changing in a desperate search for self-definition. So if he joins a group, for example, then after a short time he may feel that he has to act negatively towards other members of the group (either by being obstructive or by joining a rival group), because he feels that the group is 'holding him back' and preventing him from finding himself.

In both of these ways the negativism is not at the base of the problem, but tends to play an important part in the way in which it is expressed—and perhaps to compound the problem by making it more difficult to attain *both* a satisfactory sense of distinctiveness *and* a satisfactory sense of continuity.

(b) Self-negativism

In the process of constructing a clear 'Me', through negativism, the 'Me' is alienated further from the 'I' in the sense that it becomes more clearly objectified, and takes on some of the attributes of other objects within the phenomenal field. To the extent to which this alienation occurs, it is possible for the 'I' to act negativistically towards the requirements of the 'Me', just as it can towards the requirements of other sources which it can identify. This possibility may be turned into actuality where the expression of negativism against all external sources is frustrated; in this case, the negativism may be displaced onto the 'Me'. The example was given earlier of soldiers who cannot act against their own superiors, and do not construe their fighting as a form of negativism because they do not fully identify with their own group; reckless disregard for personal safety and even 'heroism' may then result, the negativism being expressed in this way being negativism against the 'Me's' need for survival. Masochism may also be a form of self-negativism generated in this way, as may asceticism, celibacy, and even in some cases the self-damaging behaviour of alcoholism, drug-addiction and gambling.

It is ironic that a process which helps to establish a strong sense of identity in the course of development can later be used to undermine it, sometimes with disastrous consequences for the person concerned.

(c) Hypernegativism

In some people, negativism may 'get out of hand', in the sense that it becomes a stereotyped reaction to a wide range of eventualities, or in the sense that the behaviour which stems from it is unnecessarily vicious and damaging. The latter form of 'hypernegativism', which appears to be displayed frequently by psychopaths, is pathological both from a social point of view (since the behaviour is detrimental to others) and from the point of view of the individual himself or herself, since extreme negativism of this kind is clearly maladaptive and typically leads to unpleasant consequences.

There are a number of possible reasons for this type of psychopathic behaviour, and here, as elsewhere, the negativism which is generated is not necessarily a response to identity threat. Nevertheless, at least some psychopaths seem to have special difficulties in gaining or sustaining a clear sense of selfhood and one may suppose that their exaggerated negativism is a response to these difficulties—and one which is frequently successful. My colleague Dr. K. C. P. Smith, who is a prison psychiatrist (and coauthor of the theory of psychological reversals which sets the context for the present paper) has reported many examples of statements made to him by psychopathic criminals in the course of interview which lend weight to this view. For example: 'I spent more money from the "job" I did than you will ever earn in a lifetime'; 'I have done things which are so exciting that most people would not even dream of them'; 'I don't take orders from anybody'. Many of these criminals express great pride in their 'achievements' which they contrast contemptuously with those of 'ordinary people'. They remember with pride how they were the centre of attention in court and cherish their press cuttings. In other words, through their negativistic behaviour they are able to feel themselves to be distinctive from other people and strong enough to defy the forces which as they see it push most people into living humdrum and commonplace lives. It is, of course, far from being the case that all criminals or all psychopaths present this kind picture of themselves, but enough do to make it a recognizable syndrome. Clearly, though, although such negativism may lead to successful identity formation, the extreme measures taken imply that establishing a sense of selfhood would otherwise have been problematic; and these extreme measures may be highly damaging to the person concerned in other respects.

In dealing with some problems which arise from negativism we have been considering what might be thought of as 'side-effects' of the negativistic state of mind. It should not be supposed, however, that these are *always* detrimental. Thus creativity necessarily involves at some stage a rejection of some aspect of what has gone before, and any deliberate negativistic attempt to overturn some orthodoxy stands the chance of producing original and fruitful results (in this respect see Dreistadt, 1970). Furthermore, at the level of society it might be argued on cybernetic grounds (consistent with the 'law of requisite variety' first propounded by Ashby, 1956) that negativism in the members of a society is essential for that society to have sufficient variety within itself to adapt successfully to changing conditions. These themes are altogether too large to pursue further in the present paper (but see Apter, 1982).

The thesis of this chapter, then, is that the propensity for negativism is fundamental to human nature: Man can only become fully himself, which means aware of himself, when he can deliberately and knowingly say 'No'. To be human means to possess the capacity to 'stand outside oneself' and break the rules which govern one's own behaviour. If Freud was right in supposing that some of the major myths of mankind express important psychological insights, then no better support could be found for the ideas being put forward here than the Biblical myth of the Fall of Man—since in this account Man becomes Man through a primal act of disobedience, the effect of which is to establish a degree of autonomy and distinctiveness unknown to the rest of creation. Nor is this the only mythical story to come down to us from antiquity which links Man's identity indissolubly with the defiance of larger forces. Indeed, in the long perspective of the history of human thought it would hardly be possible to identify a less original theme than the one which I have been pursuing here.

NOTES

[1] There is a sense in which these three features of identity tie in with the three Aristotelian Laws of Thought. Thus the Law of Contradiction ('A' is not 'not-A') relates to the sense of distinctiveness, the Law of the Excluded Middle ('A' is either 'B' or 'not-B') to the sense of continuity, and the Law of Identity ('A' is 'A') to the sense of autonomy. The nature of this third correspondence is perhaps not so obvious as the other two. But a connection can be made through the argument of Ayn Rand that 'The Law of Causality is the Law of Identity applied to action' since 'The nature of an action is caused and determined by the nature of the entities that act . . .' (Rand, 1957). If an

entity that acts is aware of itself it would follow that, through this extension of the law of identity, it would feel its actions to stem from its own nature—and this is another way of saying that it would feel itself to be autonomous. (In this respect, see Branden, 1969.)

[2] There are, of course, some semantic problems here, since it would be perfectly possible to say that one saw oneself clearly to be anonymous, vacillating, and weak; that is, one could have a strong, but in these respects unflattering, self-concept. Using this terminology, one could be said to have a clear or strong self-concept but a vague or weak sense of identity. The lines of the argument here should be clear, however, whichever way one wishes to define a clear self-concept. I shall continue to use the terms in a way that implies that a clear self-concept is related to distinctiveness, continuity and autonomy i.e. to a strong sense of identity.

[3] The 'negativistic' and 'conformist' states may be regarded as 'metamotivational' since they are about the way in which an individual interprets his own motivational experience. Together they constitute a pair of 'metamotivational states', one or other of which is always operative at a given moment. With Dr K. C. P. Smith, I have developed a general theory of metamotivation, in which a number of pairs of metamotivational states have been identified, the negativism–conformity pair constituting one example. Since reversal (i.e. switching) is always possible between members of a pair of such states, and since this phenomenon is of central interest in the theory, the theory is referred to as 'reversal theory' (Smith and Apter, 1975). We have attempted to elucidate the conditions under which such reversals occur, and the implications of reversals for experience and behaviour. From this perspective, then, the present chapter may be seen as developing one aspect of reversal theory. An extensive account of the theory in all its aspects will be found in Apter (1982) and a summary of some of the main arguments in Apter (1979). The interested reader might also like to consult Apter and Smith (1977, 1979, 1980) and Murgatroyd *et al*, (1978).

[4] My argument, at this point, is not inconsistent with Erikson's views about what happens during adolescence. Erikson, however, emphasizes the continuity aspect of identity. Indeed, he defines identity as a 'subjective sense of an invigorating sameness and continuity' (Erikson, 1965). And although he recognizes that negativism may be used during identity formation through choice of what he calls 'negative identity' (Erikson, 1956), negativism is not assigned the central and all-pervasive role that I am assigning to it.

[5] In this Presidential Address to the British Psychological Society in 1974, entitled 'On taking sides', Brian Foss raised as one of his principal questions that of '. . . why, when one does take sides, (is one) not only *for* one side but *against* the other' (Foss, 1974). It is this question which I am trying to answer here.

REFERENCES

Apter, M. J. (1979). Human action and the theory of psychological reversals. In: G. Underwood and R. Stevens (eds.) *Aspects of Consciousness, Volume I: Psychological Issues*. London, Academic Press.

Apter, M. J. (1982). *The Experience of Motivation: The Theory of Psychological Reversals*. London, Academic Press.

Apter, M. J., and Smith, K. C. P. (1976). Negativism in adolescence, *The Counsellor*, **23/24**, 25–30.

Apter, M. J., and Smith, K. C. P. (1977). Humour and the theory of psychological reversals. In: A. J. Chapman and H. C. Foot (eds.) *It's a Funny Thing, Humour*. Oxford, Pergamon Press.

Apter, M. J., and Smith, K. C. P. (1979). Sexual behaviour and the theory of psychological reversals. In: M. Cook and G. Wilson (eds.) *Love and Attraction—an International Conference*. Oxford, Pergamon Press.

Apter, M. J., and Smith, K. C. P. (1980). Psychological reversals: some new perspectives on the family and family communication, *Family Therapy*, **VI**, **2**, 89–100.

Ashby, W. R. (1956). *An Introduction to Cybernetics*. London, Chapman and Hall.

Bancroft, A. (1978). *Modern Mystics and Sages*. London, Paladin.

Bleuler, E. (1912). *The Theory of Schizophrenic Negativism*. Nervous and Mental Diseases Monograph Series No. 11. New York, The Journal of Nervous and Mental Disease Publishing Co.

Binet, A., and Simon, T. (1905). Méthodes nouvelles pour le diagnostic du niveau intellectuel des anormaux, *Année Psychologique*, **11**, 191–336.

Branden, N. (1969). *The Psychology of Self-Esteem*. New York, Bantam Books.

Brehm, J. W. (1966). *A Theory of Psychological Reactance*. New York, Academic Press.

Bridges, K. B. (1931). *The Social and Emotional Development of the Pre-School Child*. London, Routledge.

Dodson, F. (1971). *How to Parent*. London, W. H. Allen.

Dreistadt, R. (1970). Reversing, using opposites, negativism, and aggressiveness in creative behaviour in science and philosophy, *Psychology*, **7** (Pt. 2), 38–63.

Erikson, E. H. (1956). The problem of ego identity, *Journal of the American Psychoanalytic Association*, **4**, 54–121.

Erikson, E. H. (1965). *Childhood and Society*. Harmondsworth, Penguin.

Foss, B. M. (1974). On taking sides (Presidential Address), *Bulletin of The British Psychological Society*, **27**, 347–351.

Fromm, E. (1978). *To Have or to Be*? London, Jonathan Cape.

Holmes, T. H., and Rahe, R. H. (1967). The social readjustment rating scale, *Journal of Psychosomatic Research*, **11**, 213–218.

James, W. (1890). *The Principles of Psychology*. New York, Holt.

Klapp, O. E. (1969). *Collective Search for Identity*. New York, Holt, Rinehart & Winston.

Laing, R. D. (1959). *The Divided Self*. London, Tavistock.

Leed, E. J. (1979). *No Man's Land: Combat and Identity in World War I*. Cambridge, Cambridge University Press.

Lowen, A. (1975). *Pleasure: A Creative Approach to Life*. New York, Penguin.

Mead, G. H. (1934). *Mind, Self, and Society*. Chicago, University of Chicago Press.

Murgatroyd, S., Rushton, C., Apter, M. J., and Ray, C. (1978). The development of the Telic Dominance Scale, *Journal of Personality Assessment*, **42**, 5, 519–528.

Rahe, R. H. (1975). Life changes and near-future illness reports. In: L. Levi (ed.) *Emotions—Their Parameters and Measurement*. New York, Raven Press.

Rand, A. (1957). *Atlas Shrugged*. New York, Random House.

Reynolds, M. M. (1928). *Negativism of Pre-School Children: An Observational and Experimental Study*. Contributions to Education, No. 228. New York, Bureau of Publications, Teachers College, Columbia University.

Rogers, C. R. (1965). *Client-Centred Therapy*. London, Constable.

Smith, K. C. P., and Apter, M. J. (1975). *A Theory of Psychological Reversals*. Chippenham, Picton Publishing.

Wallon, H. (1959). Psychologie et éducation de l'enfance, *Enfance*, **3–4**, 195–449.

Wallon, H. (1963). Buts et méthodes de la psychologie, *Enfance*, **1–2**, 5–171.

Wallon, H. (1976). *Lecture d'Henri Wallon: Choix de Textes*. Paris, Éditions Sociales.

Threatened Identities
Edited by G. Breakwell

Threat and the Scientist

FAY FRANSELLA

Threat comes in many forms and many guises. It is no respecter of persons, affecting as it does both rich and poor, powerful and powerless, individuals and groups of individuals. A conference on *Models of Man* (Chapman and Jones, 1980) provided an unusual opportunity to observe threat in action within a scientific community. Over the four days of conference activities, groups of psychologists argued the case for their own interpretation of 'science' and 'model of man' (or 'person' as I prefer to say). In so doing, they were also defending the sort of psychologists they saw themselves as being. As the merits and demerits of the various positions were spelled out, and the issues unfolded, I became very aware of the very real nature of the threat. It seemed that it was not only the model of the person that was being defended by its proponents, but the very self-identity of the individuals themselves.

For some there appeared to be no problems. Those, for instance, who took an eclectic approach and had constructed their own models to make their own particular point, seemed to be insulated from the controversial issues inherent in adopting an existing orientation. Such theorists appeared to have little commitment to a model of science or a model of the person beyond their own. Such personally erected models have roots only in their originators. These psychologists have chosen elements from other theories to suit their own purposes. Because of this, such persons are unlikely to be threatened *by* others, nor are their idiosyncratic theories likely to be a threat *to* others—at least, not until they acquire some followers. Exponents of the artificial intelligence framework likewise seemed to pose little or no threat to other psychologists. Perhaps this approach is still too much of a newcomer on the scene to be seen as a challenge of threatening proportions.

It is the others I wish to discuss, both threateners and threatened, both in terms of their involvement as persons and their commitment as psylogists. It became plain to me that some people were seeing a dichotomy, or at least an orthogonal relationship, between personal involvement and psychological commitment. This was neatly summed up in Wetherick's discussion of Howarth's paper:

> It seems to me that you have advanced a theory of everything except psychology. As a human being my wish is that resources are put to the best use, by me and by the rest of humanity. But this is not what I am concerned with as a psychologist: I want to participate in the construction of a science (Chapman and Jones, 1980).

For others at the conference, the superordinate constructs relating to the 'self' and the 'psychologist' appeared to be as one.

Personal involvements became particularly apparent when issues centred on the nature of the person in relation to scientific inquiry, and on the nature of scientific inquiry itself. Here sparks truly flew. I want to argue that many of the psychologists who were in hot debate at that conference retreated to entrenched positions because their whole personal psychology and personal identity were threatened. Further, that such threat would be found in all scientists and indeed in all persons if we were to look upon them 'as if' they were also scientists, as Kelly (1955) suggests we might.

ONE VIEW ON THE NATURE OF THREAT

There are many ways of defining threat; the prospective from which I am describing what I saw as happening at the conference stems from the psychology of personal constructs. In personal construct theory, a threatening situation or person is one which makes us aware, at some level, of imminent change in the ways in which we see ourselves. We are threatened if we anticipate that present events will lead us to play a role we devalue; the possibility of losing an argument with someone we look down on might result in our seeing ourselves as 'stupid'. We are threatened if events move too quickly for us; a patient may be threatened if the symptom looks as if it is disappearing before he or she is ready to be 'a person without a symptom'. Landfield (1954) hypothesized that a person can be threatening to us if he or she exemplifies or expects from us some important way of behaving which we have outgrown but one which is still possible; thus, a person who espouses a new theoretical position may be 'at risk' when brought face to face with someone who is committed to the now rejected position; adolescents are readily threatened if parents or important adults expect from them outgrown 'childish' behaviours. Threat thus occurs whenever we perceive, at some level of awareness, imminent change in some central personal commitment, in some cherished view of ourselves.

EVIDENCE FOR PERSONAL INVOLVEMENT AND COMMITMENT IN SCIENTIFIC INQUIRY

Those who think of the scientific enterprise as being carried out by the dispassionate investigator are sorely misguided as many statements about and by scientists show. For instance, Watson in '*The Double Helix*' (1969) asks: 'Would we *have* any science if truth did not inspire passionate devotion in the researcher?'. And Mahoney (1976) quotes Albert Einstein as saying: 'The state of mind which enables a man to do work of this kind is akin to that of the religious worshipper or lover. The daily effort comes . . . straight from the heart.' Yet others have commented on the degree of emotional involvement and commitment they have found in the course of their research. Mitroff (1974), for instance, carried out a study on a group of scientists who were involved in five Apollo space missions. Mitroff suggests that:

> . . . strong emotions—the hostile feelings between various types of individuals, the intense commitment to particular preferred positions—are not themselves necessarily detrimental to the ideal of scientific objectivity. It may well be . . . that every scientist must be committed to his ideas if he is to be able to engage in particular types of observations, and that if emotional commitment blind the scientist from seeing some things, then without it would not be able to see other things. Some scientists are keen observers precisely because of their commitments, not ın spite of them . . . to eliminate strong emotions and intense commitments may be to eliminate some of science's vital sustaining forces (Mitroff, 1974).

At the risk of labouring the point, I would like to give one further quotation. Dwelling on this issue is partly for my own sake as, for a long time, I was one of those who felt that scientific inquiry was, and should be, a cold, calculating affair. I have changed my views quite radically, but find from conversations with fellow psychologists that many still hold to the former view. This seems particularly to be the case with those I would categorise as following a behavioural approach to problems. My last quotation is from Polanyi in his paper 'Logic and Psychology':

> . . . the relation of the scientist to his surmises is one of passionate personal commitment. The effort that led to a surmize committed every fibre of his being to the quest his surmizes embody all his hopes.
> Such investments add up with frightening speed to the whole professional life of the scientist. To think of scientific workers cheerfully trying this and trying that, calmly changing course at each failure, is a caricature of a pursuit consuming a man's whole person. Any questing surmise necessarily seeks its own confirmation (Polanyi, 1968).

TYPES OF SCIENCE

It is a truism now to say that, to a scientist, his or her view of science is of great significance. But there were at least two models of science being debated at 'Models of Man'. One seemed to be more or less based on Newtonian science and the other on quantum mechanics or, as Zukav (1979) calls it, the 'new physics'. Zukav sums up some of these differences nicely as follows:

Newtonian physics	*Quantum mechanics*
Assumes an objective reality 'out there'	Does not assume an objective reality apart from our experience
Assumes we can observe something without changing it	Assumes we cannot observe something without changing it.
Claims to be based on 'absolute truth'; the way that nature really is 'behind the the scenes'	Claims only to correlate experience correctly
Aims to predict events	Aims only to predict probabilities

Our conception of reality and the nature of our access to it becomes of vital importance in our scientific quest. It seems that many psychologists espouse the Newtonian view and assume there actually is a reality 'out there' and one on which we can somehow get our hands. To illustrate the other viewpoint, Albert Einstein likened the external world to a watch, the workings of which we can only guess at:

> Physical concepts are free creations of the human mind, and are not, however it may seem, uniquely determined by the external world. In our endeavour to understand reality, we are somewhat like a man trying to understand the mechanism of a closed watch. He sees the face and the moving hands, even hears its ticking, but he has no way of opening the case. If he is ingenious he may form some picture of a mechanism which could be responsible for all the things he observes, but he may never be quite sure his picture is the only one which could explain his observations, He will never be able to compare his picture with the real mechanism and he cannot even imagine the possibility of the meaning of such a comparison (Einstein, 1938, in Einstein and Infield, 1971).

The nature of the scientific endeavour and the very nature of psychology itself was on trial at the 'Models of Man' conference. For some, the expressed aim was to accumulate *facts* to support a theory, for others the aim was more akin to a striving for *understanding*.

Perhaps because of his original training in physics and mathematics, Kelly (1955) clearly differentiated between these two scientific strategies. For the former position he coined the term *accumulative fragmentalism*—facts or 'truths' are collected like golden nuggets in the belief that they will all add up to a coherent whole come the Day of Judgment. The latter approach he described from the standpoint of the philosophy which underpins his whole psychology—that of *constructive alternativism.* This position does not say that one should not collect information, but rather that one might regard the present 'fact' as a stepping stone toward the erection of yet another experimental hypothesis; one that may explain the existing information in a better way—and so on. He says:

> While constructive alternativism does not argue against the collection of information, neither does it measure truth by the size of the collection. Indeed, it leads one to regard a large accumulation of facts as an open invitation to some far-reaching construction, which will reduce them to a mass of trivialities (Kelly, 1970).

An examination of Einstein's view of the nature of reality and of physical concepts likens him to a constructive alternativists as he faces the closed watch.

Kelly then continues his discussion of the two approaches to science by suggesting how exponents of each approach may deeply threaten the other:

> A person who spends a great deal of his time hoarding facts is not likely to be happy at the prospect of seeing them converted into rubbish. He is more likely to want them bound and preserved, a memorial to his personal achievement. A scientist, for example, who thinks this way, and especially a psychologist who does so, depends upon these facts to furnish the ultimate proof of his propositions. With these shining nuggets of truth in his grasp, it seems unnecessary for him to take responsibility for the conclusions he claims they thrust upon him. To suggest to him at this point that further human reconstruction can completely alter the appearance of the precious fragments he has accumulated, as well as the direction of their arguments, is to threaten his scientific conclusions, his philosophical position, and even his moral security. No wonder, then, that, in the eyes of such a conservatively minded person, our assumption that all facts are subject—are wholly subject—to alternative constructions looms up as culpably subjective and dangerously subversive to the scientific establishment (Kelly, 1970).

Thus, contradictory information or 'facts' are no threat in themselves to the 'constructive alternativist', they merely provide grounds for reconstruction and further experimentation. But for the 'accumulative fragmentalist', it could mean a major revision of his or her whole scientific way of life and theoretical base.

THE PSYCHOLOGISTS AND THEIR MODELS

All discussions at the 'Models of Man' conference were recorded and transcribed. As a participant, I received copies of these transcripts and it seemed an interesting idea to go through them to see if there were any ways in which a reason could be found to explain why the 'warring factions' (Reid, 1980) never made contact. Perhaps, as Du Preez (1972) found when analysing South African political party debates, they were disagreeing on some fundamental issues.

What I ended up by doing was going through the discussions in the transcripts and underlining repeated themes. I am not intending to present what follows as scientific data. There is, for instance, no reliability check. The underlying themes I sensed at the conference clearly influenced my approach to the typescripts. So I therefore read through the pages with some preconceived notion of what might be going on and selected those statements that seemed to exemplify a theme. I then searched for something that seemed to be the opposite point of view that was being argued. From the personal construct psychology standpoint, all constructs are regarded as bipolar. As in war, there are two sides. Gray (p. 32) spelled this out early when commenting on Shotter's paper:

> I am going to sound a note of warfare, because I think that what you talk of is something very different from scientific explanation and something actually not as important or valuable as scientific explanation. You offer us description and, as description, it is very good. But does it offer anything that we could not have got from a good novelist a hundred years ago? Secondly, if explanation is offered, you do not offer any means of testing your explanation. Of course, testing is the cardinal feature of scientific work through which we can descard theories which are proved useless; and so we can make progress. The danger in your approach is that we may go round in circles (Gray, 1980).

Table 1 Some constructs used by the 'Mechanists' at the Models of Man Conference (Chapman and Jones, 1980)

THE SCIENCE OF PSYCHOLOGY: THE SCIENTIFIC STUDY OF MAN	
Scientific study of man	Nonscientific study of man
Mechanism/Empiricism	Humanism/Theorizing
The person is his/her brain	(No obvious alternative)
Man studied biologically and and behaviourally	Man studied 'PSYCHOLOGICALLY'
Involves quantification of observable behaviour	Involves analysis of qualitative data from-unobservable events
Produces scientific explanations	Produces descriptions
Are testable	Often not testable
Is useful	Is not useful if not testable
Accumulate predictive laws	Accumulate nothing
Make scientific progress	Go round in circles

Thus, Table 1 shows some bipolar constructs which seemed to me to centre around the discussions of what psychology was about which came from those referred to as 'the mechanists'. All references to people and pages in this section refer to the published report of the conference in *Models of Man* (Chapman and Jones, 1980).

In a similar way, Table 2 shows the bipolar constructs that were extracted from the discussions exemplyfying some of the ideas coming from the 'humanists'. The ordering of the constructs does not represent any hierarchical relationships.

Table 2 Some constructs used by the 'Humanists' at the Models of Man Conference (Chapman and Jones, 1980)

What *is* the person?	The person as an object for study
Humanism	Mechanism
The person has purposes, intentions and performs actions	The person has behaviour
Should study the body of knowledge we possess as persons—experience	Should study behaviour
The person cannot be studied objectively	Psychology is the objective study of organisms
Reality is invented by people	Reality exists to be studied
Man is self-creating	Man is a mindless bureaucrat
This psychology leads toward larger possibilities for human beings—increases their capacity to alter the course of their lives	This psychology leads toward narrower possibilities for human beings—they are largely determined
This is a moral and political issue	

One thing that is apparent is that both mechanists and humanists are concerned with the nature of inquiry and its methods—but each gives this a different measure of importance. Both started off with a view that human beings were legitimate objects for study, but they differed radically in how this should be done. The mechanists took as their starting point the proposition that the science of psychology should concern itself with *the study of* individuals of groups. The humanists, however, said 'we do not want to start from there'. They were concerned with individuals as persons and seemed to want psychology to be asking a question, such as 'what *is* the person?' This confusion was voiced by Weinreich-Haste (p. 307) toward the end of the conference but it never became a central issue for discussion. she said:

Are we confusing models of science and models of person? We should try to tease out our implicit assumptions about the nature of the person and our implicit assumptions about what are legitimate and effective ways of doing research. As it is, there are examples of people doing essentially mechanistic-type research in humanistic fields and humanistic-type research in mechanistic fields (Weinreich-Haste, 1980).

While the nature of the scientific process was the most clear-cut issue for debate, the issue of the nature of the human person was never far away. But they can, in fact, be related if one examines the difference between the Newtonian and the 'new' physics. In the latter, the person is an integral part of the scientific procedure—'we cannot observe something without changing it'.

Another major issue that arose from time to time but was never fully spelled out concerned the relationship between psychology, society and politics. It seems from reading the transcripts that this might be linked to the models of science/person confusion and have something to do with reflexivity. That is, the extent to which psychologists see themselves as independent of the environment in which they exist and which they seek to influence. Some of the ideas expressed can be seen in Table 3.

There were those who dwelt on the nature of science and the role it should play in relation to society, and there were those who wished to talk about the ways in which psychologists, as the model makers, might have their views unconsciously influenced by society and the implications of this. There were also clear concerns expressed about the political effects of our

Table 3 Some constructs concerned with reflexivity used by participants at the Models of Man Conference (Chapman and Jones, 1980)

PSYCHOLOGY AND REFLEXIVITY	
Model stamped with views, myths etc. of society	Model not stamped with views, myths etc. of society
Restricts what psychology can achieve	Does not restrict what psychology can achieve
Cannot transcend society	Science can and should be independent of society
Cannot create any radical changes in society as other sciences have	Psychology can create radical changes as other sciences have
Model may threaten the ideological prejudices of society—what then?	Role of psychology is not to solve political problems
Psychological model may be the ideology which justifies the existing economic system	

actions. Harré (p. 213), for instance, commented that 'psychologists themselves are part of the devices by which the world is constructed: everything they do filters out into the world and creates its own facts'. Discussing the nature of 'the war', Frude (p. 12) said 'If there is a war, or a need for war, it is because our various models of man are locked into our political endeavours'. And Shotter (p. 127) amplified Broadbent's view that a psychological model may be the ideology which justifies the existing economic system, by remarking that 'the danger is that applied psychologists are merely satisfying the demands placed upon them by their clients or society at large. Hence they simply produce models which satisfy those demands and leave it at that'.

Having suggested that scientists are involved in, and committed to, what they are doing and presented some soft data to suggest some of the issues which concern some psychologists, I now want to return to the notion of threat and discuss some of its implications.

THREAT AND GUILT

Threat is defined as an awareness of the need to reconstrue our identity in some radical manner if events proceed as they are doing. Now, if events *do* continue in this threatening way, we may be persuaded by them and so be dislodged from our perch of self identity and experience guilt. Thus, scientists who adhere to a well-established approach may well experience guilt if truly and successfully threatened.

Kelly's definition of guilt contains no value judgment. It is a wholly personal experience. The criminal is just as likely to experience guilt when he finds himself helping an old lady across the street as is the saint who finds himself being irritated by a sinner. Both may perceive that they are *apparently dislodged from their core role structures*. For Kelly, a role is a course of activity based upon our interpretation of the thinking of those with whom we are enacting that role. Our core roles are those that concern our identities.

Take the hypothetical case of a psychologist who has spent a great deal of his life playing the science game to the advantage of himself, science and his colleagues. Part of his identity or core role structure, perhaps a large part, concerns his adherence to his work, his colleagues and his beliefs about the nature of science. For years he and his colleagues have had the field to themselves. There have been a few opposite views expressed, and when these happen they have been little more than voices crying in the wilderness. But, they find that, for no apparent reason, these voices are becoming more strident, people are beginning to listen to them, some articles are beginning to appear in valued learned journals. If our scientist, even for just a moment, entertains the idea that these voices are a force which may bring him and others to question his life's work—he will first experience *stress*—that is, he will be aware of potential threat. He is, however, only fully threatened if he then really does question his own worth, his own standing in the eyes of others as well as in his own eyes. If he discovers he has indeed been wrong all these years, his identity is affected.

> 'Guilt is psychological exile from one's own core role, regardless of where, when, with whom, or in what scenes the part has been played' (Kelly, 1955).

There are several ways in which he could deal with this guilt. He could simply decide that the zeitgeist is such that these new-fangled ideas are going to become popular and will, in time, partially eclipse his own group. Accepting the inevitable would result in his leading a less meaningful professional life—less acceptance of journal papers, more difficulty in obtaining research grants, fewer eager PhD students hammering on his door. But he may shrug his shoulders and say 'that is life and the nature of science'.

Or our psychologist may not be able to passively accept the situation. He cannot shut out the new ideas. As he finds them more and more persuasive he becomes aware that he is going to have to change quite radically. In the end he deals with this guilt by reconstruing himself and his science. He may be the perfectly non-personally involved researcher, dedicated to objectivity and truth. But I find myself inclined to agree with Agnew and Pyke (1969) when they say 'Perhaps there are researchers like that. We haven't met enough to fill a phone booth'.

Yet others may accept this idea that these 'humanists' have a point in putting their emphasis on, say, the importance of 'intentions' in the person, but find the implications of that acceptance too profound, requiring too deep and extensive changes in ways of construing themselves and the whole scientific enterprise to be wholly accepted. This latter person is the one who is likely to become *hostile*.

THREAT AND HOSTILITY

Kelly views hostility, as all other constructs within his theory, from the standpoint of the person. What does the hostile person think he or she is doing? The hostile person is actively extorting evidence to support a view that has already been seen to be a failure. This does not mean consciously worked out. But it means that, at some level of awareness, it is recognized that to change one's current standpoint would involve far too many other changes, and so events that would precipitate this extensive change cannot be allowed to continue. The hostile person has to cook the books. We refuse to acknowledge the importance of the new data that contradicts our position—we denigrate the researcher; we ignore the newcomers and say that ours is the only 'true' psychology and so on and so forth.

This does not only apply to psychologists. Mitroff (1974), for instance, comments that the scientists he studied during the series of space missions were prejudiced, dogmatic and sometimes unable or unwilling to change their views and would try to discredit evidence that contradicted their own hypotheses. Agnew and Pyke (1969) put it in more poetic terms:

> Since any experiment is open to criticism, the theorist always has a way out in rejecting unwelcome data. The rejection of a theory once accepted is like the rejection of a girl friend once loved—it takes more than a bit of negative evidence. In fact, the rest of the community can shake their collective heads in amazement at your blindness, your utter failure to recognize the glaring array of differences between your picture of the world, or the girl, and the data (Agnew and Pyke, 1969).

THE THREAT OF AGGRESSION

So much for those who are threatened and who may suffer guilt and some of their responses. What about those who do the threatening? During the 'Models of Man' discussions, Reid (p. 11) commented that, if one must use a warlike metaphor, then, in the battle between the two camps 'the missiles tend to come from one direction—the humanist camp'. Kelly defines aggression as that which we do when we are actively elaborating our construct system. In this sense, the humanists were certainly being aggressive and were perceived to be so. They were actively elaborating their views of themselves and of their view of psychology—with the emphasis on 'active'. It is the taking of the initiative to change oneself and the world around one—or both. In doing this, we disrupt others—we threaten their comfortable life style. This is never more obvious than in the case of the adolescent aggressively defining himself in his world and causing severe disruptions and threats to adults around and about. It was thus that the humanists at the conference were seen by the others to be aggressive, whereas from their own point of view, they were actively seeking to push against the obstacles they saw laying in their path—and the mechanists in general were countering this aggression by being hostile. In a few cases, however, it did seem as if some real attempts were being made to use another way to counter threat—by reconstruing.

NORMAL VERSUS REVOLUTIONARY SCIENCE

I would now like to broaden the discussion by suggesting the role threat may play in the history of science. It seems to me that what I am describing as having occurred at the previous conference is a good example of the dichotomy Kuhn draws between normal and revolutionary science. Those indulging in normal science are content; all's well with the scientific world. Of course, psychology does not have a single paradigm. But I think it can be argued that some psychologists act as if it did. They are those who adhere to the scientific-study-of-man model, with its emphasis on the scientific method, they act 'as if' this were the only paradigm for a 'proper' psychology. This has resulted, amongst other things, in the exclusion of Freud's theory as a legitimate area for study because of the supposed 'untestability' of most of its concepts. It certainly does not include the humanists' concern with the study of the person (although some have attempted to bring this within the paradigm, for example, Rychlak (1977) in this book *The Psychology of Rigorous Humanism*.

Only future observers of science will be able to state whether or not psychology is witnessing the crisis prior to the revolutionary phase of science—or even whether we are in the revolutionary phase already. But Kuhn's seems a useful model to apply to the activities of psychologists at the 'Models of Man' conference. Toward the end of the discussions, Hargreaves (p. 308) related this to our need to philosophize:

> I think that one descriptive point that Kuhn makes is that when science is proceeding normally the philosophers of science are ignored. When crisis occurs between paradigms it is then that their views are sought. It is perfectly clear that some people here are in crisis—others not! The others then are with us under sufference to some degree, and they are saying, 'What is all the fuss about?' Those in crisis are saying, 'Come on, let's get some philosophizing done'.

Science can thus be seen as advancing, to some extent at least, by the ability of the 'newcomers' to deal with and overcome the threats roused in their adversaries. Using the concept of threat in relation to hostility makes it easier to understand comments such as those of Mahoney (1976).

> The revolutionary phase of scientific growth is often long and fitful. When the new paradigm has ascended to some degree of popularity, this does not automatically result in the concession of the old guard. Paradigm clashes may continue for centuries—with cold wars, frequent skirmishes, and occasional head-on confrontation. In one sense, then, old paradigms seldom die a quiet, dignified death—their demise is often marked by prolonged groans of atrophy and unmistakable conceptual sclerosis (Mahoney, 1976).

The physicist Max Planck talked in similar vein in 1949:

> A new scientific truth does not triumph by convincing its opponents and making them see the light, but rather because its opponents eventually die, and a new generation grows up that is familiar with it (Planck, 1949).

We thus have our normal scientists in psychology with their philosophy of accumulative fragmentalism; their belief in conventional research

Table 4 The contrast or implicit poles of constructs used by the 'Humanists' against the emergent poles of constructs used by the 'Mechanists'

Humanists are against:	Mechanists favour:
The person as an object for study	Scientific study of man
Mechanism	Mechanism/Empiricism
The person has behaviour	The person *is* his/her brain
Should study behaviour	Man studied biologically and behaviourally
	Involves quantification of observable behaviour
Psychology is the objective study of organisms	Produces scientific explanations
Reality exists to be studied	Are testable
Man is a mindless bureaucrat	Is useful
This psychology leads toward narrower possibilities for human beings—they are largely determined	Accumulate predictive laws
	Make Scientific progress

Table 5 The contrast or implicit poles of constructs used by the 'Mechanists' against the emergent poles of constructs used by the 'Humanists'

Humanists favour:	Mechanists are against:
What *is* the person?	Nonscientific study of man
Humanism	Humanism/Theorizing
The person has purposes, intentions and performs actions	(No obvious alternative)
Should study the body of knowledge we possess as persons experience	Man studied 'psychologically'
	Involves analysis of qualitative data from unobservable events
The person cannot be studied objectively	Produces descriptions
Reality is invented by people	Often not testable
Man is self-creating	Is not useful if not testable
This psychology leads toward larger possibilities for human beings—increases their capacity to alter the course of their lives	Accumulate nothing
	Go round in circles

methods which also determine the sorts of questions that it is legitimate to ask and their personal involvement in maintaining the status quo, put 'at risk' and threatened by those hammering on the door. Those who seek to change all this are only themselves likely to be threatened if they start to doubt that they are on the right path.

Looking again at the constructs extracted from the 'Models of Man' discussions, it is important to note that the humanists have something which they are clearly against—it is those mechanists (see Table 4). The mechanists, however, seem to be in a much more difficult situation, for it looks as if the only opposite conception they have to their own position is something that is 'not psychology' (see Table 5).

It is no wonder, if this is the case, that any personal doubts about their own position caused by the strident voices of the humanists would be profoundly disquieting—for these voices are threatening not only their particular model of psychology, but the whole of psychology itself. And, if they are personally involved in being a psychologist, their personal identity can indeed truly be said to be threatened.

REFERENCES

Agnew, N. M., and Pyke, S. W. (1969). *The Science Game.* New Jersey, Prentice Hall.

Chapman, A. J., and Jones, D. (eds.) (1980). *Models of Man.* Leicester, British Psychological Society.

Du Preez, P. (1972). The construction of alternatives in Parliamentary debate: a psychological theory and political analysis, *S. Africa. J. Psychol.*, 23–40.

Einstein, A., and Infield, L. (1971). *The Evolution of Physics.* Cambridge, Cambridge University Press.

Kelly, G. A. (1955). *The Psychology of Personal Constructs*, Vols. 1 and 2. New York, Norton.

Kelly, G. A. (1970). A brief introduction to personal construct theory. In: D. Bannister (ed.) *Perspectives in Personal Construct Theory*, London, Academic Press.

Landfield, A. W. (1954). A movement interpretation of threat, *J. Abn. Soc. Psychol.*, **40**, 529–532.

Mahoney, M. J. (1976). *Scientist as Subject: the psychological imperative*, Cambridge, Mass., Ballinger.

Mitroff, I. I. (1974). *The Subjective Side of Science*, New York, Elsevier.

Planck, M. (1949). Scientific autobiography, and other papers, with a memorial address on Max Planck by Max von Lane, translated from the German by Frank Gaynor. New York, Philosophical Library.

Polanyi, M. (1968). Logic and psychology, *Amer. Psychologist*, **23**, 27–43.

Rychlak, J. (1977). *The Psychology of Rigorous Humanism.* New York, Wiley.

Watson, J. D. (1969). *The Double Helix*, New York, New American Library.

Zukav, G. (1979). *The Dancing Wu Li Masters* New York, Hutchinson.

Section B: Threats to the individual as group member

Threatened Identities
Edited by G. Breakwell

Social Identity and the Half-Asian Child

Peter Hitch

Writings on social identity can generally be grouped under a number of themes: the nature of social identity, and in particular its importance as part of the individual's psychological structure (the Self, and I and so on). Then there are theoretical and empirical works on the development of primary social identity, notably sexual and ethnic. Also included are enforced changes of identity, e.g., to that of prisoner or retired person. Finally, there are the less straightforward areas where a person's social identity is neither uncomplicated nor acquired without trouble. Studies in these areas tend to concentrate on the experience of migrant groups and minority cultures.

Less frequent, but becoming more common, are considerations of what happens when a person's identity comes under threat. This might occur where a migrant changes cultures and is confronted with a minority status definition of himself. The challenges to existing identities and the ways of coming to terms with these challenges need to be seen as more than oddities or deviant cases. They also have practical significance when attempting to understand the position of second-generation immigrants in Britain, and it is in the area of identity confusion that some of the most interesting current work is being done.

However, for all the recognized difficulties involved in moving from one culture or group to another, there are cases which represent a more extreme degree of maladjustment than identity confusion. This is the situation where a person is socially assigned to a group, but does not wish to be a member. What is more, the members of that group also reject him and would not admit her to membership even if he wished to join. In addition, the group to which she feels she belongs is also denying him membership. She is rejected by both groups and belongs nowhere. Lest this calamitous situation be thought to be a figment of an abstract imagination, it is suggested that there is a social category—the word 'group' begs the question—for which this situation is a reality. The members of this category can be expected to have severe problems in placing themselves psychologically and socially.

This chapter will review the state of knowledge about this category, and ascertain to what extent its existence puts to the test theories and concepts about the nature of the self-concept and of identity.

CHILDREN OF MIXED RACE

Children of mixed race, although numerically small in Britain in relation to the coloured migrant population, are significantly over-represented in statistics of social problems. In one British urban community the rate of juvenile crime among half-Asians during the years 1970–1972 was twice as high as among nonAsians, and five times as high as among full-Asians, (Batta, McCulloch and Smith, 1975). The children are more likely to come into care, to come in earlier and to stay longer than other ethnic groups McCulloch, Batta and Smith, 1979). They are over-represented in Local Authority day nurseries and among cases in Child Guidance Clinics, in marked contrast to the situation of Asian children who appear especially protected within the family situation (Mawby and Batta, 1980).

At first sight, aetiological explanations would not be hard to find as they would seem to lie in the circumstances of early childhood. Half-Asian children are usually the result of unstable liaisons between Asian men and white women. The Asian community discourages male relationships with white women and under this pressure many desert their common law wives and any children and return to their own kin. If the mother, facing considerable hostility from her family, is impelled to reject the child physically or psychologically, it may be that she had already been partly estranged from her own community at the time of her relationship with an Asian. Such children are thus especially likely to experience a broken home, with all the ensuing problems.

However, this is only one aspect of the problem. The early familial environment of the child will be steering it towards membership of the white English culture. Partly, this is the natural result of being close to the main caretaker, who is white. This is compounded by the traditionally distant role of Asian fathers *vis-a-vis* infant care. In Bradford, the child will learn English with a Yorkshire accent, will have little or no knowledge of the language of the father and will not be exposed to Asian media like ethnic television programmes or films. In short, the half-Asian will see herself as English, like her mother.

When those whose physical features differ from the white norm begin to meet the outside world of the street and the school or, very often, the Children's Home, they find that other English children do not regard them as one of them. Instead, they treat them as if they were Asian, coloured, black, 'wog' and so on. This is a situation of great threat and it is hardly surprising that children become very sensitive about the contradiction between what they see as their group membership and their colour.

Some illustrations extracted from case files of social service agencies bear this out:

(i) When I am classed as being black then I go into a raging fury because I am not. Just because I am more brown than white does not mean to say that I am a foreigner (child in care).

(ii) *X* is the only mixed-race child in the family . . . his half-sister has been vindictive and vicious, refers to black animals and has suggested that they be sent back to the jungle (social worker).

(iii) *C* is very conscious and sensitive of his colour. Mother states that he hates the fact that he is coloured and claims that since he was two to three years old he has shown resentment by stealing and damaging articles that belong to her. When he was younger, if he had a wound and picked the scab, his skin did not return to its former colour, and he said that he hoped he would develop spots all over so that he could become white (social worker).

(iv) Of twenty-one cases of mixed-race children at a Classifying School, ten were reported as being 'colour sensitive', to the degree that it was regarded as worthy of report.

In the last case, it was interesting to find that colour sensitivity was more marked in those children who came from stable households, i.e., where there was no neglect, abandonment or marital disharmony. This is not to say that colour self-consciousness is not a symptom of psychological stress resulting from domestic upsets. However, this is not the only cause.

The final element in the identity problem is that there is no hope of recognition by immigrant communities. The half-Asian child, in particular, has few if any usable kinship links. He will not have an Asian language for conversation. In short, she will lack nearly all the cultural attributes necessary for acceptance by the Asian community. It should be emphasized that one is not generalizing to children of mixed race as a whole. In a study by Wilson (1981) using a sample of children, one of whose parents (usually the father) was African, Afro–Caribbean or Afro–American, nearly three-quarters saw themselves as 'brown' or 'mixed'. It is perhaps only when colour and culture are operating in the same direction that the problems become acute. Thus it is probable that the identity difficulties are concentrated among half-Asians.

Faced with this distressing phenomenon, it is worth while enquiring to what extent current theories of social identity are adequate to encompass it.

There are two ways of relating a concrete phenomenon to a grand theory. The first is to reduce the macrotheoretical postulates and concepts to lower order hypotheses and then to test them against the concrete phenomenon.

This deductive way assumes that all phenomena will be within its frame of reference, and that all middle-range concepts are derivable from the main theory. The alternative way is to derive concepts from the phenomena themselves and then to work upwards to determine what theory or theories would best encompass such concepts. The latter method will be used at first since social scientists have proposed lower order concepts which, it has been maintained, describe the condition of some children of mixed race.

MARGINAL MAN

If there is any social category into which the half-caste has been placed it is that of 'marginal man'. This term has now almost become a cliché and one, until recently, unchallenged in the literature. Before investigating its relevance, it is therefore worth spending some time evaluating the concept in its own terms.

Although the term was invented by Park (1928), it was Stonequist (1937, 1942) who gave it its first full elaboration. In 1937, he pictured the marginal man as someone who 'leaves one group or culture without making a satisfactory adjustment to another, and finds himself on the margin of each and a member of neither'. However, Stonequist was not entirely consistent, and his 1942 definition refers to a different conception:

> '... an individual who lives in, or who has ties of kinship with, two or more interacting societies between which there exist sufficient incompatibility to render his own adjustment to them difficult or impossible. He does not quite 'belong' or feel at home in either group'.

Such a person cannot really be said to have left one group to join another. If he has, then his leaving is only partially successful, for he still has significant ties with that group. An example of the difference between the two concepts can be seen in the hypothetical cases of two persons who are upward socially mobile but are not secure in their new status. The former has left his working-class culture or disowned her parents, but has failed to become integrated into middle class society. On the other hand, the latter has, for some reason, never severed himself from his roots. Precisely because she is trying to live in two worlds at once he is unable to live in either. His is not a case of leaving one group and *then* not being able to make a satisfactory adjustment. On the contrary, there is an implication that she cannot adjust because he has failed to leave her group of origin. She may move freely in the higher circles and be fully accepted, yet whenever he goes back to her old family, pub or community feels his old identity being re-awakened by something which is more than nostalgia. According to Green (1947), this is the quintessence of marginality.

Because of the differing nature of these two definitions, it is difficult to know which to apply. Many subsequent writers have drawn on a mixture of both. McDavid and Harari (1968) picture the marginal man as one who lives in a no-man's land between the subculture of his origin and that of his later position. Generally speaking, writers portray a social and psychological situation, rather than describe how this came about. This is just as well, seeing that there is a further ambiguity about what it means to leave a group. It is possible to do so in three ways: physically, socially and psychologically, and it is by no means certain that one always leaves a group in all three, let alone simultaneously. The exile or deportee will have left his homeland physically, she may have no social contacts yet still retain his internalized ethnic or cultural identity, as witness the anguish of exiles from Ovid onwards.

Less extreme example of these types of incongruity would include a career army officer who is cashiered, or a long-serving prisoner who is released. A normal occurrence is a person who retires from a work situation where he has closely identified himself with the group. The blow can be softened by 'anticipatory resocialization', or, as more commonly termed, 'preparing for retirement'. The same is done by having predischarge groups of long-stay mental patients; here snags can occur if these groups generate a warm atmosphere that makes leaving all the harder.

On the other hand, it is not necessary to be oneself a migrant to experience the dilemma of living in two cultural worlds. Second generation immigrants are particularly held to have this problem (Green, 1947; Krausz, 1971). Further, the dilemmas may be caused by not being allowed to leave a group. An adolescent who feels the physical and psychological tug of adulthood, yet who is still expected to play the role of child *vis-a-vis* his significant adult others, will be in a marginal position, if he has also internalized the self-conception derived from this role. If half of her feels an adult and half a child, he will be in an ambiguous position of true marginality. It is clear that there are many ways of not leaving, or only partially leaving, a group.

There may equally be as many ways of not joining another group. It may, for example, be through indifference. This is exemplified by the case of the Pakistani peasant who comes to Britain with so much of his culture surrounding him that he can be said to be relatively immune from the influences of his host culture, except where enshrined institutions have a quasi-legal constraint on his behaviour (Hitch, 1977). On the other hand, the immigrant's daughter who wishes to have social relations with white male adolescents may find herself challenged by the representatives of her culture of origin. The dutiful daughter, on the other hand, will experience little overt conflict, though her exposure to the classroom norms in a mixed-sex school will undoubtedly give her some feeling of marginality.

A more complex situation arises where the second-generation immigrant copes with culture conflict by participating with other peers in a 'marginal culture', one which is '... a complete and unitary culture poised between two other cultures, and for that reason described as marginal. For the individual concerned ... it is not marginal but normal' (Goldberg, 1941). Another coping strategy, adopted by many Asian teenagers in Britain, is to 'get by' in the British teenage culture, at the same time retaining a firm Asian ethnic identity (Ballard, 1975).

Next, there is the case of the person who seeks to join a group but is not allowed to enter it. This experience will be particularly stressful to someone who has already internalized the values of the group, the point being that the values of other groups have been rejected, or not internalized. Therefore, it is not a question of culture conflict, and the crisis is entirely due to an abnormal relationship to the group of aspiration. As Green (1947) says, 'it is those Negroes and second-generation immigrants whose values and behaviour most approximate to those of the dominant majority who express the most personal crises'. Finally, there is the case which Green considers to be the quintessence of marginality, where an individual, being unable to leave totally the group of orientation becomes identified with *both* groups, and is thus psychologically prevented from truly joining either.

This need not be problematic. It is possible to run with the hare and hunt with the hounds, and fence-sitting can be a psychological trait as well as a piece of political strategy. However, if allegiance to one group implies, logically or materially, the rejection of the other to have psychological ties with both groups is painful. It is not easy in Northern Ireland to be half-Catholic and half-Protestant. One must therefore agree with Green that marginal man is essentially a psychological concept, and that for two cultures to clash they must both have been internalized.

The essence of Stonequist's concept, which runs through subsequent reformulations of Goldberg (1941), Green (1947) and Antonovsky (1956), is of a person who cannot be fully and unambiguously a member of one culture. But, as many writers have pointed out, it is possible to belong to a culture without being regarded by other people as a member of the group possessing the culture. Marginal man may have difficulty placing himself, but marginality can also arise from a person's being excluded from groups to which he thinks he belongs. Indeed, it was that which Merton (1968) saw as the condition of marginal man. 'Qualitative descriptions of the behaviour of marginal men ... can be analytically recast as that special and restricted case of reference group behaviour in which the individual seeks to abandon one membership group for another to which he is socially forbidden access.'

Essentially the same definition had been given by Kerkhoff and

McCormick (1955), a marginal man being 'one who uses a nonmembership group as a reference group ... who has internalized the norms of a particular group ... but he is not completely recognized by others as being a legitimate member of that group'.

The value of this term is that it concentrates simultaneously on both sides of a particular relation between a person and the social world. Its starting point is the individual who is a member of one group and wishes to leave this group (socially and psychologically) and to join another. Entry is somehow prevented, perhaps by the negative attitudes of the group towards the individual, or perhaps by the fact that the necessary qualifications and credentials are for some reasons unattainable. It becomes of crucial importance if the group to which entery is sought is crucial to the individual's values, for then psychological distress will occur. Groups which are psychologically important in this respect have been termed 'reference groups' and a discussion of this 'middle-range' concept is relevant.

MARGINALITY AND REFERENCE GROUP THEORY

The term has a number of meanings. Its founder, Hyman (1942), used it in the sense of a group one uses as a bench mark against which one judges one's own status, experience and performance. Merton (1968) termed this a 'comparative' reference group, and added the concept of 'normative' reference group, denoting the source of values assimilated by individuals *who may not be members of the group*. This last clause is important. It is possible to be an active member of one group but consciously list another group as reference.

Newcomb (1961) in a study of female students at an American College found that many of them had prior allegiances to their families. They were psychologically participating in two groups, but since only one of them had any meaning for them, they could hardly be said to be 'marginal women'. They did not share the current political attitudes, and generally their participation in the student culture was less than wholehearted.

If reference group is not to be regarded as coterminous with membership group, the same applies to its relationship to role. A woman may occupy a primary role like that of wife or mother without identifying herself with it psychologically or with other women in the same role. Similarity of *behaviour* with other similar role players does not imply commitment or even approval. Role behaviour, as used sociologically, is a function of others' expectations and structural constraints rather than the actor's attitudes. Rose (1962) cites the case of 'a Negro who hates being a Negro but is obliged by his Negroness to act in accord with the expectations for Negroes' behaviour'.

On the other hand, Merton's marginal man has internalized the values of a group to which he is denied access. Even though Merton assumes that a group has been discarded beforehand this is not essential to the concept. Nor is it vital that marginal man be seen as having two reference groups in the way that Mann (1969) claims when he states that 'marginality is the condition of being caught between two conflicting reference groups'. Indeed, the marginal man has no conflicting group loyalties. He has exchanged all his pounds for francs but the French will not accept his currency. The half-Asian children we described earlier are precisely in this position. They have whites as their reference group, but they are not admitted to this group when outside the family. Instead they are assigned at best to the 'group' of half-castes. This is not a group but a category and so there is no culture. either marginal or 'straight'. The category of half-castes in Britain does not form a community, nor does it provide a source of values for its members.

The refinement of the concept of 'group' led to yet another consideration in the already bewildering notion of reference group analysis. Leaving aside the fact that one can refer to a unit which is difficult or impossible to designate as a sociological unit, like a philosophy (Pollis 1968), one can have psychological allegiances to collections of people who are not organized in any social, or indeed psychological, way. Sherif and Sherif (1969) use the term 'reference set' in relation to such units as women, a social class, and an ethnic situation. (As the word 'set' has other meanings in psychology, it seems preferable to speak of reference *category*.) So half-coloured do not form a group but a category, and there is no culture, either marginal or 'straight'. The category of half-Asian, let alone half-coloured, does not form a community nor does it provide a source of values for its members.

Even more striking is the fact that the reference group is the one in which the half-Asian children have been socialized from birth. They take it for granted that it is their membership group until they meet real-life members who effectively deny them access. Yet it is the only group they know, and this makes them essentially different from the migrant or social climber. To be denied access to a group of which you have considered yourself to be a member since birth is a frightening experience, and one that is not usually thought of in connection with either Stonequist's or Merton's formulation.

In the specific context with which this discussion is concerned there is an additional disqualification preventing a marginal person joining his membership group. This concerns language, a factor which is important in two ways. Without going to the extremes of linguistic derminism, there is little doubt that language influences and restricts the range of categories used in the structuring and transmission of experience, and provides common frames of reference for members of a group sharing a particular language. Along with other, more normative, cultural factors, language will be important in differentiating the ways of life of Urdu and English speakers. So the half-Asian children who have been brought up with English as their mother tongue will by virtue of this inhabit a different social world from their Asian counterparts. The second point needs no elaboration; a child who cannot speak another language is *ipso facto* excluded from a group which uses that language in day-to-day affairs.

The relevance of both these considerations is that it is not necessary for a marginal man to be excluded from a group by that group's decision. He can have excluded himself by not possessing the language skills that enable her to participate in the life of the group, and by not sharing in those aspects of the culture that are linguistically influenced. This, therefore, adds another complication to the concept of marginality.

In Merton's terms, a marginal man is a person who aspires to belong to a reference group but who is ineligible. He is 'apt to be rejected by his membership group for repudiating its values'. But the half-Asian child is labelled by whites as being a member of a nonwhite group. He was not repudiated the values of the half-Asian group because she has never belonged to it. So he has not psychologically abandoned one group to join another.

These complications make it all the more difficult to apply the description of American mulattoes given by Stonequist in the British context. In America, the labels black and white do not have such strong *cultural* referents as they do in Britain, and language is not a factor. Recent American writing has portrayed mulatto children as racially ambiguous with an ability to 'move more easily between racial groups than other blacks or whites', (Schafft, 1976). Research on race relations in Britain only recognizes two colours, and so there is no research on half-Black. Leaving aside the additional linguistic and cultural problem faced by the half-Asian child there is no evidence that the half-West Indian does not experience being assigned what she feels to be an incorrect colour. (Some of the examples cited earlier were of half-West Indian children.) British society in racial matters is not exactly 'tolerant of ambiguity'.

To be fair, it must be recorded that the application in America has not gone unchallenged either. Wirth and Goldhamer (1944) assert that 'the modern mulatto is brought up in a *Negro* home, surrounded by *Negro* relatives, in a *Negro* community'. They believe the Anglo-Indian, as depicted by Hedin (1934), to be the only true ideal-type marginal man.

> During the British Raj, the Eurasian was seen as a member of the colonized by the colonizers and of the colonizers by the colonized. No matter whose definition the Eurasian accepted, the resultant self-image would be invalidated by rejection.' (Breakwell, 1978.)

Up to this point, the discussion has been on the point of marginality, rather than its psychological consequences. This is partly a consequence of staying within a sociological frame of reference and partly due to confusing marginal position with marginal experience. There seems to be a consensus that certain pathological traits are a direct consequence of marginality. Park (1928) wrote of 'spiritual instability, intensified self-consciousness, restlessness and malaise'. Kerkhoff and McCormick (1955) presented a composite picture derived from several descriptions to be found in the literature:

> 'The marginal man is said to be characterized by serious doubts about his place in any social situation. He is conscious of his relationships with friends and acquantances and is fearful of rejection . . . (he shows) characteristic sudden shifts in mood and an inability to make up his mind to act decisively. . . . He is painfully self-conscious in the presence of other people. . . . His hypersensitivity is seen in his excessive worry about the future . . . a restless feeling that gnaws at him. . . . All of the above leads him to be highly critical of other people and to feel that others treat him unjustly (p. 52).'

In their own study of children on an American Indian reservation, the authors found that those Indian children who identified with the white group showed marginal personality traits which tended to be more pronounced with an increase in the amount of resistance encountered from the white group (degree of resistance was used as an independent variable since 'total impermeability' was not encountered, but this would of course not apply in a more overtly racial situation).

Such feelings of isolation will only be vague if the situation is that type of marginality where there is an ambiguity of cultural belonging or a clash in cultural frames of reference. It will happen if there are multiple reference groups which fight for supremacy within the individual, as in the case of the 'frustrated' career-woman housewife. Conflicts of a more conscious nature will arise where there is a conflict between reference group and membership group. Reference has been made earlier to people who cannot break psychological ties with the group they have left, and here again reference group theory can be an alternative and perhaps more useful framework of analysis than marginality.

For the half-Asian child who is denied access to his reference, problems are more acute still. The child who had assumed that she is white now finds herself not accepted by whites as one of them. It is not that his company is shunned; he will be accepted but only essentially to the extent that full Asians are accepted in white peer groups, though language will clearly be a factor in his favour. It is that she will have to fight harder for recognition and it may well be that she finds access only to deviant juvenile groups and 'volunteers' to take on the more hazardous roles; hence the high conviction rate mentioned earlier.

The stresses are nothing to do with a clash of multiple reference groups as as there is only one. Neither can one say the child is on the margin of two cultures since he has been firmly socialized into white culture, and the culture of nonwhites means nothing to him. What we have here is not ambiguity of reference but a denial of identity.

THEORIES OF SOCIAL IDENTITY

It is thus pertinent to explore macrotheories of the nature of identity. There is a tendency to link the social disconfirmation of identity with its social creation. There is in fact no logical connection between the two. The fact that schizophrenia can be 'cured' by phenothiazine injections does not prove that the illness has purely biochemical origins. Similarly, although identity needs to be confirmed in social relationships, and can indeed be destroyed in them, its origin could conceivably lie elsewhere. However, the crucial dependence of identity on its social context is argued most strongly by sociologically-oriented social psychologists. In other words, to assess whether such a threat to one's social self-conception would be painful, it is important to discover not only how crucial is the social origin of identity but also how stable or inflexible it is (depending on one's point of view).

In spite of a long history of theoretical and research endeavour, the depiction of these aspects of a person's self-image which relate to membership of a community is not exactly a coherent one. This is partly due to differing views of the nature of the self and its structure. The self is seen either as unified or made up of separate components like the jewels in a crown, each having its own moment of display according to where the light falls (or differentiation may be a phenomenological question, the answer varying for each individual (Gergen, 1971)). Other disputes concern its intrinsic versus its situationally determined nature. However, the main difficulty has been in giving recognition to the fact that a person lives in a society which is itself structured, not only into roles but also into groups, institutions and membership categories. Once one gets beyond the fact that, to put it simply, a person's self-concept is bound to be affected deeply by the perceptions held by those who are close and influential, one comes up against the problem of the two social psychologies. The social psychology which takes its orientation from social psychology is at its happiest when dealing with aspects of the self which can be seen as individual attributes or qualities, like temperament, prowess at sports or intellectual pursuits and possession of habits. These tend to have a high emotional loading either simply in terms of self esteem (for example, Coopersmith, 1967) or more subtly in terms of evaluation, potency and activity (Osgood *et al.*, 1957). In effect, many self-concept scales are attitude scales turned inwards. Sometimes the range of aspects is enlarged to include sex-related characteristics and social roles. The crucial point, however, is that they are given the same dynamic status as psychological characteristics. 'I am a black' is often included as being in the same category scheme as 'I am sometimes shy'.

A basic distinction is made between organized and other/social selves (Burns, 1979). The social self is seen as the self as the individual believes others see and evaluate him/her. Since this uses exactly the same range of characteristics, social categories and roles have no particular special place. One's consciousness of one's position in the vertical and horizontal social order does not appear to warrant a special place in the self-constellation. Primary or core identity has been highlighted by the humanistic psychologists, but primary or core *social* identity is only in the sidelines.

It would be expected that sociological social psychologists would have more to say about social aspects of the self-concept. Unfortunately from the early days, theorizing took the form of sociological imperialism, where everything is regarded as social in origin. For G. H. Mead, the self is formed in the same way as other objects—through the 'definition' made by others, chronologically and essentially others come first. The individual's self-conception will contain the characteristics and values that others attribute to him.

One awkward question that arose during the development of symbolic interaction was 'who are these others?' If the self is the 'generalized other' does this mean that it represents some sort of conversational stew of internal voices? Or does it assume that all that all the voices will say the same (which would be hotly denied by conflict-theory sociologists)? Or perhaps some people are more important than others? The last question relates to Mead's use of the term 'significant others', a term not used by Mead and which remained vague for many years. It carried the implication that it was individuals who were crucial and diverted attention away from higher-order phenomena such as groups, social classes and cultures. It also seemed to deny the individual any choice in the matter. It was not until the invention of the concept of 'reference group' that active subjectivity began to have a place. This demanded giving more substance to the 'I' than Mead had ever done, and divided symbolic interactionists into two camps, those following Herbert Blumer and those associated with Manford Kuhn.

Basically, theories of identity held by sociologists are more social than sociological, and although their ideas seem still largely ignored by psychologists, they are to be seen as an alternative psychology rather than a link between psychology and sociology. Thus 'social' means something more than the influence of other people, and identity means more than a self-description in terms of qualities. What may be termed 'social identity' is that aspect of the cognized self which refers to membership of a group, or category, of social significance. The list in the literature is endless: student, prisoner, Protestant and so on. Frequently quoted is the self-labelling of Lyndon Johnson, the former U.S. President, as 'a free man, an American, a United States senator, a Democrat, a liberal, a conservative, a Texan, a taxpayer, a rancher, and not as young as I used to be nor as old as I expect to be'. All these are social in that by using them one places oneself in a particular position in the world of other people, a world that is patterned and structured.

President Johnson had not been all these things since birth, and consequently his social identity underwent change. Not all the changes would have had fundamental implication for the self. Getting married or retiring will be more important than joining the Social Democratic Party. All the same, this has to be empirically tested—being a member of a working man's club could conceivably be more important than being a husband. Just as there are primary and secondary roles, so there are primary and secondary social identities. The distinction between the two is again a matter for empirical testing, but it cannot be assumed that this will be elicited by survey-type questions. Using an open-ended instrument, Mulford and Salisbury (1954) found that sex and age identities were only rarely mentioned. The answer is that these are more likely to be part of the 'taken for granted' world that ethnomethodologists attempt to uncover. And one wonders if only 10 per cent of women would mention sex identity in 1981!

If membership of a particular group or category is salient and is either terminated from outside, threatened, or disputed this must have clear implications for social identity. Beginning with a discussion of Mead, and the problems arising from his formulation, attention will be focussed on work which attempts to clarify those aspects of reference group theory which are crucial to social identity.

SYMBOLIC INTERACTIONISM AND THE STABILITY OF THE SELF

Mead's views of the self, mostly contained in a collection of lectures (Mead, 1968), came about as a result of asking the question: how is cooperative behaviour possible? People respond to each other, not in a mindless stimulus-response way, but by psychologically interpreting each other's actions. When one makes a request for an action to be done, the requester must have an image of the act being done and the respondent must also have the same image. Society is only possible where people can imaginatively recreate the intentions behind the 'gestures' that other people make. In addition this entails the 'ability of the human being to respond to his own gestures. This ability enables different human beings to respond in the same way to the same gestures, thereby sharing one another's experiences' (Meltzer, 1978).

If one can respond to one's own gestures, then this implies one has a *self*, which the owner can praise, blame, punish and so on. One can thus direct actions at oneself. Meltzer's statement of how the self is created is more succinct than Mead's:

> The mechanism whereby the individual becomes able to view himself as an object is that of role-taking, involving the problems of communication. . . . It is only by taking the role of others that the individual can come to see himself as an object. The standpoint of others provides a platform for getting outside oneself and thus viewing oneself. The development of the self is concurrent with the development of the ability to take roles.

Through these roles and the internalization of gestures that goes with them, the child builds up a composite internal picture of herself based on the various expectations held by role partners. This Mead terms the 'generalized other', a generalized role or standpoint from which the child views himself and his behaviour, and which represents the set of standpoints shared by members of the group.

One major difficulty with this conception is that it seems to imply that the self is continually changed according to the social context. Although it may be fallacious to take the commonsense view that personal identity is something that is gained in childhood, reworked in heat in adolescence and stays unaltered for the duration of life, there is, nevertheless, something intuitively unsatisfactory about the idea of the self as being fundamentally unstable. This is due, in part, to the emphasis on interaction and behaviour which are relatively fluid and variable. Mead called his theory 'social behaviourism', and any behavioural theory of the self has to answer the charge of positing an identity which is chameleon-like. It is true that Mead considered that at some stage the child's self-development comes to an end when the interaction of the generalized other has been achieved. But Mead never developed a full theory of child development, nor did he explore the paradox of an identity which arises out of society and yet can transcend all the varieties and vicissitudes of different norms and cultures, like the English Colonial Civil Servant dressing for dinner in the wilds of Africa.

There is indeed recognition by some theorists that there is a stable core which prevents a person from being a totally malleable victim. Lindesmith and Strauss (1968) say that 'the generalized other . . . is not a mere incorporation into the person; it is an assimilation attended . . . with anguish, anxiety, concern and care'. Berger (1966), too, admits that transformation of the self cannot occur *ad infinitum*: 'transformability of the self depends not *only* on its social context, but also on the degree of habituation to previous identities, and perhaps also on certain genetically given traits'. In neither case are the ideas amplified to any extent, and it is not surprising that what undergraduates most remember of symbolic interactionism are the fundamental changes in identity involved in becoming a convict (Berger, 1966), or a mental patient (Goffman, 1970).

These examples are impressive precisely because the change in social situation is total in more senses than one. A prisoner's situation is deliberately contrived to prevent his having any meaningful contact with his previous life, so that the two environments are separated not only by space but also by time. There is a 'life before' and a 'life now'. Given this two-dimensional separation, identity transformation is, in one sense, a relatively smooth process. The individual does not have two identities confronting each other. The attention of the reader of those accounts is drawn to the integration of the social system in which his identity is changed. There are, however, also indications that the previous existence shared these qualities. 'The recruit comes into the establishment with a conception of himself made possible by certain stable arrangements in his home world' (Goffman, 1970). The causes of this stability are not explored, but according to the theory, they can only lie either in a perfectly integrated social organization or in an identity which can, to some extent, overcome the vicissitudes of changing roles and social circumstances.

Hiller (1947) saw the answer in the fact that certain statuses are more salient than others in the formation of personal identities. If this is so, then it becomes a matter of empirical investigation as to which statuses are the key ones. Quite apart from posited factors of individual predisposition, much will depend on the extent to which various role partners can impose the salience of a particular role. Once this is conceded, the way is open to all kinds of psychological explanation in terms of reward/punishment, identification and so on. Primacy alone would be insufficient. So, for example, a mother may, be restricting a child's after-school activities, stress the status of son as opposed to that of playmate. A conflict of salient roles may occur in adolescence where the role of offspring may conflict with that bestowed by the significant others of the peer group.

However, in both these cases flexibility is possible, in theory at least. Partners are free to choose, to submit, to impose. In a very different category come statuses which are ascribed to the point of being immutable. Age is one, and race is another. In a social system where race is important in determining life chances and social status, an individual's basic social position is therefore fixed at birth. This position cannot be changed in his own lifetime, apart from the occasional opportunity for light-skinned 'blacks' to pass as whites. Speaking of American society, Berger (1966) concludes 'thus a man's conduct, ideas and psychological identity are shaped by race in a manner far more decisive than they commonly are by class'. This too, is a matter for empirical validation, and more recently, Wellman (1971), has found that the salience of race in the identity of U. S. Negroes varies with the social situation, e.g. the racial mixture of the school. On the whole it appears to be assumed that individuals will take the role connected with the ascribed status, and that attempts to take the identity of a different racial group will be seen in deviant terms, in the face of the immutable facts of biological existence.

It is also assumed that role conflict is only experienced in less immutable roles. One's identity as an employee may conflict with that assigned by one's marital role partner. Such a situation may be uncomfortable to the incumbent, but the pressures for consistency are strong both externally and internally. Externally, roles tend to be segregated, so that the individual can select the appropriate identity at any given time. For him to be able to do this, one must once more assume that if there is such a thing as a central core of identity it is not called into question. There are also internal pressures towards consistency, based according to Berger (1966) on 'very profound psychological needs to perceive oneself as a totality', thereby once more introducing a psychological frame of reference at a key point.

If roles can be segregated along with their appropriate identities then this means that either identity is by its nature fragmented or partial, or that there is a stable base of unknown origin upon which the partial identities are mere superstructures. The same occurs with those varieties of reference group theory which link values to identity. The question then arises whether some reference groups are more important than others for the formation of identity.

THE ORIENTATIONAL OTHER

The inherent discontinuity between symbolic interactionism and reference group theory was noticed by Kuhn (1964), who proposed adding the concept of *orientational other* to the repertoire of symbolic interactionism. It consists of four attributes:

1. The term refers to the others to whom the individual is most fully, broadly and basically committed, emotionally and psychologically.
2. It refers to the others who have provided him with his general vocabulary, including his most basic and crucial concepts and categories.
3. It refers to the others who have provided and continue to provide him with his categories of self and other and with the meaningful roles to which such assignments refer.
4. It refers to the others in communication with whom his self-conception is basically sustained and/or changed.

An interesting feature of such a category system is that it shows how a salient reference group can be crucial in the formation of a core self-image. This contrasts with the view of Denzin (1972) who believes that the self becomes gradually differentiated in the transition from home to home-plus-school. Regression to earlier modes will occur from time to time, when conceptions which are taken for granted in the home become problematic in nursery school. Yet one would have thought that such a situation would be far more than just problematic, it would amount to a *disconfirmation of self*, even though the child will be able to learn how to reconcile two social worlds.

The fact that such situations are nothing more than problematic makes it necessary to explore a little further the meaning of racial identity in early childhood. It is suggested that the salience of such an identity cannot be seen in terms of the wider social system because the child is shielded from the effects of this in psychological terms (though of course not in material terms) until his social relationships go beyond the family circle. Its significance is due to the fact that it is taken for granted until challenged. Many aspects of normal cognitive development concern the shift in nature of the view of reality as a result of socialization or experience.

The identity adopted through an orientational reference group is not open to negotiation. It is too deeply rooted in emotional identification with the significant others for that to happen. So, in terms of this analysis the half-caste child adheres to the culture, and the identity, of what he considers to be not only his reference group but also his membership group. Since membership of this group is bestowed by other members on a perceived racial basis his membership is denied him. His identity is disconfirmed.

As these deviant cases are not to be found in the sociological literature, one has to turn to psychiatric writings. It is principally in the writings of Laing (1961) where recognition is given to the idea that 'a person's identity . . . is the complex of those aspects of his being whereby he and others identify him'. On the same page he writes: 'a person will have considerable difficulty in establishing a consistent definition of himself in his own eyes if the definitions given by others are inconsistent'.

Laing also writes of 'disconfirmation', though here he tends to stress it as the denial of the validity of the person's own experience. There is, however, no reason why the use of the term could not be extended to cover the cases mentioned above, where one's self-conception is being denied; in fact, Laing (1961) does this in the case of Brian. Like all good psychoanalysts, Laing sees intrafamilial relationships as the most crucial in identity formation, yet it could be argued that disconfirmation from outside the family could be equally traumatic, and lead to identity confusion, though of course not necessarily to schizophrenia in every case.

It is clear that the concept of marginality, in its original and most of its subsequent formulations, does not encompass the position of the half-

Asian child. There is no question of ambiguity of membership, nor is there anywhere the desire to forsake one group for another. The child believes himself to be a member of the majority society as a birthright; his socialization has fitted him for no alternative. What matters is that this is his reference group—more than that, his group of orientation. The majority society rejects him and assigns him to a group of which he is not a member by any criteria save skin colour, and which he has no desire to join. The group to which he technically belongs by birth has no social or psychological meaning.

ATTEMPTED SOLUTIONS

There are three areas in which any initiative could arise, either to help an individual solve his problems or to create a situation where the problems do not arise.

(a) Attitudes of the white community

This is a question of altering public opinion and can only been seen as operating within a very long term perspective. It is difficult to improve attitudes towards a group which only barely exists, and is in an entirely different position from West Indians, Irish or Vietnamese.

(b) Individual attempts

The most obvious solution is that of 'passing', a process whereby the individual attempts to conceal her origins or else play them down. This will depend on what physical characteristics are salient. It may be that possession of a lightish skin may put the texture of the hair in a different perceptual context. It usually involves erasing traces of one's social background, e.g. accent. In the case of half-Asians this will already have been done. 'Passing' has sometimes been seen as a legitimate deceit and obviously would be so for a person who knows he is black attempting to become accepted as white. The half-Asian on the other hand believes she has been white all along. If the individual has been accepted as white in early social life then the problems described in this chapter will not have arisen. It should be emphasized that 'passing' usually means moving from one *established* group to another as in the case of moving from coloured to white in South Africa.

It may also be possible for an adult to move into a situation of social anonymity or where race is less salient. In many inner-City areas there are heterogeneous subcommunities, consisting of deviants, the downwardly socially mobile and those who find it difficult to live in communities with rigid social structure and norms. This may well be a solution chosen by many, but the rest of society would regard it as a failure.

A second strategy, mentioned by Breakwell (1978), is that of self-delusion. However, the individual is not attempting to delude himself that he is white because she has been so from birth. Self-delusion is a matter of individual identity and fantasy life but is not likely to succeed in the social world.

(c) Creating group support

This solution has been used by members of subordinate, deprived or stigmatized groups such as Jews and gays to raise their status so that the social bonds need no longer be clandestine and furtive but open and worthy of respect. The difference between these groups and half-Asians is that they have always been something more than categories: Jews are bonded by religion and kinship, homosexuals by definition are socially active. More pertinent in the International Year of the Disabled (1981) is the case of the physically handicapped. Many special groups like the blind have had pressure group organizations for years which have not only fought discrimination, but also have sought the psychological acceptance of handicapped people as being 'normal people with a bit of a problem'. For those who cannot get full acceptance networks of relationships have been set up. On the other hand, half-Asians are one stage behind; they are not identifiable as a significant category in the British population as contrasted with mestizos or mulattoes. It is also a split group; being a question of colour and not of race, problems are only experienced by those who cannot 'pass'.

Nevertheless, if one accepts that all individuals need some sort of social belonging and that to be able to rest on one's individuality alone is restricted to those of exceptional spiritual development, then it is only by the creation of a sense of group identity that any advancement can take place. It needs not only the help but the initiative of adults in some guidance role (teachers, or social workers). It is fraught with dangers: it institutionalizes the black/white dichotomy, it may well have the effect of finally destroying the illusion that individuals have of their whiteness; and one is, in effect, bringing together marginal individuals into a marginal group. Perhaps the aim should be modest—a group for the benefit of its members rather than a group wishing to change the world. Some ideas of the possibilities can be seen in the organization called 'Harmony', a loose knit organization consisting of people who have crossed national or racial boundaries in marriage.

Perhaps the first task is to restructure the cognitions of those who are in caring or counselling positions. The reactions of welfare-oriented liberals often seem governed by the stimulus of colour alone. A recent report on black children in care stated:

> If they must spend their childhood in care they need practical help to be proud to be black ... they need black care staff ... they need help to keep a toehold in their community of origin ... at the very least they need social contacts with their ethnic group (ABAFA/Runnymede Trust, 1979).

The writers of this report are not to be criticized. British society recognizes the distinction between black and white. It will also, in certain circumstances, subdivide black into ethnic-cultural categories. But there is only a vague category for the half-coloured, and none for the half-Asian. There is even less likelihood of the category referring to a group in any psychological or social sense. There is no such institutional tradition as there is in South Africa.

Perhaps we have been taking an excessively circuitous route to come to the conclusion that there is a class of people in society who are rejected by the group to which they belong, and consequently do not belong to any group. More understanding of the nature and significance of primary social identity can be gained by finding out how such people come to make their personal existence meaningful.

I am greatly indebted to Mr. David Batta for making available the social work records used as material in this chapter, for elaborating on the results of his own research, and for many meaningful discussions. I also wish to thank the Editor for commenting on an earlier draft.

Peter Hitch,
School of Applied Social Studies,
University of Bradford

August 1981

REFERENCES

Association of British Fostering and Adoption Agencies/Runnymede Trust (1979). *Black Children in Care*. London, A.B.A.F.A. (mimeo).

Antonovsky, A. (1956). Towards a refinement of the 'marginal man' concept, *Soc. Forces*, **35**, 57–62.

Ballard, C. (1975). Culture Conflict and Young Asians in Britain. Paper presented to International Congress on Transcultural Psychiatry, Bradford, United Kingdom.

Batta, I. D., McCulloch, J. W., and Smith, N. J. (1975). A Study of juvenile delinquency among Asians and Half-Asians, *Brit. J. Crim.* **15** (1), 32–42.

Berger, P. (1966). *Invitation to Sociology*. Harmondsworth, Penguin Books.

Breakwell, G. M. (1978). The trouble with marginal identity. Paper presented at Colloquim on Identity, University of Rennes. (December 1978.)

Burns, R. B. (1979). *The Self Concept*, London, Longman.

Coopersmith, S. (1967). *The Antecedents of Self-Esteem*. San Francisco, Freeman.

Denzin, N. (1972). Genesis of self in early childhood, *Sociol. Quart.* **13** (3) 292–314.

Gergen, K. I. (1971). *The Concept of Self*. London, Holt, Rinehart & Winston.

Goffman, E. (1970). *Asylums*. Harmondsworth, Penguin Books.

Goldberg, M. M. (1941). A qualification of the marginal man theory, *Amer. Sociol. Rev.* **6**, 52–58.

Green, A. W. (1947). A re-examination of the marginal man concept, *Soc. Forces*, **26**, 167–171.
Hedin, E. L. (1934). The Anglo-Indian Community. *Amer. J. Sociol.*, **40** (2), 165–179.
Hiller, E. T. (1947). *Social Relations and Structures.* London, Harper.
Hitch, P. J. (1977). Culture, structure and the explanation of migrant mental illness, *Mental Health and Society*, **4**, 136–143.
Hyman, H. (1942). The Psychology of Status, *Archiv. Psychol.*, **38**, 269.
Kerkhoff, A. C., and McCormick, T. C. (1955). 'Marginal status and marginal personality, *Soc. Forces*, **34** (1), 48–55.
Krausz, E. (1971). *Ethnic Minorities in Britain.* London, McGibbon & Kee.
Kuhn, M. H. (1964). The Reference Group Reconsidered. *Sociol. Quart.* **5**, 6–21.
Laing, R. D. (1961). *The Self and Others.* London, Tavistock.
Lindesmith A. R., and Strauss, A. L. (1968). *Social Psychology.* London, Holt, Rinehart & Winston (Third Edition).
Mann, L. (1969). *Social Psychology.* Sydney, Chichester, Wiley.
Mawby, R., and Batta, I. D. (1980). *Asians and Crime: The Bradford Experience.* Southall, Middlesex, Scope Communications.
McCulloch, J. W., Batta, I. D., and Smith, N. J. (1979). 'Colour as a variable in the Children's Section of a Local Authority Social Services Department', *New Community*, **7** (1), 78–84.
McDavid, J. W., and Harari, H. (1968). *Social Psychology.* London, Harper & Row.
Mead, C. H. (1968). *Mind, Self and Society.* Chicago, Univ. of Chicago Press.
Meltzer, B. M. (1978). Mead's Social Psychology. In: J. G. Manis and B. N. Meltzer (eds). *Symbolic Interaction: A Reader in Social Psychology.* London, Allyn & Bacon (Third Edition).
Merton, R. K. (1968). *Social Theory and Social Structure.* Glencoe, Free Press (Third Edition).
Mulford, H. A., and Salisbury, W. W. II (1964). Self-conceptions in a general population, *Sociol. Quart.*, **5** (4), 5–22.
Newcomb, T. H. (1961). *Personality and Social Change: Attitude Formation in a Student Community.* London, Holt, Rinehart & Winston.
Osgood, C. E., Suchi, G. T., and Tannenbaum, P. H. (1957). *The Measurement of Meaning.* Urbana, Univ. of Illinois Press.
Park, R. E. (1928). Human migration and the marginal man, *Amer. J. Sociol.*, **33**, 881–893.
Pollis, N. P. (1968). Reference group re-examined, *Brit. J. Sociol.*, **19**, 300–307.
Rose, A. (1962). A systematic summary of symbolic interaction theory. In: A Rose (ed.) *Human Behaviour and Social Processes.* London, Routledge & Kegan Paul.
Schafft, G. E. (1976). Racially Ambiguous Children: Brokers for Change. Paper presented to the Annual Meeting of the American Anthropological Association, U.S.A., Washington D.C. (November 16–20.)
Sherif, M., and Sherif, C. W. (1969). *Social Psychology.* New York and London, Harper & Row.
Stonequist, E. V. (1937). *The Marginal Man.* New York, Scriveners.
Stonequist, E. V. (1942). The marginal character of the Jews. In: I. Graeber and S. H. Brett (eds.) *Jews in a Gentile World.* New York, MacMillan.
Wellman, B. (1971). Social identities in black and white, *Sociol. Inquiry*, **41** (1), 57–66.
Wilson, A. (1981). Mixed race children: an exploratory study of racial categorisation and identity, *New Community*, **9** (1), 36–43.
Wirth, L., and Goldhamer, H. (1944). The hybrid and problems of misgenation. In: O. Klineberg (ed.) *Characteristics of the American Negro.* New York, Harper.

Threatened Identities
Edited by G. Breakwell

Self-conception Among Young British–Asian Muslims: Confutation of a Stereotype

TOM KITWOOD

> 'The group discussed the problem of identity-confusion ... two measures were necessary to eliminate or at least diminish the feeling of identity-confusion: firstly, the teaching of mother-tongue in schools, and secondly, inclusion of Asian history and culture in the school curriculum so that Asian children may not only appreciate their own history but also identify with their national heroes.'
> Report of a Conference on Ethnic Minorities in Bradford, 1979.

There is a stereotype of children who are ethnically Asian, but who have been brought up in this country: those who are, in the language of two popular images, 'between two cultures' and a 'half-way generation'. It is that they live in a tension between two conflicting systems of meaning and value, and therefore experience a problem of 'personal identity'. A superficial analogy can be made between their predicament and that of the offspring of racially mixed marriages, who might also be supposed liable to 'identity-confusion'.

I have not made a systematic study of this stereotype, though it seems to be especially prevalent among those whose taken-for-granted knowledge includes a smattering of humanistic psychology, and those whose informal theory of social change has a component of technological determinism (who have no qualms over such notions as 'modernization' and 'cultural lag'). The stereotype is very appealing, since it appears to explain so much. And it receives strong commonsensical corroboration, for example, in the way British–Asian adolescents often anglicize their first names, or in such recent stylistic phenomena as young Asians going 'Afro' and Pakistani punk.

The stereotype is reinforced by association with certain other ideas, though it is not necessarily dependent upon them. One is that the culture of the host society is genuinely and crucially inconsistent with that of the migrants; another is that the former is sufficiently strong to pose a serious challenge to the latter. The stereotype is sometimes linked to a general theory of assimilation ('identity-confusion' is a natural concomitant of the assimilation process). The whole idea also fits well with a conception of the person as relatively passive, an object moved by external forces, rather than as active and constructive. Some of these views may well be incorrect, or at least require qualification; in particular the general theory of assimilation, which underlay the idea of America as a great cultural melting pot, has been challenged by many kinds of evidence since the seminal work of Znaniecki early this century. At a theoretical level, moreover, the question of 'personal identity' among young British–Asians has not (so far as I am aware) been properly resolved.

It must be emphasized that this discussion refers only to one broad group: the offspring of Muslim parents who came originally from the regions of the Punjab and Mirpur in what is now Pakistan, and who settled in the centres of textile industry in the North of England during the 1950's and 1960's. (Hereafter, for the sake of brevity, I shall refer to them as 'Muslim adolescents' or 'young Muslims', and the particular Asian community in which they find themselves as the 'community'.) It would not be justified to extend the characterization offered here to all young British–Asians, regardless of their geographical and cultural background and their place of settlement in Britain. Even among those whom we are considering here there is considerable diversity.

A brief description of the method of research on which this paper is based has been published already (Kitwood and Borrill, 1980). It will suffice here to point out that the approach is highly eclectic and opportunistic, drawing on a wide range of historical and cultural material. The primary data have been collected from interviews and group discussions with about 50 young British–Asian Muslims in Bradford and Manchester, in which the participants were given the opportunity to give accounts of the meaning and significance of certain aspects of their social world. The aim is then to advance explanations and interpretations that are consistent with the data, though not derived from them by simple induction, as in more positivistic approaches.

A THEORY OF 'PERSONAL IDENTITY'

The stereotype which I have outlined receives its strongest support from a body of theory which has become highly respectable, even an orthodoxy in some circles. It was used for about two decades as one of the main resources for understanding adolescence in industrial societies; a cohort of social workers was trained on the assumption of its validity.

Its origins are in Freudian psychotherapy, particularly as this developed during the period following the First World War. Some workers, notably Karen Horney (1937), found that their clients were presenting symptoms of a kind to which the original theories of Freud could not easily be applied. The pernicious activities of the superego were less in evidence, whereas the problems of ego-development appeared to have become mush more important. Many of the new symptoms were to do with a sense of emptiness, meaninglessness and deadness, and the inability to develop a consistent or coherent style of life. In some cases, the client's complaint could be summed up in the words 'I do not know who I am'. Hence arose the conception of a general area of psychological malaise, commonly known as that of 'personal identity' (*pace* the philosophers, who have engaged in a virtually unrelated debate under the same name).

The concept of 'personal identity' in the psychological tradition is most closely associated with the research of Erikson. His major works (1965, 1968) were the fruit of over thirty years of practice in psychotherapy, combined with excursions into the field of anthropology. Perhaps Erikson's most important contribution was his attempt to show in detail how individual psychology was related to broader social and cultural conditions. In his mature work he claimed that the problem of 'personal identity' was not just characteristic of a minority, the typical neurotics of the industrial era, but something universal. Erikson proposed an eightfold developmental scheme for the life of the individual. During each stage there is a specific 'task' to be accomplished. The scheme is cumulative, in that the satisfactory completion of one task is held to be necessary before the next can be attempted. The fifth stage, adolescence, is concerned with the establishment of 'personal identity'; this is the precondition of the next, early adulthood, which involves the capacity to form intimate and enduring relationships.

Much of Erikson's work was soon forgotten, though his theory of adolescence was widely accepted. Perhaps it resonated in some way with the manifestations of youthful rebellion and uncertainty that were such a striking feature of the 1960's. It is a difficult theory to interpret, because though rich in insight it lacks definitional and methodological precision. Erikson deliberately abstained from offering stipulative definitions of his principal terms, preferring to let his readers sense meanings through induction. In his cumulative scheme 'identity-formation' seems to involve the acquisition of a consistent style of organization of experience, entailing a restructuring of childhood 'identifications' and an incorporation of some of the roles offered by society. The adolescent may well engage in tentative 'identifications', symptoms of which are intolerance and gross stereotyping of others. There may be a state of 'identity-confusion', during which the person is unable to establish a clear basis of consistency. Occasionally there may be an 'identity crisis', though a crisis in the ordinary sense is not to be expected in the majority of cases. If the community's characterization of the person can be brought into accord with the emerging self-definition the task of 'identity-formation' is likely to reach a satisfactory conclusion; if not, the person may well face psychological difficulties in early adulthood, or their delayed outworking at some later point of stress or change. According to this theory, then, there is a danger in bringing adolescence to an end too early, since this might force a person into a premature and inadequate 'identity'. Sufficient time must be allowed for the necessary experimentation, free from long-term commitment, for a genuine 'identity' to be established. Erikson was remarkably emphatic about the state of affairs at the end of 'normal' adolescence; for he wrote of a 'final identity', fixed by early adulthood, and of adolescence being 'conclusively complete when identity is discovered'.

Because of its strong intuitive appeal it is easy to accept Erikson's theory as offering a general or even universal account of adolescence. If so, his ideas seem well suited to explaining the predicament of the children of Asian migrants into industrial societies. As adolescents, the theory suggests, they would be likely to find it extremely hard to develop a consistent style of life and a unity in their ordering of experience. They are required to act within two very contrasting cultural frameworks. They might be supposed to have a particularly strong tendency to reject identifications with parents and others in the Asian community, while perhaps having insufficient contact with the kind of people with whom they could realistically identify elsewhere. Such roles as are objectively available in the host society may be unfamiliar or unacceptable. Personal experimentation is severely restricted because of the traditions of the Asian family. There is a common tendency, for girls especially, for the period of adolescence to be curtailed by withdrawal from school at the first opportunity, or by early marriage. Thus if any group could be held, *prima facie*, to exemplify Erikson's theory in its negative aspect—the probability of failure to complete the 'task' of adolescence—it is this. And 'Muslim adolescents', because of the radical incompatibility of their parents' outlook with Western ways, might be expected to show 'identity-confusion' to a marked degree.

Close inquiry, however, suggests that this is not the case.

THE PROCESSES OF SELF-CONCEPTION

Had Erikson's theory been current coin at the time when Popper was struggling with the problem of how to demarcate scientific knowledge, it might have proved a useful example of non-science; but of that rich and significant kind that would later give rise to genuinely scientific insights.

Progress, however, requires that self-conception be analysed more precisely than Erikson's scheme allows. And here it is probably mistaken to start with static concepts that describe the results of processes; it may be wiser to focus attention on the processes themselves, while leaving open the question of that to which they give rise.

A useful summary of (mainly American) work in this field is given by Wegner and Vallacher (1977). Their treatment is logically flawed at several points, particularly in the naive use that is made of experimental data, and their examples tend to be facetious or trivial. Nevertheless, their reframing of the topic of social cognition as the study of implicit and everyday psychological theory is valuable and illuminating. I shall use their discussion of 'implicit self-theory' as a basis for what follows. Here three processes are hypothesized by which a person comes to obtain information pertaining to the self.

The first is 'social feedback', or making inferences from the reactions of others. Presumably, it is through this process that a child first acquires the sense of being a person at all, and then gradually comes to learn from significant others the kind of person he or she is supposed (in the double sense) to be. Social feedback continues to be used as a source of data throughout life, though possibly diminishing somewhat in importance with age. Through experience a person grows in sophistication, learning how to draw inferences not only (to use Goffman's terminology) from the signs that others 'give', but also from those they 'give off', thus taking into account reactions that are merely conventional.

The second main process is 'social comparison', whereby a person relates his or her performance to that of others. In straightforward physical or intellectual tasks it may be fairly simple to obtain comparative data; but the greater the extent to which social interaction is involved in the performance the more likely it is that a person will use data from the first process too, comparing the feedback given to others with that conveyed to the self.

The third process is 'self-attribution', or drawing direct inferences without the mediation of others. Wegner and Vallacher place their main emphasis here on the attribution of attitudes and values to the self through assessment of behaviour, apparently conflating this matter with that of how a person comes to know the name of an inner state. More broadly, it is plausible to suppose that a person might make inferences both from his or her behaviour (particularly in novel situations) and mental states (particularly when these are persistent or recurrent) and so might come to attribute certain dispositions to the self.

Self-conception is highly problematic, since none of these processes yields clear and consistent data. Social feedback is difficult to evaluate because it requires an estimation of others' sincerity, and because of problems of interpretation when differences of class or culture are involved. We have found in work with English adolescents (Kitwood, 1980) that use is often made of a special kind of social feedback, which might be termed 'espionage': that is, a person asks a trusted friend to find out how he or she is faring socially, and to report back. It is hoped that the information obtained thus will be more reliable than that derived from direct engagement, though there is still the possibility that the assistant may be incompetent or treacherous. In some respects social comparison is less fraught with difficulty than making inferences from others' reactions. Even here, however, ambiguities of data are unavoidable, and there is the problem that suitable others for social comparison may not be available. Self-attribution is extremely problematic. A person might, for example, infer the existence of a trait without giving due weight to situational factors, or make inept appraisals due to variation in mood. Moreover, even if all the data from these processes were absolutely clear, the person might not order them correctly, recognize important lacunae, or be logically precise in the drawing of inferences.

Although there are some parallels, there is a great difference between forming conceptions of others and of the self. In the latter case, as many theorists have pointed out, the one who is known is also the knower. 'Objective' data about the self are limited to such rare instances as glimpses in a reflecting surface, or hearing a tape recording. Data pertaining to others often seem to be more easy to interpret, though they are restricted in scope; data pertaining to the self are available in great abundance, but tend to ambiguity or contradiction. It is this that makes the development of a coherent self-concept so difficult. Stability is gained through greater differentiation, but resolution of the problem of the resulting complexity requires integration through a process of second-order reflection.

That is a summary of Wegner and Vallacher's position, together with my own glosses and additions. These authors, and the sources they cite, generally take an industrial society as the backcloth for their theorizing, and in this respect their treatment is limited. The theory looks rather different if one retains the three processes of self-conception as having general validity, but also takes into account the variety of human societies.

Under the conditions of modern industrialism, it certainly seems to be the case that some people participate in several different social life-worlds, each with its *mores* and implicit meanings; that some who live thus experience such discrepancies or uncertainties in the data pertaining to themselves that they 'do not know who they are'; and that some kind of resolution to this problem may be possible through a higher-order synthesis. In a closely integrated community, however, the situation is very different. There may well be a single social life-world within which production, leisure, entertainment, morality and religion form a unity, with little privacy for the individual. Roles may be sharply demarcated, and life-history divided into distinct stages, yet all is enacted in one social arena. There is interpersonal variation, to be sure, and the form of existence calls for many different skills. But knowledge about each member is shared to a large extent within the group, through discussion and gossip, leading to a coherent and publicly shared opinion. From the individual's point of view there is abundant opportunity for checking and cross checking hypotheses about the self; and this can be done concretely, often almost unconsciously, without the need for second-order reflection. Under these conditions the 'problem of personal identity' associated with the fragmentation of life that can occur in industrial societies does not exist; it may well be literally inconceivable.

FORMATION OF MUSLIM ASIAN COMMUNITIES IN THE NORTH OF ENGLAND

Much has been written about the background to the migration of Asian workers to Britain (e.g. Allen, 1971), and I will make only the briefest comment on this topic. The society from which the Muslim migrants came was predominantly agricultural, steeped in tradition, and based on small communities: *gemeinschaft* in an almost ideal-typical sense. Links between members were established at many levels, primarily through extended ties of kinship, but also through the owning and renting of land and through the interdependence of the different occupations. The family system was one which gave great authority to the father, and in a subsidiary sense to the sons as they grew older. The maintenance of male honour was of great importance. A man's wife was under contractual obligation to provide certain services. While having a distinctly subordinate position, she was granted her own areas of control, and was able to enjoy a great deal of companionship among her own sex. The closest bonds of affection were usually between the mother and her children, the father remaining somewhat aloof. Marriage was by arrangement, in some cases negotiated while the parties were still children. There was a strong tradition of marriage between first cousins, and it was common for two or more families to be interlinked over several generations. The family took full responsibility for the care of its older members.

It was natural that the migrants should try to recreate this social world in their new environment, though in this they were only partially successful. The housing was cramped and the climate was harsh. Hours of work were long and often inconvenient, making it difficult to maintain the integration of family life. The women could not engage in the open-air conviviality to which they had been accustomed. The prevailing disposition of the British was one of incomprehension, breaking out from time to time into open or even violent hostility. The communities that formed under these conditions tended to be somewhat rigid and defensive, fearful of accommodation to the new situation. Being concerned to be acceptable to the host society, and perhaps rendered docile through the effects of Imperial rule in their homeland, they remained politically quiet. Their view of the British educational system was ambivalent. On the one hand, they approved of erudition and were eager for their children to do well at school; on the other, they deplored the apparent decadence and permissiveness of British *mores*, and were fearful that their children might be subverted. When times were very bad they could console themselves with the thought of returning to Pakistan.

The children of the migrant generation, however, were confronted with new problems and possibilities. They had a strong sense of belonging to the 'community', yet as they grew up they thought of Britain as their natural and rightful home. They were bound, moreover, to participate in the life of the host society on its own terms, in a way which their parents never were. This is the context in which their self-conception is to be understood.

SELF-CONCEPTION AMONG 'YOUNG MUSLIMS': THE CHILDHOOD BACKGROUND

The early socialization of 'young Muslims' is very different from that of their British counterparts in the North of England. Since it is not seen, and is rarely discussed outside the 'community', it tends to be under estimated or forgotten by observers.

The child of a Muslim family has, from the very first, a strong sense of being part of a wide net of relationships: mainly that of the extended family, but also that of others who migrated from the same area of Pakistan, and the 'community' as a whole. It is possible that this early experience of being bound together with others is more intense in Britain than it would have been in Pakistan, because of the defensive stance taken by (or forced upon) the migrant generation. A 'young Muslim' becomes aware, moreover, of occupying a unique position in the social group; no-one else has precisely the same relationship to mother, father, brothers, sisters, uncles, aunts and cousins. This conveys a definite sense of individuality, though not in a characteristically Western or Eriksonian sense. Thus from a variety of sources, through social feedback and social comparison, the child acquires a definite sense of who he or she is; and as in any *gemeinschaft* environment, the messages which others convey to any individual tend to correspond. Putting it another way, the child is able, within the 'community', to gain a great deal of evidence pertaining to the self, together with its corroboration. Simple and direct learning is all that is generally required; self-conception occurs through a series of concrete operations.

The child learns also about appropriate kinds of behaviour, but far more through the performance of specific duties than through the application of general or abstract principles. There is no clear distinction between morality and custom. Life in the family is highly structured according to roles, even if some traditional practices have to be modified a little because of such exigences as shift-work or drawing the dole. There are definite patterns of authority, mutual support and respect, and favoured forms of communication. While the integrity of family life is of overwhelming importance, there is also, and not clearly demarcated from it, the fulfilment of at least some of the external requirements of Islam: occasional visits to the mosque, the (at least partial) observance of Ramazan, the celebration of Id-ul-fitr. Day-to-day existence is given a structure, based on clear prescriptions for action. Each individual belongs not only to a human collective, but also to a pattern of life. This is the basis of ontological security for the individual.

A 'young Muslim' in Britain is, however, required to leave the 'community', even if only to a limited extent, from an early age. The most important aspect of this is going to school, which is at first like entering a foreign country. Some of the customs are unfamiliar or surprising; the linguistic milieu, even if superficially comprehensible, possesses many strange connotations. From the very beginning, 'young Muslims' sense that they are, in some profound way, different, however hard the school authorities try to avoid discrimination. Of course, there are some obvious reminders also, such as attending special classes for those with language difficulties, or being bussed to school. Asian children are sometimes forced by others to play together, or even not to use the playground at all. These experiences may be unpleasant or frightening, but are not a source of inner bewilderment. For the social life of the 'community' is subjectively much more real; it is this that provides security and the basic categories for interpreting events in the world outside.

From the first point of entry into the life of the host society a 'young Muslim' is likely to face racist attacks or insinuations. A boy or girl may be called 'Paki', 'Wog', 'Curry' or 'Chapatty-face' as early as the infant class at school. By the time they leave primary school, many boys have been involved in fights with racial connotations. The school also, in the insensitivity of its arrangements (meals, P. E., assembly, recording of names), may have conveyed subtle racist messages. Even this is not particularly damaging, because it is plainly so crude and ignorant that it cannot be taken seriously. Racism simply becomes an accepted part of the world in which 'young Muslims' live, something to be handled with skill. They receive an abundance of messages that they are valued, from those whose testimony is trusted.

Thus 'young Muslims' on the threshold of adolescence are already integrated, in powerful and mutually reinforcing ways, into an intelligible and closeknit social order. It makes strong demands, and by modern Western standards may seem to be rigid or oppressive. But it conveys to each individual a profound sense of belonging: to a family, to a community, and in a broader sense to the Islamic world. At the same time, 'young Muslims' have had a progressive introduction to that alien territory, British society, and have begun to learn how to operate within it. This experience does not undermine their sense of who they are; rather, it tends to enhance it. If they had been cloistered within the 'community' until the age of 13 and then were thrown suddenly into British society, the position might be very different. As it is, a kind of inoculation process takes place. They learn over about seven years how to live in two worlds, and are ready for the much more challenging encounter with the host society that occurs during the early teens.

'MUSLIM' AND INDIGENOUS ADOLESCENTS: A BROAD COMPARISON

If my argument is correct, it means that by the time 'young Muslims' reach the beginning of the period conventionally defined as adolescence, their ontological basis is far more secure than is the case with the majority of their British contemporaries. The consequence is that during adolescence they process self-relevant information differently, even when displaying behaviour that might be judged typical of a British teenager. If this is not taken into account, it is easy to misconstrue their personal development during the early teens.

Among British adolescents from a social class background comparable to that of the Muslims in the North of England, one main pattern seems to be this. When they reach the age of about 12 there become available social life-worlds that are neither distinctively childish nor adult, and which have evolved as adaptations to the specific conditions of that age-group in industrial societies: notably, long periods of unstructured time, and shortage of money. Many boys and girls are drawn into these new worlds and psychologically 'move out' from home; the main locus of their social being becomes those of their own age and a few years older. Although this 'move' entails exposure to an uncertain and hazardous environment, there is the opportunity to acquire social and other skills, and abundant scope for learning through immediate perception of success and failure. Here both social feedback and social comparison are extremely important, sometimes leading to considerable personality changes. When high-quality interaction with nonpeers is available in such context as a job, the pursuit of a hobby, or even the classroom, it also is highly valued. After the age of 16, several modes of integration with the adult world become possible. Many boys and girls are eager to take up roles with clear prescriptions (for example in work or marriage) finding there a certain security. Forms of cultural adaptation to long-term unemployment are evolving slowly, but many of those who cannot find work face considerable *anomie*.

Although this is a great simplification, it does serve to show the contrasting position of 'Muslim adolescents'. However much they participate in the teenage social life-worlds of their contemporaries, and however impeccable their performances there, they do not 'move out' psychologically. Many 'Muslim' boys are allowed considerable personal liberty during their early teens; they are able to go to amusement arcades, cinemas and discos, to stay out fairly late in the evenings, to try their success with a British girl friend, to visit pubs. Parents sometimes deliberately overlook what their sons are doing, provided there are no gross misdemeanours and family respectability is not compromised. Girls are far more restricted, and the penalties for misbehaviour severe (the ultimate sanction being to be 'sent back') but even so are able to make brief undetected ventures. During this period, however, most 'Muslim adolescents' remain firmly integrated into the 'community'. They use their new experiences to reassess, relativize or rework aspects of their background, while keeping its fundamentals intact. This process, moreover, is not always in the direction of Westernization. It may involve discovering the 'truth' about colonialism, a positive assertion of Asian or Islamic values, a serious critique of the decadence of the host society, or developing a radical political consciousness. It is very rare indeed for 'Muslim adolescents' to throw themselves, psychologically, at the mercy of those of their own age, or to allow themselves to be profoundly reformed through peer-group interaction. Even such apparently dramatic denials of their background as involvement in punk or rastofarianism should probably be construed as unusually bold but short-lived experimentation from an established base; and not as a sign of serious 'identity-confusion'.

At present, by far the majority of those who leave school at 16 tend to be reabsorbed rapidly into the 'community' as young adults. Many girls stay at home for a few years before marriage, helping their mothers. Boys who find work discover new ways of coping with the demands of life in Britain, but return to find their place of ease among those of their own culture. Those who are unemployed still have social support, and often there is work of a kind for them to do within the 'community'. Boys and girls who stay on at school or who go into further education can prolong the period of reworking of their background; though it is rare, even then, for them to challenge it fundamentally.

'MUSLIM ADOLESCENTS': THE PROCESSES OF SELF-CONCEPTION

Let us now look at the matter more closely, in relation to the three processes outlined in the second main section of this paper.

(i) Social feedback

Broadly speaking, 'Muslim adolescents' are able to gain information from a wider variety of others' reactions than are their indigenous counterparts. Relatively less is from peers and more from those who provided so much feedback during childhood.

Among their own age-group the most significant source of feedback is those of similar background. Here school has an important function, in extending the range of friendships among 'young Muslims' beyond the immediate locality. This is reinforced where the system of bussing is in operation, and where interethnic relations at school are poor. School, moreover, enables activities to take place that would not be allowed in the home context. It is even possible for a boy and girl to be 'going out' together, this perhaps meaning no more than taking a brief walk during the lunch hour, or meeting on journeys to and from school. Brothers and sisters can be used as agents in the business of 'espionage' and in the conduct of secret liaisons. Of course the feedback that individuals receive has both positive and negative aspects; but—to use an analogy from wireless—these are the modulations, while the carrier-wave still bears the message of being a 'young Muslim'.

During the early teens, 'young Muslims' come into more extended contact than before with boys and girls of different ethnic and cultural backgrounds. By this time, they have generally acquired sufficient skill to interact acceptably, knowing that few accommodations are likely to be made in their direction. Thus the anglicizing of first names may be interpreted as part of a realistic and even cynical tactic to facilitate communication. Where social feedback is unfavourable it can be resisted. 'Muslim adolescents' have had several years within which to become inured to racist insinuation; uncomplimentary feedback that is not racist can, moreover, be treated as if it were, and so be discounted. On the other hand, any feedback that is positive in tone can be taken at face value.

Whereas many indigenous boys and girls 'move out' during their early teens, the contribution of their families to their self-conception tending to decline in importance, this does not appear to be the case with 'young Muslims'. Their families watch anxiously over their development during a period of extended exposure to influences which they consider both noxious and potent. They attempt, so far as is realistic, to ensure that their children remain securely within the family and the 'community', and teach them the responsibilities fitting for their age. From the boys' and girls' point of view, of course, not all the social feedback is acceptable, especially as their sophistication increases. The prevailing parental style, particularly that of the father, is not one of negotiation, and tends to persistent moralization. Some 'Muslim adolescents' may, indeed, become critical or distrustful of their parents, perceiving them on occasions as hypocritical, ignorant or servile. This, however, does not necessitate a total rejection of the feedback they convey: simply that certain components be filtered out.

One further aspect must be mentioned: social feedback in a more literal sense. The network of kin and community among Muslims in the main city areas of the North of England is so integrated that news and gossip travel very fast. The activities of the younger generation are being monitored constantly, and misdemeanours are quickly reported back. A boy who enters a pub or a girl who accepts a lift runs the risk of being confronted with the fact, duly embellished and distorted, within a couple of days. These attempts at social control have an ambivalent character to those who are the targets. On the one hand, they are resented as an intrusion, and seen as a challenge to ingenuity; on the other, the fact that such a system exists enhances their sense of belonging.

(ii) Social comparison

The theory of social comparison, or at least the version to which I have made reference, suggests that the most significant data are obtained from those who are similar in some important respect. Information derived from such sources will be more richly textured, more reliable and useful. 'Muslim adolescents', then, make their most significant social comparisons with others from the same kind of cultural background.

In this respect, it is worth comparing their situation with that of the offspring of racially mixed marriages. For the latter, there is a dearth of people who are precisely similar, since interethnic marriages are rare; it is conceivable that this could, in certain circumstances, cause ontological insecurity. The 'young Muslims' with whom our research is concerned do not, however, have this problem. They belong to a large cohort, and there is plenty to assure them that their situation, for all its difficulties and ambiguities, is not unique. To use another jargon, they do not lack a clear reference group.

The main resource for social comparison, then, is other 'Muslim adolescents' who are known through the extended family, and those who have become friends through the 'community' and through school. It seems that besides such general bases for comparison as temperament, appearance or achievement, a number of constructs have evolved that are specifically relevant to their situation: the relatively traditional versus the 'modern', the devout versus the irreligious, those who are aware of Asian culture versus those who are not, those who are allowed freedom versus those who are restricted, those who take a stand on racist issues versus those who are quietistic. Thus within any large group of 'Muslim adolescents' there tends to be a number of clusters, and even factions. The broader framework within which this differentiation occurs, however, is not on the agenda for questioning.

There are several other aspects of social comparison, which I shall mention only briefly.

With the gradual increase in affluence among Asians in the North of England, visits to Pakistan are becoming more frequent. Several of those we interviewed had been there for short periods. Some were shocked or dismayed by what they found, though they were surprised at the extent to which Westernization had taken place. The most common conclusion is that though their ultimate roots are in Pakistan, that country could never be their home. In other words, their sense of being in a historically new category, that of 'British–Asians', is confirmed. In due course, this reaction passed on to others, and becomes part of the stock of common knowledge.

A 'young Muslim' in this country is likely to be placed by the host society into the same category as other Asians from different backgrounds. In the ordinary course of life in the 'community' contact with such people might be rare, especially because of residues of the conflicts on the Indian sub-continent. The school system is relatively undiscerning, however, treating all 'Asians' as the same for some purposes. Outside the classroom, Asians may be forced into association through lack of other friends, or even to band together in self-defence. When this occurs, it helps a 'young Muslim' to a greater understanding of the common ground between different Asian cultures, and to a recognition of what is distinctively Islamic.

Adolescence also provides the opportunity for a much closer and many-sided encounter with boys and girls of different ethnic backgrounds. Many 'young Muslims' make close friendships with their British contemporaries during their early teens, though relatively few do so with West Indians. Whatever may be the appearances in the short term, it is doubtful whether these friendships are a major force towards assimilation, far less towards 'identity-confusion'. But they do have an important function, in giving young Muslims first-hand knowledge of actual British people, the chance to discover what is and what is not held in common, to break down false or second-hand impressions. The fact that Asian minorities are the subject as well as the object of stereotyping can easily be overlooked.

The discussion of social comparison would not be complete without reference to the place of television and cinema in the life of 'Muslim adolescents'. They watch a great deal of television, especially since they spend more time at home than their British counterparts. From it, they are able to acquire simplistic views about aspects of British life to which they have no access, and without any personal risk. It forms the basis, to use the phrase of Noble (1975), for 'pseudo-social interaction'. Since there is very little evidence for the direct behavioural influence of television, it is improbable that it undermines the self-conception of 'young Muslims'; it may well, however, confirm views that they hold already, and enhance their sense of belonging to a superior tradition. Asian films have a different significance. It is common for family groups to go to the Asian cinemas, and videotaped films are now being used extensively in homes. Many of these films convey an idealized and highly romantic image of life in an affluent sector of Indian society. A boy or girl seeing them for the first time may well believe that they convey some literal truth; but by the age of about 16 most 'young Muslims' are experienced enough to see them in a very different way, with irony and sociological sophistication. Through understanding who they are not, they have a more assured knowledge of who they are.

(iii) Self-attribution

In order to estimate the part played by this process in the self-conception of 'Muslim adolescents', one over-riding point must be considered. A *gemeinschaft* society generates a high level of consensus, and tends to discount private intuitions which go against the collective opinion. Thus there is a tacit cultural value which implies that self-attribution should be taken as relatively unimportant among the sources of evidence pertaining to the self. Whereas a British teenager with existential courage and a strong sense of individualism might use self-attribution to deny or modify drastically an existing self-concept, this is far less likely to happen with those whom we are considering here.

One of the most important functions of self-attribution during adolescence is in relation to experiences that are fundamentally new. Here a person may have no clear evidence from the first two processes, and will tend to make direct inferences from actions and inner states. 'Muslim adolescents', because they have been sheltered during childhood, may indeed face more such occasions than their British counterparts: the first time of being out after dark alone, the first real challenging of parental authority, the first opportunity to act on feelings of sexual attraction, the first perusal of forbidden magazines, the first really ugly racist episode, the first taste of 'the devil's piss'. After experiences of this kind a person's reaction may well be 'I did not know I would feel like that', or 'I did not know that I had it in me to behave like that'. We have no grounds for thinking that 'young Muslims' do not engage in such reflection, either privately or in discussion with their friends. But it is doubtful whether this kind of evidence, subjective and transient as it appears to be, would be sufficient to challenge their sense of who they are, which is so firmly and socially grounded.

Our earlier research with British adolescents suggests that frequently there is a discrepancy between how they are feeling and how they are required to act, particularly in the presence of their peers. Some only become consciously aware of this when making disclosures about themselves under conditions where there is no pressure to conform to others' expectations. It is possible that this unawareness is even more marked among 'young Muslims', both in their peer-relations and within their families, since the necessity to follow conventions of behaviour has been inculcated from a very early age. From the standpoint of Western psychiatry, with its concern to 'liberate' the individual, this might be viewed as engendering repression, and therefore unhealthy; the remedy would be 'personal growth' through greater awareness and acceptance of inner states. It must be remembered, however, that other fundamental conceptions of the person are possible, and that in some societies the majority have lived out their time happily enough with high levels of repression.

(iv) Attempts at integration

Thus far I have indicated some of the resources for self-conception among 'young Muslims', placing particular emphasis on factors that work against 'identity-confusion'. The main hypothesis has been that during childhood they receive strong, many-sided and self-corroborating evidence pertaining to the self; that during adolescence the processes of social feedback and social comparison mainly promote greater differentiation at the periphery of the existing self-concept; and that self-attribution, for cultural reasons, is not taken to provide crucially important evidence.

But do 'Muslim adolescents' ever work towards some kind of broader synthesis of their experiences as participants in two cultures? Does their self-conception ever involve second-order reflection, and with what results?

There are some boys and rather more girls who, so far as we can discern, reflect but little on the anomalies of their existence. They have had to make forays into British society for as long as they can remember, and have established a sufficient competence in those areas where it is needed, such as school work and basic social relations. They remain, however, firmly rooted in the 'community', perhaps perceiving no alternative; this is their meaningful social world, whereas much that goes on outside it remains mysterious. In relation to their self-conception, then, the greater part of the information available in the wider society simply is not processed, because the constructs by which to do so have never been developed.

There are others who reflect sufficiently far to realize that their situation is remarkably different from that of most British teenagers, and that they are perceived by those outside the 'community' as being in a paradoxical situation. Thus a girl describes her existence as being like that of full-time actor: going to school requires the putting on of one set of theatrical robes and performing a definite role, while going home means relinquishing that role, changing costume, and taking up another. Accounts such as this give evidence of an attempt at synthesis, but at a concrete level. The fact of being an 'actor' is not in itself a source of personal discomfort or dissonance.

Some 'Muslim adolescents', particularly among those who stay in education several years beyond the age of 16, attempt to make sense of their situation at a deeper level, including working out some higher-order guidelines for action. One form of synthesis is through fresh appraisal of what it means to be a Muslim. Islam claims to be a way of life that transcends all barriers of race and nation; it enables a person to make the desired assertions 'I am not a Pakistani' and 'I am not British', but still to have an overriding self-description. The modern proponents of Islam declare, moreover, that their beliefs are not antagonistic to science and technology, and thus that there is nothing anti-progressive in their attitude, even if the so-called progress of the West deserves censure. It seems probable that a reworking of Islam, involving fresh examination of its teaching on crucial issues, will increase. Another form of synthesis is through political involvement. A growing number of young British–Asians are becoming conscious of their rights as citizens, and the extent to which they are subjected to structural and procedural injustice. In contrast to the migrant generation, they are prepared to engage in collective action. For 'young Muslims' this usually (but not always) involves rejection of the specifically religious dimension of Islam, while retaining the associated sense of solidarity. It sharpens their understanding of their unique historical situation, and makes possible a powerful assertion of who they are.

I have pointed here to a range of reactions and possibilities. The striking thing is that generally 'young Muslims' do not find the fact of existing 'between two cultures', and of being a 'halfway generation' intrinsically problematic. It would be so, one might hypothesise, for those whose underlying conception of the person was based on a strong form of Western individualism, which required personal consistency of behaviour. But this, as I have tried to show, is not the case with those we are considering here. Thus it would require a profound metaphysical change rather than a superficial encounter with British people and institutions before their predicament was experienced as one of 'threatened identity'.

THE ERIKSONIAN CASE

This paper has done little more than indicate general patterns, and inevitably it has been promoting stereotypical views to which there are many exceptions. I wish now to point to one kind of case in which self-conception is thrown into serious disarray. It does not seem to be common among 'Muslim adolescents', but it is important for the completion of the picture.

The case is that of a person who tries to escape from that Asian-ness and Muslim-ness in which his or her self-conception was originally grounded, in order to participate in the host society on its own terms—but who fails. Typically, such a person breaks most ties with the 'community' and aspires to British middle-class ways. Perhaps the hope is that success in gaining qualifications and entering a professional career will be a passport to social acceptance in the new milieu. Those who do this wholeheartedly are taking a great risk with their self-conception. They are effectively discounting the processes by which they were formed as social beings, abandoning the network of human relationships which gave them such strong ontological validation; implicitly, they are in process of rejecting one metaphysic of the person and taking up another. If they succeed they become little more than Western individualists with a brown skin. During the change they have to pass through a period of great vulnerability while new processes of social feedback, social comparison and self-attribution are being established.

For those who fail, the position is indeed serious. They have exiled themselves from the social milieu in which they might have been sustained, and obtained in return mainly evidence with damaging implications: that they are not liked or accepted, that they have not 'made the grade'. They have no clear place in society, and their inner world is in disarray. Erikson's theory of 'identity-confusion', and even that of 'identity crisis', might indeed provide an accurate description of their case. It must be emphasized, however, that this phenomenon is vary rare among the present cohort of 'Muslim adolescents' in the North of England. It might perhaps be more common among those of Asian background for whom the 'community' is less cohesive, or in a time of greater economic opportunity.

A CASE OF MISATTRIBUTION

If the argument of this paper is substantially correct, we are left with a final question. How has the stereotype arisen that Asian adolescents in Britain are liable to 'identity-confusion'? No doubt, some of the general processes involved in stereotyping, and those particularly associated with the misperception of adolescents, have come into play. But I wish to offer an additional speculation.

Anyone who meets 'Muslim adolescents', but only superficially, has to deal with two conflicting sets of data. On the one hand, some aspects of their presence are definitely foreign, even mysterious or exotic: notably their physical appearance and their use, on occasions, of unintelligible tongues. On the other hand, they often adopt interactional styles virtually indistinguishable from those of their British contemporaries, including speaking English with impeccable regional accents. Most British people trying to make sense of these two sets of data have no clear basis for doing so, either in theory or experience. One solution which, while not logically dependent on the evidence, provides some kind of explanation, is to attribute to these boys and girls a 'problem of personal identity'. The ground has been prepared by the incorporation of Eriksonian ideas into middlebrow commonsense psychology; the attribution is not falsified because the interaction remains on a superficial level. In reality, it is not the 'Muslim adolescent' who is confused but the observer. Even if the former does not have a problem of 'identity', the latter does have a problem of 'identification'. Serious inaccuracies of perception can occur when people make uncritical use of resources from their own taken-for-granted world.

In cases such as the one we have been considering, there is an obvious solution. It is to get to know some of the people concerned personally, to understand the objective conditions of their existence, and to listen carefully to what they have to say. Our research method is based on this simple but largely untried idea.

ACKNOWLEDGEMENT

I would like to express my thanks to Sundar Kanta Kapila (Walker), Nadira Mirza and Carol Borrill for their help given when this paper was taking shape.

REFERENCES

Allen, S. (1971). *New Minorities, Old Conflicts.* New York, Random House.

Erikson, E. H. (1965). *Childhood and Society*, New York, Norton.

Erikson, E. H. (1968). *Identity: Youth and Crisis.* London, Faber & Faber.

Horney, K. (1937). *The Neurotic Personality of Our Time.* London, Routledge & Kegan Paul.

Kitwood, T. M. (1980). *Disclosures to a Stranger. London*, Routledge & Kegan Paul.

Kitwood, T. M., and Borrill, C. S. (1980). The significance of schooling for an ethnic minority, *Oxford Review of Education*, **6**, 241–253.

Noble, G. (1975). *Children in Front of the Small Screen.* London, Constable.

Taylor, J. H. (1976). *The Half-way Generation.* Slough, National Foundation for Educational Research.

Watson, J. E. (ed.) (1977). *Between two cultures. Migrants and Minorities in Britain.* Oxford, Blackwell.

Wegner, D. M., and Vallacher, R. R. (1977). *Implicit Psychology.* New York, Oxford University Press.

Threatened Identities
Edited by G. Breakwell

Emerging from Threatened Identities: Ethnicity and Gender in Redefinitions of Ethnic Identity

PETER WEINREICH

INTRODUCTION

This chapter is concerned with processes of identity development in circumstances that pose *threats to identity*. It is further concerned with processes of self-redefinition by which individuals attempt to *emerge from threatened identities*.

Identity is defined in Personal Construct Theory (PCT) terms. The psychodynamic concept of *identity conflict*, with its connotations of threat to identity, is critically examined. Certain ambiguities in the concept of an individual's *identification with another* are resolved. Related definitions are presented in which the individual's personal construct system provides a core component, and through which their psychodynamic meanings are clarified. The resultant theoretical framework, a synthesis of certain aspects of psychodynamic theory with key concepts of PCT, is used to derive propositions concerning self-concept change under circumstances which may be regarded as posing psychological threats to traditional identities, specifically those giving rise to ethnic identity conflict in which major redefinitions of self not only involve ethnicity but also gender roles.

Rapid social change challenges our understanding of how individuals come to redefine themselves and renegotiate their relationships with others in situations of flux. Such individual redefinitions, that is, changes in self-concept and identity, are especially acute concerns of people in transitional positions in society. The present theoretical exposition is presented in general terms, but the empirical data and case study analyses are drawn from an arena of intergroup and interpersonal relations which is likely to command people's attention into the forseeable future. This arena is that currently labelled *race relations*. By concentrating attention on the particular characteristics of identity development in young people of immigrant background, the dynamics of various kinds of self-concept development are brought into high relief. By comparing modes of identity development in immigrant offspring with those of indigenous adolescents, their interrelationships are clarified. The different symbolic functions that members of one group have for another are made manifest.

Integral to attempts to resolve ethnic identity conflicts are redefinitions of *gender* roles, since these core features of people's identities are closely bound to the specific cultural milieux of ethnic groups. The symbolic use of others across ethnic boundaries may play an important part in new definitions by adolescents of their gender roles. The interplay of gender and ethnicity in an ethnically mixed society becomes a significant consideration in adolescent self-concept development (one which may be exploitative and, on occasion, vicious, but which may more frequently involve a valued recognition of the integrity of other people's life-styles).

The offspring of immigrants represent a category of people for whom redefinitions of self, and renegotiations of relationships with others, are particularly salient concerns in their lives. Whilst all individuals have to invest a degree of psychological effort in their identity development, immigrant offspring have to contend with often uncomfortable transactions between themselves as *members-of-a-minority-ethnic-group* and people of the indigenous population. Empirical procedures[1] used with adolescents from two minority ethnic groups ('West Indian' and 'Asian')[2] and with indigenous adolescents will, in this chapter, serve the dual function of demonstrating the usefulness of the concepts defined here in understanding processes of self-concept change, and of establishing the significance of ethnicity and gender in their unfolding.

The chapter is divided into three parts. The first consists of a brief theoretical analysis of identity development from which is derived two fundamental postulates concerning processes of self-concept change. Conceptions of identity conflict and their limitations are examined in the light of empirical evidence. Further definitions elucidate the meaning of identity conflict. In the second part, the power of the resultant conceptualization is demonstrated in an empirical analysis of ethnic identification conflicts and associated characteristics in adolescents from three ethnic groups growing up in the city of Bristol in England. The patterns of identification conflicts differ between the groups, but whilst these may be regarded as attributes of *threatened identities* in terms of some idealized unchanging prototypical identity, there is, in general, no evidence of widespread self-devaluation relating to a subordinate ethnic status as such. Third, theoretical propositions concerning redefinitions of ethnic identity by ethnic group members are derived from the foregoing analysis of identity development. They are illustrated by two studies of individuals who, in their particular cases, *are* emerging from threatened identities.

1. IDENTITY DEVELOPMENT

Kelly's basic concept, the personal construct, acknowledges individual variation in people's definitions of themselves and others. His theoretical orientation emphasizes individual change (Kelly, 1955). As Bannister and Fransella (1971) say 'People interpret and reinterpret themselves and their situation. The whole of construct theory is based upon this fundamental idea that a person's psychological processes are channelled by the ways in which he successively construes events'. Kelly's construct theory therefore provides a sound basis upon which the theoretical conceptualization of self-concept development and change can be built. It is used in this chapter, in conjunction with the psychodynamic approach to identity formation, in order to elucidate the relationship between the individual's conception of himself in the past and his construal of what he aspires to be.

An important aspect of self-concept development is the continuity between past and present self, despite changes which may have occurred in the intervening period. But, as will be seen, the nature of the continuity is not necessarily self-evident. What is required is a definition of identity which conceptualizes the continuity of the person's current self-image with his past and also conceptualizes his potential for change.

Definition of identity

The following definition of *identity* acknowledges change in self-concept development, whilst also recognizing continuity. It is derived from definitions by Erikson (1958, 1965) and Laing (1961) but it gives the *process of construal* a central place:

> One's identity is defined as the totality of one's self-construal, in which how one construes oneself in the present expresses the continuity between how one construes oneself as one was in the past and how one construes oneself as one aspires to be in the future.

In this definition of identity, the nature of the continuity between the person's self construal in the past and as self aspires to be in the future is not specified. However, it is precisely this that a theory of identity development and change must be capable of explaining. What is the nature of the continuity and how is that continuity related to the determinants of change? What is the nature of the continuity in the absence of change and what are the antecedant conditions which inhibit change?

The resynthesis of childhood identifications: two fundamental postulates of identity development

Erikson (1968) presented the task facing adolescents in their identity formation as one of resynthesizing their childhood identifications in order to form a coherent identity. Failure to form such an identity he characterized as *identity diffusion*.

Established empirical procedures by Marcia and others (Marcia, 1966, 1967; Marcia and Friedman, 1970; Waterman and Waterman, 1971; Waterman, Geary and Waterman, 1974; Constantinople, 1969, 1970; Hauser 1971, 1972; Hauser and Shapiro, 1973), have identified uniformities in identity development, but these investigators do not elaborate on the process involved in the resynthesis of childhood identifications. As Erikson observes, these processes are central to identity development, and it is to these that the current conceptualization is directed. They provide the key to understanding the continuity in change in self-concept development.

If all childhood identifications were compatible one with another, there would be no problem in 'synthesizing' them and there would be no need to consider their *resynthesis*. A resynthesis implies a rearrangement or realignment of previous identifications with perhaps an acceptance of some and a rejection of others, or a redefinition of them in part. Erikson stresses that identifications with others tend to be partial rather than wholly with them, and that they are not necessarily compatible with each other. In general, therefore, there will be incompatibilities in identifications and, in the course of time, individuals will develop many conflicts in their identifications with others. Erikson would maintain that this is especially true of adolescents, given the rapidity of their biological and psychic development, hence his stress on identity formation being an adolescent task. The reason for the resynthesis of identifications is to be found in these identification conflicts, which are likely to be more pervasive during adolescence than at other periods during the life cycle though arguments could readily be put forward for any transitional period in the life cycle necessitating such resyntheses. This brief analysis forms the basic derivation of two fundamental postulates of identity development, which, with appropriate empirical procedures, make it possible to designate the nature of the continuity between the person's construal of self *in the past* and that *aspired to be in the future*.

POSTULATE 1

Resolution of conflicted identifications

When one's identifications with others are conflicted, one attempts to resolve the conflicts, thereby inducing re-evaluations of self in relation to the others within the limitations of one's currently existing value system.

POSTULATE 2

Formation of new identifications

> When one forms further identifications with newly encounted individuals, one broadens one's value system and establishes a new context for one's self-definition, thereby initiating a reappraisal of self and others which is dependent on fundamental changes in one's value system.

It follows from this second postulate that, as one forms new identifications with others, one becomes particularly vulnerable to self-doubt, since at the time of incorporating new values and aspirations one will, in most instances, lack the skills for their implementation and therefore downgrade one's self-evaluation in these respects, until such time that one has acquired the relevant mastery.

Conceptions of identity conflict: some empirical evidence

In order to demonstrate the practical utility of this analysis, it is necessary to define the terms *identification* and *identification conflict with another* explicitly. However, before doing so, a discussion of the ubiquitous but ambiguous term *identity conflict* is required in order to demonstrate the necessity for a more molecular analysis of a person's conflicts in identifications. Especially relevant social contexts for these concepts are those encompassing cultural discontinuities, such as between ethnic groups, or across social class, religious, or generation barriers, or a combination of these. Consider the case of adolescents of immigrant parentage.

With widespread migration, significant minority ethnic communities become established within nation states. Two major sociopsychological factors affects the socialization of the young in such circumstances. One is the nature of the relationship between the indigenous population and the minority groups. The other is the creation of the plurality of cultural values, or the differences between ethnically distinct communities in their folklores and customs. The empirical evidence presented in this chapter will concern adolescent self-concept development when the relationship is one of exploitation of, and discrimination against, the minority groups. The plurality of cultural values will be represented chiefly by 'West Indian' and, to a lesser extent, by 'Asian' communities within the city of Bristol in England.

Two concepts concerning identity development are prevalent in the literature on discrimination and on the clash of cultural values. They are *identity conflict* and *culture conflict*. The first more usually refers to the proposition that those experiencing discrimination internalize the derogatory images of themselves projected by the discriminators.[3] Culture conflict refers to the proposition that the offspring of ethnic minorities are 'between cultures' and internalize conflicts between the values of the one culture and those of the other.[4] Both propositions posit the existence of social problems *within* the ethnic minority groups. We will question whether these are valid inferences.

Discrimination and negative identity

One proposition which has had wide currency in the literature on ethnic relations is that discrimination results in self-devaluation, in which it is argued that the oppressed group internalizes the negative images of their group held by the oppressors. The consequence of this internalization is that members of the oppressed group have devalued self-images. It has been held that this is true of minority ethnic groups and of women. Latterly, this proposition has been criticised. While minority or 'oppressed' group members may share some of the dominant group's images, they do not necessarily have low self-esteem as a consequence.

One of the outcomes of the Bristol study has been a confirmation of these criticisms. Adolescents of school leaving age were randomly sampled at low frequency from schools in Bristol with catchment areas which included concentrations of offspring of 'West Indian' and 'Asian' parentage. The sample consisted of 37 indigenous English (15 boys and 22 girls), 32 of 'West Indian' background (14 boys and 18 girls), and 13 of 'Asian' background (7 boys and 6 girls). They participated in the study on an individual basis, each person being interviewed by researchers from the three ethnic backgrounds represented in the sample, and subsequently being given individually tailored rating sheets of bipolar constructs so that they could construe themselves and significant others. A separate manual (Weinreich, 1980) gives the data collection procedures followed, the definitions of the concepts used and their algebraic equivalents, and instructions on the use

DISCRIMINATION/SELF-DEVALUATION PROPOSITION

Table 1. Degree to which English adolescents devalue minority ethnic groups

On a scale of evaluation ranging from − 1.00 to + 1.00, English adolescents devalue:

'Asian' adults compared with English adults by	0.54*
'Asian' boys compared with English boys by	0.39*
'Asian' girls compared with English girls by	0.42†
'West Indian' adults compared with English adults by	0.32*
'West Indian' boys compared with English boys by	0.37*
'West Indian' girls compared with English girls by	0.37*

*$p < 0.01$; † $p < 0.02$ (related t-tests).

of the IDEX computer program (Weinreich et al., 1981) to compute the indices referred to in this chapter.

As a generalization, the *discrimination/self-devaluation* proposition does not receive empirical support.[5] Discrimination on the grounds of 'race' does not result in self-devaluation by 'immigrant' adolescents, nor does discrimination on the grounds of sex result in self-devaluation of girls

DISCRIMINATION/SELF-DEVALUATION PROPOSITION

Table 2. English and 'West Indian' adolescents' evaluation of their own ethnic groups. On a scale of evaluation ranging from −1.00 to +1.00:

(i) With respect to their OWN SEX PEERS, mean evaluation:

By:	
English girls of English girls is	0.40 (16)
'West Indian' girls of 'West Indian' girls is	0.33 (16)
English boys of English boys is	0.53 (13)
'West Indian' boys of 'West Indian' boys is	0.44 (12)

Irrespective of ethnicity, girls have a lower evaluation of their own sex than boys of theirs ($F = 5.100$; *df* 1,53; $p < 0.05$).
The factor of ethnicity is nonsignificant.

(ii) With respect to their OPPOSITE SEX PEERS, mean evaluation:

By:	
English girls of English boys is	0.27 (16)
'West Indian' girls of 'West Indian' boys is	0.17 (18)
English boys of English girls is	0.49 (13)
'West Indian' boys of 'West Indian' girls is	0.43 (14)

Irrespective of ethnicity, girls have a lower evaluation of the opposite sex than do boys ($F = 11.249$; *df* 1,58; $p < 0.01$).
The factor of ethnicity is nonsignificant.

(iii) With respect to ADULTS, mean evaluation:

By:	
English girls of English adults is	0.35 (14)
'West Indian' girls of 'West Indian' adults is	0.28 (17)
English boys of English adults is	0.58 (12)
'West Indian' boys of 'West Indian' adults is	0.47 (13)

Irrespective of ethnicity, girls have a lower evaluation of adults than do boys ($F = 5.304$; *df* 1,52; $p < 0.05$).
The factor of ethnicity is nonsignificant.

Note: Sample size varies as indicated by *N*'s in brackets due to instances of incomplete information.

DISCRIMINATION/SELF-DEVALUATION PROPOSITION

Table 3. Self-esteem by ethnicity
Self-esteem: range −1.00 to +1.00

Boys and girls combined†	(*N*) English	(*N*) 'West Indian' and 'Asian'
Including cases of 'defensive high self-esteem'	(37) 0.375*	(45) 0.512*
		(32) 0.475 'West Indian' (13) 0.605 'Asian'
Excluding cases of 'defensive high self-esteem'‡	(37) 0.375 *NS*	(39) 0.470 *NS*
		(28) 0.434 'West Indian' (11) 0.563 'Asian'

* The difference between these means is significant $p < 0.05$ (analysis of variance). 'Immigrant' adolescents have higher self-esteem than English.
† Analysis of variance indicates no significant gender differences in self-esteem.
‡ Four 'West Indian' and two 'Asian' adolescents are identified as exhibiting 'defensive high self-esteem'.
NS Not significant in the absence of cases of defensive high self-esteem.

compared with boys. The relevant evidence is presented in three tables (Tables 1, 2 and 3). It is clear that, while English adolescents devalue adults, boys and girls of 'Asian' and 'West Indian' origin, 'West Indian' boys and girls do not subscribe to these devalued images. In addition, 'West Indian' and 'Asian' adolescents in the sample do not in general devalue themselves compared with their English counterparts. Their mean self-esteem is, if anything, somewhat higher than that for the English though this is bolstered by instances of *defensive high self-esteem*, a concept which is discussed later on in the chapter. With respect to girls there is also no evidence of lowered self-esteem compared with boys. It should be noted that these conclusions are derived from indices of evaluation which are based on the value systems to which the individuals themselves subscribe, rather than on ones externally imposed through the use of standard scales of questionaire items.

The argument of self-devaluation as a consequence of discrimination has also included the view that there are basic similarities between being black and being female. Again, data from this sample does not support this. Girls do not have lower self-esteem than boys, but they do have lower evaluations of their own sex than boys of theirs. However, they also have lower evaluations of the opposite sex and of adults than boys do. Furthermore, boys do not devalue girls; on the contrary, it is girls who have a poor view of boys. In brief summary, it appears that minority group adolescents do not hold to a devalued group image, but that girls do devalue their own sex compared with boys without, however, internalizing this as a devaluation of self. Evidently, ethnicity and gender contribute to self-concept development in different ways. Irrespective of ethnicity, girls in this sample generally form less positive views of large segments of their social world than do boys, an indication perhaps of a more realistic or cynical orientation towards society.

Culture conflict

It will now be appreciated that strong assumptions have been made in previous literature about the relationship between discrimination, self-image and identity conflict. It is no longer apparent what precisely 'identity conflict' means. The fact that there are considerable differences between the values held by different ethnic groups does suggest that those children who grow up experiencing two quite distinct cultures are likely to internalize values from both. This means that their identifications will not be confined solely to their ethnic groups of origin and that conflicts in their identifications are to be expected. In other words, the meaning of identity conflict in the case of cultural discontinuities is to be found in the person's *conflicts in identifications with others* dependant on successive identifications with, in the early years, parents, siblings and other kin representing the one culture, and, later on, with various charismatic others in society at large representing the other.

In order to carry this analysis to empirical test, it is necessary both to precisely define what is meant by a conflict in identification with another and to develop a procedure for assessing such conflicts in a person. Since the assessment procedure should be valid for use with people holding widely differing value systems, the definition must take the person's value system into account. Personal construct theory provides a helpful conceptualization for this, namely, that individuals possess systems of bipolar constructs whereby they construe themselves and others, and which represent, amongst other things, their differing value systems.

Further requirements for the assessment procedures are that they will:

(a) Provide a measure of the overall extent and magnitude of people's identification conflicts (to be called the degree of *identity diffusion* characterizing a person).
(b) Locate within their self-concepts those others with whom their identification conflicts are greatest in magnitude (that is, to be able to establish the ways in which one's distribution of identification conflicts differs from another's).

(c) Indicate the nature of the relationships between their identification conflicts and their self-evaluations (that is, to be able to simultaneously assess a person's self-esteem and 'identity conflict' without interpreting *a priori* 'identity conflict' to mean a negative self-evaluation or low self-esteem).

Conflicted identifications with others: definitions

Before defining what is meant by a person's conflict in identification with another, the term *identification* itself requires clarification. Identifications with others are generally partial rather than absolute. People tend not to identify in an all or none fashion with the values and characteristics of various groups and individuals. The definitions that follow will therefore include statements about the *extent* of a person's identification with another.

Furthermore, two distinct meanings of *identification* can be distinguished. The one concerns the person's recognition of commonality of qualities with another, which may be referred to as *empathetic* identification. The other emphasizes the person's wish to become like another whom he or she admires, that is, *role model* identification. In the first sense, the other is experienced as having things in common with self, whether these be good or bad. In the second, the other represents qualities which have become incorporated into the person's ideal self-image. This conceptual distinction is crucial to the definition of a person's identification conflict with another. The two senses will therefore be considered separately.

A definition of identification in the empathetic sense is straightforward. With a person's current self-image as reference point:

> the extent of one's *current identification* with another is defined as the degree of similarity between the qualities one attributes to the other (whether 'good' or 'bad') and those of one's current self-image (me as I am now).

The other use of the concept refers to people's ideal self-images. It relates to their reference models or groups, either as ones whom they wish to emulate, or as ones forming contrasting standards for comparison. Two definitions follow corresponding to the distinction between emulation and contrasting standards:

> the extent of one's *idealistic-identification* with another is defined as the degree of similarity between the qualities one attributes to the other and those one would like to possess as part of an ideal self-image (me as I would like to be);

> the extent of one's *contra-identification* with another is defined as the degree of similarity between the qualities one attributes to the other and those from which one would wish to dissociate.

People's idealistic identifications constitute their positive value systems associated with their more positive reference models, whilst their contra-identifications are linked with their contravalue systems and their more negative reference models.

An explicit definition of the term *identification conflict* can now be given. One's conflict in identification with another is both a function of the extent of one's current identification with the other and one's simultaneous wish to dissociate from certain characteristics of the other. Consider an adolescent Asian girl who strongly identifies with the Asian culture's emphasis on duty and obligations, but who, having adopted Western concepts of love, dissociates from the Asian institution of arranged marriages. She perceives that her parents are committed to orthodox Asian values and in many respects empathetically identifies with them, for example, with their shared commitments to duty and obligations, but she also wishes to dissociate from their belief in arranged marriages. Her identifications with her mother and father are therefore conflicted. Identification conflict involves the person's simultaneous *current-* and *contra-*identifications with another:

> the extent of a person's *identification conflict with another* is defined as a multiplicative function of that person's current- and contra-identifications with the other.

As the person's current- and contra-identifications with the other simultaneously increase so will that person's conflict in identification become greater.

Personal Construct Theory forms the basis for the translation of these definitions into empirical measuring procedures. In practice, individuals are asked to use their own bipolar constructs, presented one at a time, to construe their significant others (including groups of people). In addition, they are asked to construe their current and past self-images (*me as I am now* and *me as I used to be*) and their ideal self-image (*me as I would like to be*). For example, using the construct *believes in law and order—believes in each man for himself* a person may categorize father as believing in each man for himself, but mother as believing in law and order. With the use of a centre-zero interval scale the extent to which the person feels these polar attributes are true of father and mother can be indicated (Weinreich, 1980).

Positive value systems are determined by reference to people's construal of their ideal self-images. Positive values are defined as those characteristics attributed to how one would like to be. Contra-value systems are assumed to correspond to the polar contrasts of these attributes. For example, if in using one's construct *studies for something worthwhile—works just for the money* one applies the first pole to one's ideal self-image, *studying for some-*

thing worthwhile is defined as an element of one's positive value system and *working just for the money* as an element of one's contra value system.

The degree of a person's current identification with another is determined by the extent of overlap between that person's current self-image construal and that of the other. Contra-identification with the other is given by the extent to which the person attributes contra-values or characteristics to that other. The magnitude of the person's conflict in identification with that other is then expressed as the product of the degrees of self's simultaneous current- and contra-identifications with the other. These procedures can be used to estimate the magnitude of the person's identification conflicts with each of self's significant others in turn. They therefore fulfil the requirements stated earlier for assessing identification conflicts in people with differing value systems. They enable a person's specific pattern of identification conflicts to be established, and to be differentiated from another person's pattern. Since self-evaluation can be computed as an appropriate summation of the positive and negative characteristics attributed to self, the specific relationship between self-esteem and pattern of identification conflicts can be ascertained (Weinreich, 1980).

The broad dispersion of identification conflicts with many others when these are considerable in magnitude is regarded as the analytic equivalent of Erikson's clinical description of identity diffusion (Weinreich, 1979a). The incompatibilities in identifications in such instances corresponds to a high lack of synthesis of identifications. Analytically, therefore: the degree of a person's *identity diffusion* is defined as the overall dispersion of and magnitude of that person's identification conflicts. Evidently, people characterized by high levels of identity diffusion may be differentiated one from another in terms of their specific patterns of conflicted identifications.

The procedures described in the manual referred to earlier (Weinreich, 1980) enable one to compute a quantitative index of the degree of a person's identity diffusion that is related to the quantification of the person's identification conflicts with named others. As we have seen from the analysis of the data from the Bristol study, indices of self-evaluation and evaluation others are also computed. It can be demonstrated, both theoretically and empirically, that high identity diffusion, as defined in the above analysis, may accompany a range of self-evaluations from negative to positive. It would therefore seem prudent to restrict Erikson's term *identity crisis* to only those states in people characterized by widely dispersed and high levels of conflicted identifications, when these are accompanied by *low* self-evaluations. This restrictive use would be compatible with Erikson's vivid clinical descriptions of highly demoralized adolescents, whilst avoiding unwarranted implications when the term is used indiscriminately to refer to any instances of identification conflicts.

2. EMPIRICAL EVIDENCE OF ETHNIC IDENTIFICATION CONFLICTS

Applying this mode of analysis to the data from the Bristol sample, it is found that ethnicity is, as expected, an important feature of self-concept development in adolescent boys and girls from the two ethnic minorities (see data in Table 4). In very nearly all cases of the 'West Indian' and 'Asian' adolescents, conflicts in identification with general representatives of their own ethnicity are salient, despite other differences between the ethnic

Patterns of identification conflicts

Table 4. Conflicts in ethnic identifications

Distribution of high identification conflicts in English, 'Asian' and 'West Indian' adolescents is given in terms of percent of such conflicts present (percent present + percent absent = 100 percent*) in relation to:

(*N*)	Parents	Own ethnic group (English people)	'West Indians'	'Asians'
(15) English boys	47	47	60	40
(22) English girls	32	55	59	45
(37) Together	38	51	60	43
(*N*)	Parents	Own ethnic group ('Asian' people)	English	'West Indians'
(7) 'Asian' boys	14	100	57	43
(6) 'Asian' girls	17	83	50	83
(13) Together	15^{L}	92^{HH}	54	61
(*N*)	Parents	Own ethnic group ('West Indian' people)	English	'Asians'
(14) 'West Indian, boys	21^{L}	79^{HH}	86^{HH}	29^{L}
(18) 'West Indian' girls	55^{H}	95^{HH}	39^{L}	28^{L}
(32) Together	41	87	59	28

Chief characteristics which differentiate the groups at a statistically significant level: HH = high presence; H = moderately high; L = low.

Reading across L v HH, $p < 0.001$; H v HH; $p < 0.01$.

Reading down ('West Indian' boys and girls) L v HH; $p < 0.01$; L v H, $p = 0.055$.

* The distribution of high identification conflicts for an individual is obtained in the following manner. Indices of identification conflict with the following targets are calculated by the IDEX computer program: parents, representatives of own, and other, ethnic groups, and a miscellaneous category. The five highest values for identification conflicts occurring for the person are selected and then distributed between the target categories. One or more entries in a target category designates the presence of high identification conflict, whilst a null entry designates an absence.

groups. This common feature can be explained as the outcome of a process of dual socialization. First, children form identifications within their parent cultural group during early primary socialization. Then they become increasingly altered to the indigenous culture through secondary socialization by way of schooling and the mass media. Over a period of time, they form part-identifications with, and adopt some of the values of, indigenous people encountered at school and elsewhere. This leads to the development of varying degrees of conflicts with some of those earlier identifications which were grounded during primary socialization.

To this extent, 'identity conflict' is shown to be related to growing up 'between cultures'. However, the empirical results qualify the culture or identity conflict view of self-concept development in two ways. Firstly, these ethnically related conflicts in identification do not imply devalued self-images. Secondly, the specific pattern of ethnic identification conflicts varies according to ethnicity and gender. Our studies show that 'Asian' boys and girls have a very low incidence of identification conflicts with their parents. For 'West Indian' adolescents there are sex differences, boys having a low frequency of identification conflicts with parents and girls having a high frequency. In another respect, 'West Indian' boys stand out from the other 'immigrant' adolescents in that they have by far the highest proportion of identification conflicts with the English.

Identity diffusion

'Identity conflict' is therefore an imprecise term to use to describe the effects of discrimination or dual socialization on self-concept development, and, when it is used in these contexts, its negative connotations can be grossly misleading. However, whilst there is no evidence that these 'immigrant' adolescents' ethnic identification conflicts are accompanied by systematic

PATTERNS OF IDENTIFICATION CONFLICTS

Table 5. Identity diffusion in English and 'immigrant' adolescents

Mean extent of identity diffusion (range 0.00 to 1.00):

	(*N*) boys	(*N*) girls
English	(15) 0.29	(22) 0.31*
'Immigrant' ('West Indian' and 'Asian')	(21) 0.27†	(24) 0.35*†

* The predicted higher identity diffusion for 'immigrant' compared with English girls was significant at $p < 0.05$, one tail t test, but did not hold for boys.

† The unexpected difference in identity diffusion between 'immigrant' boys and girls was significant at $p < 0.01$, two tail t test.

devaluations of the self, it is argued that 'dual socialization' will result in *greater* identification conflicts. This gives rise to the hypothesis that boys and girls of immigrant parentage will exhibit greater degrees of 'identity diffusion' than indigenous boys and girls. This hypothesis was found to hold for girls, but not for boys (see data presented in Table 5). This unexpected finding for 'immigrant' boys prompted the question of what *mechanism* they were using to diminish their identity diffusion, especially since 'immigrant' girls exhibited substantially higher levels than they did.

Defensive high self-esteem: a variant of identity foreclosure

At the individual level there were some adolescents who exhibited exceptionally low levels of identity diffusion, together with high levels of self-esteem. They did not give a differentiated view of the social world, but tended to see themselves and most others in globally favourable terms. By this means they were able to avoid acknowledging identification conflicts with others. Their posture was one of denial of conflicts and presentation of a *defensive high self-esteem* (Silber and Tippett, 1965; Binder *et al.*, 1974; Rios-Garcia and Cook, 1975). Was it possible that 'immigrant' *girls* acknowledged greater overall levels of conflicted identifications with others, and *boys* tended towards a defensive denial of them? On the basis of quantitative criteria, all cases in the sample of *defensive high self-esteem* were identified. Likewise, all cases of *high identity diffusion* were noted. When instances of *defensive high self-esteem* and *high identity diffusion* were taken together, their combined frequency was significantly greater for 'immigrant' than for English adolescents in the Bristol sample. Cases of *defensive high self-esteem* tended to be 'immigrant' boys whilst those of *high identity diffusion* tended to be 'immigrant' girls. This corroborates the finding of significantly higher levels of identity diffusion in girls of immigrant parentage compared with boys (see data in Table 6).

Defensive high self-esteem is one variant of an identity state classified as *identity foreclosure*, which represents an unchanging state of development in which the person has foreclosed prematurely on a particular self-conception (Erikson, 1965; Marcia, 1966; Hauser, 1971). By not allowing conflicts in identification into awareness, the antecedent conditions for change do not at the time obtain. In one sense, then, there is here evidence of 'threatening circumstances' to identity affecting these adolescents of minority ethnic parentage, in which some develop states of high identity diffusion, whilst some others appear to defend themselves against such threats by foreclosure: in total they account for about one-third of the 'immigrant' sample. However, as demonstrated by the empirical evidence cited earlier, these identity states are not accompanied by general self-devaluation.

PATTERNS OF IDENTIFICATION CONFLICTS

Table 6. 'Defensive high self-esteem' and 'high identity diffusion' in English and 'immigrant' adolescents

	Number of cases of			
(*N*)	'Defensive high self-esteem' (*A*)	'High identity diffusion' (*B*)	(*A*) and (*B*) combined	Remainder
In English:				
(15) Boys	0	0	0	15
(22) Girls	0	3	3	19
In (37) English adolescents	0	3	3*	34*
In 'Immigrant' ('West Indian' and 'Asian'):				
(21) Boys	5	3	8	13
(24) Girls	1	7	8	16
In (45) 'Immigrant' adolescents	6	10	16*	29*

* Combined frequency of 'defensive high self-esteem' and 'high identity diffusion' is significantly higher for 'immigrant' than for English adolescents ($p < 0.01$).

The quantitative criteria designating:

(a) An instance of 'defensive high self-esteem' are: for the IDEX index of self-esteem, 0.70 or greater; and for the IDEX index of identity diffusion, less than 0.20.

(b) An instance of 'high identity diffusion' is: for the IDEX index of identity diffusion, 0.40 or greater.

Reference models

If the circumstances for some adolescents of 'immigrant' parentage are indeed threatening to their identity development, what other factors in general enable them to maintain positive self-evaluations? Is the answer to be found in the support that they might receive from their parents and other authority figures in the community, such as teachers, and in their own orientations towards them? Or is it be found in their relationships with their peers? The people principally involved in the socialization of adolescents are obviously likely to be important to their identity development. Additional analyses deriving from the conceptualization introduced in this chapter (see Weinreich, 1980, for an extended treatment) enable one to answer two further questions. Firstly, how intensely involved are these adolescents with

Table 7. 'Asian', 'West Indian' and English adolescents' ego-involvement with 'authority figures' (mum, dad, and teachers)

Ego-involvement with (scale: 0.00 to 5.00 max)			
Analysis of variance			
No interaction effects			
A1 *Targets* main effect	$F = 20.32$; df 2,216; $p < 0.01$		
	Mum	Dad	Teachers
For:			
All boys and girls	3.97	3.96	3.20
I.e. irrespective of ethnicity, boys and girls are less ego-involved with their teachers than with their parents.			
A2 *Sex* main effect	$F = 4.64$; df 1,216; $p < 0.01$		
	'Authority figures'		
For:			
All boys	3.87		
All girls	3.62		
I.e. irrespective of ethnicity, girls are less ego-involved with 'authority figures' than boys.			
A3 *Ethnicity* main effect	$F = 3.58$; df 2,216; $p < 0.1$		
	'Authority figures'		
For:			
'Asian' boys and girls	4.05		
'West Indian' boys and girls	3.72		
English boys and girls	3.63		
I.e. 'Asian' boys and girls are more ego-involved with 'authority figures' than are 'West Indian' and English boys and girls.			

NOTE: *Ego-involvement and idealistic-identification*

The results of statistical analyses of indices of ego-involvement and idealistic-identification in the Bristol sample of adolescents are presented in the same format in Tables 7 to 14. The data are analysed in segments. Thus, Tables 7 and 8 refer to ego-involvements and idealistic-identifications with *authority figures*; Tables 9 and 10 to these indices for *adults in general from their own and other ethnic groups*; Tables 11 and 12 likewise for *peers*; Tables 13 and 14 to idealistic-identifications with their *most favoured sibling* and *most favoured same sex friend* respectively (ego-involvements, being constancies for these targets, are not included in Tables, but are cited in the text).

Each Table represents the results of an analysis of variance performed on these indices, in which there are three factors: (1) the targets of the adolescents' construals (e.g. mum, dad, and teachers in Tables 7 and 8); (2) the sex of the adolescents; and (3) the adolescents' ethnic group membership (i.e. *targets*, *sex*, and *ethnicity* respectively). Only statistically significant results are presented in detail, in which significant *interaction effects* between the factors are given first, followed by *main effects* for each factor. *Degrees of freedom* (df) vary between pairs of Tables, because not all targets for construal were relevant for all individuals in the sample. Tables 15 and 16 are concerned with further specific comparisons.

their parents, siblings, teachers, peers and others from their own and other ethnic groups: that is, how great is their *ego-involvement* with these people? Secondly, to what extent do such significant others feature as their positive role models: that is, what is their degree of *idealistic-identification* with them?

Table 8. 'Asian', 'West Indian' and English adolescents' idealistic-identifications with 'authority figures' (mum, dad, and teachers).

Idealistic-identification with (scale: 0.00 to 1.00 max)

Analysis of variance

A23 *Sex* by *ethnicity* interaction effect: $F = 10.11$; $df\ 2{,}216$; $p < 0.01$

For:	'Asian'	'Authority figures' English	'West Indian'
Boys	0.86	0.74	0.79
Girls	0.78	0.76	0.60

I.e. 'West Indian' girls idealistically identify with 'authority figures' the least.

A1 *Targets* main effect $F = 7.94$; $df\ 2{,}216$; $p < 0.01$

For:	Mum	Dad	Teachers
All boys and girls	0.77	0.76	0.68

I.e. irrespective of ethnicity, boys and girls idealistically identify with teachers less than with parents.

A2 *Sex* main effect: $F = 14.84$; $df\ 1{,}216$; $p < 0.01$

For:	'Authority figures'
All boys	0.78
All girls	0.70

I.e. irrespective of ethnicity, girls idealistically identify with 'authority figures' less than boys

A3 *Ethnicity* main effect $F = 10.27$; $df\ 2{,}216$; $p < 0.01$

For:	'Authority figures'
'Asian' boys and girls	0.82
'West Indian' boys and girls	0.75
English boys and girls	0.68

I.e. 'Asian' boys and girls idealistically identify with 'authority figures' the most.

NOTE: See note at foot of Table 7

We turn our attention first to the differences between the English, 'Asian' and 'West Indian' adolescents in their involvement with, and orientation towards, the authority figures of parents and teachers (see data in Tables 7 and 8 respectively, in which only the statistically significant findings are presented). For all of these adolescents, irrespective of ethnicity, both ego-involvement and idealistic-identification with their teachers are in general less than with their parents. However, the girls differ from the boys in that, also irrespective of ethnicity, their ego-involvement both with parents and teachers is rather less. Beyond this difference, 'West Indian' girls are exceptional in that their idealistic-identification both with parents and teachers is substantially lower than that of any other category, including 'West Indian' boys. For them these authority figures do not generally feature as positive models. A further important difference between the groups is that 'Asian' adolescents, compared with their English and 'West Indian' counterparts, are more ego-involved both with parents and teachers and also perceive them as more positive role models. In general, therefore, 'West Indian' girls in the Bristol sample have a poor orientation towards authority, and Asian boys and girls have a particularly good one.

Next, we consider these adolescents' orientations towards people within the community defined in terms of their own and other ethnic group (see data in Tables 9 and 10 for their orientations towards *adults*, and Tables 11 and 12 for *peers*). Adolescents of immigrant parentage respond more intensely than their English counterparts to adults and peers labelled in ethnic terms, whether the label is that of their own ethnic group or that of the other (the English for 'Asians' and 'West Indians'). Boys and girls,

Table 9. 'Asian', 'West Indian' and English adolescents' ego-involvement with 'ethnic group' adults

Ego-involvement with (scale: 0.00 to 5.00 max)	
Analysis of variance	
No interaction effects	
A3 *Ethnicity* main effect	$F = 4.53$; df 2,129; $p < 0.05$
	Both 'own' and 'other group' adults
For:	
'Asian' boys and girls	3.34
'West Indian' boys and girls	3.08
English boys and girls	2.68

I.e. English boys and girls are less ego-involved with adults defined in terms of ethnic labels than 'immigrant' boys and girls.

Table 10. 'Asian', 'West Indian' and English adolescents' idealistic-identification with 'ethnic group' adults

Idealistic-identification with (scale: 0.00 to 1.00 max)

Analysis of variance

A13 *Targets* by *ethnicity* interaction effect: $F = 4.63$; df 2,129; $p < 0.05$

	'Own group' adults	'Other group' adults
For:		
'Asian' boys and girls	0.78	0.67
'West Indian' boys and girls	0.61	0.54
English boys and girls	0.76	0.47

I.e. English adolescents idealistically identify with 'immigrant' adults the least, and 'West Indian' adolescents with their own group adults the least.

A1 *Targets* main effect $F = 22.65$; df 1,129; $p < 0.01$

	'Own group' adults	'Other group' adults
For:		
All boys and girls	0.70	0.54

I.e. irrespective of ethnicity, boys and girls idealistically identify with 'other group' adults less than with 'own group' adults.

A2 *Sex* main effect $F = 9.21$; df 1,129; $p < 0.01$

	Both 'own' and 'other group' adults
For:	
All boys	0.67
All girls	0.56

I.e. irrespective of ethnicity, girls idealistically identify with adults defined in terms of ethnic labels less than boys.

A3 *Ethnicity* main effect $F = 3.88$; df 2,129; $p < 0.05$

	Both 'own' and 'other group' adults
For:	
'Asian' boys and girls	0.72
'West Indian' boys and girls	0.58
English boys and girls	0.61

I.e. 'Asian' boys and girls idealistically identify with adults defined in terms of ethnic labels the most.

Table 11. 'Asian', 'West Indian' and English adolescents' ego-involvement with 'ethnic group' peers

Ego-involvement with (scale: 0.00 to 5.00 max)		
Analysis of variance		
No interaction effects		
A1 *Targets* main effect	$F = 3.55$; df 1,124; $p < 0.05$	
	'Own group' peers	'Other group' peers
For:		
All boys and girls	3.06	2.81
I.e. irrespective of ethnicity, boys and girls are less ego-involved with 'other group' peers than with 'own group' peers.		
A3 *Ethnicity* main effect	$F = 8.23$; df 2,124; $p < 0.01$	
	Both 'own' and 'other group' peers	
For:		
'Asian' boys and girls	3.29	
'West Indian' boys and girls	3.12	
English boys and girls	2.60	
I.e. English boys and girls are less ego-involved with peers defined in terms of ethnic labels than 'immigrant' boys and girls.		

irrespective of their ethnic group membership, are generally more involved with peers from their own group than from the other. Thus, whilst 'own group' peers tend to be more important than 'other group' peers for all three ethnic groups, ethnic labelling has a greater significance for 'Asians' and 'West Indians' than for the English.

English boys and girls have the least favourable orientation towards 'other group' adults and peers, which is in line with their devaluation of 'West Indians' and 'Asians' cited earlier. However, whilst this effect is especially marked for the English, boys and girls from all three ethnic groups favour their own ethnic group, both adults and peers, more than the other. The discrepancy is however the least for 'West Indian' boys and girls. Irrespective of ethnicity, girls generally have less favourable orientations towards both adults and peers than boys, a point also noted earlier and a further indication of their realistic or cynical view of the world compared with boys. 'Asian' boys and girls, consistent with their more positive appraisals of 'authority figures', have more favourable orientations towards

Table 12. 'Asian', 'West Indian' and English adolescents' idealistic-identification with 'ethnic group' peers

Idealistic-identification with (scale: 0.00 to 1.00 max)

Analysis of variance

A13 *Targets* by *ethnicity* interaction effect $F = 4.25$; df 2,124; $p < 0.05$

For:	'Own group' peers	'Other group' peers
'Asian' boys and girls	0.71	0.59
'West Indian' boys and girls	0.62	0.59
English boys and girls	0.72	0.46

I.e. English adolescents idealistically identify with 'immigrant' peers the least, and 'West Indian' adolescents with their own group peers the least.

A1 *Targets* main effect $F = 17.18$; df 1,124; $p < 0.01$

For:	'Own group' peers	'Other group' peers
All boys and girls	0.68	0.55

I.e. irrespective of ethnicity, boys and girls idealistically identify with 'other group' peers less than with 'own group' peers.

A2 *Sex* main effect $F = 16.28$; df 1,124; $p < 0.01$

For:	Both 'own' and 'other group' peers
All boys	0.68
All girls	0.55

I.e. irrespective of ethnicity, girls idealistically identify with peers defined in terms of ethnic labels less than boys.

adults, whether 'Asian' or English, compared with 'West Indian' and English boys and girls.

Finally, we turn to these adolescents' orientations towards siblings and friends. Here we find remarkable constancies across ethnic groups and sex. Constant features are their high ego-involvements with their most favoured sibling and their most favoured same sex friend (mean ego-involvements for all boys and girls in the sample are 3.66 and 3.72 respectively on the scale 0.00–5.00). These individuals are generally very positive reference models, the sibling being especially so for 'Asian' boys and English girls, and the same sex friend being a little more so for boys than girls, irrespective

Table 13. 'Asian', 'West Indian' and English adolescents' idealistic-identification with their most favoured sibling

Idealistic-identification with (scale: 0.00 to 1.00 max)

Analysis of variance

A23 *Sex* by *ethnicity* interaction effect $F = 4.87$; df 2,123; $p < 0.01$

	Most favoured sibling for		
	'Asian'	English	'West Indian'
Boys	0.87	0.68	0.78
Girls	0.73	0.80	0.73

I.e. 'Asian' and 'West Indian' boys idealistically identify with their favoured siblings more than girls from these ethnic groups do, whilst the reverse holds for English boys and girls.

Table 14. 'Asian', 'West Indian' and English adolescents' idealistic-identification with their most favoured same sex friend

Idealistic-identification with (scale: 0.00 to 1.00 max)

Analysis of variance

No interaction effects

A2 *Sex* main effect $F = 4.42$; df 1,74; $p < 0.05$

For:	Same sex friend
All boys	0.89
All girls	0.84

I.e. irrespective of ethnicity, girls idealistically identify with their favoured same sex friend somewhat less than boys.

Table 15. Frequency with which adolescents mention same and opposite sex friends

	Mention of friend of	
All adolescents (82)	Same sex	Opposite sex
Yes	80	51
No	2	31

$\chi^2 = 31.9, p < 0.01$

of ethnicity. References to friends of the opposite sex are relatively infrequent (data indicating these differences are presented in Tables 13, 14 and 15). It therefore emerges that individual same sex friends and siblings dominate as highly valued reference models, a feature that will be especially important for girls, given that others, including same sex peers as a group, do not rate highly for them.

We are now in a position to explain why adolescents of immigrant parentage maintain positive self-evaluations, even though their circumstances may be threatening to progressive identity development. Attention will be given to offering explanations for:

(a) Why the discrimination/self-devaluation proposition does not hold.
(b) Why patterns of identification conflicts differ among these minority adolescents.
(c) Why the same formal agency of socialization, the school, has differential success with 'West Indian' adolescents compared with 'Asian' and indigenous adolescents.

Discrimination/self-devaluation proposition

The discrimination/self-devaluation proposition assumes that the indigenous population form the significant others for minority group children. The above analyses demonstrate that, though ethnic labelling is a salient factor in their identities, their own ethnic group members in general feature as more favourable reference models than the English. Particularly prominant amongst these are their favoured siblings and same sex friends. For 'Asian' boys and girls, these positive orientations towards siblings and friends reinforce those towards their parents, whilst for 'West Indian' girls they compensate for their somewhat poor opinions of their parents. In all, despite differences between the minority groups in this Bristol sample, specific people within their own groups are generally more influential in their identity development than indigenous whites. When this is not the case quite different outcomes are possible. This is demonstrated in the surprising role of a friendly older white boy in a black boy's identity development, in which he helped to boost the black boy's self-evaluation, whilst unwittingly contributing to locking him into a rejection of his black skin (Weinreich, 1979a).

In addition, though English boys and girls in Bristol do devalue 'West Indians' and 'Asians' beyond the preference for one's own ethnic group shown by the other groups too, their ego-involvement with them is generally low. With individual exceptions, these English adolescents are less concerned with their minority group peers than the view that characterizes them as virulently prejudiced would assume. The data demonstrate that their impact on minority group peers, as indicated by the latter's ego-involvement with them, is somewhat less than that of other members of the respective minority groups. In particular, there is little evidence that minority group peers generally devalue themselves individually as a consequence.

Discrimination against women does not appear to be a direct issue for the adolescent girls in the Bristol sample. Their ego-involvement with authority figures is less than boys' and, in relation to their families, both parents play less of a positive role for them than for boys. For girls, therefore, relatively high prominence is given to their most favoured same sex friend. She emerges as being even more prominent, by comparison, as *the* major reference model than the same sex friend for boys, even though that friend is similarly placed in the self-concepts of boys and girls from all three ethnic groups. Girls are thus rather less likely to adopt in unmodified form the views of their elders, be they traditional stereotypes or newly projected desiderata. In the girls a degree of sceptism towards the broader social world accompanies a robustness in self-evaluation: whatever the extent of sex discrimination and how it is perceived, they do not devalue themselves in terms of their own value systems.

Patterns of ethnic identification conflicts

At an ethnically specific level, the empirical data establish that the 'Asian' boys and girls in the Bristol sample have generally more respect for authority figures than do the English and 'West Indian'. Their respect for adults, represented by their high ego-involvement and positive identification with them, transcends ethnic boundaries. The effect generalizes to their schoolteachers and other indigenous adults. It is a characteristic most strongly seen in their very positive orientation towards their parents, and explains their generally low level of identification conflicts with them.

'West Indian' girls in the sample emerge as being antiauthority. Their less positive orientation towards their parents explains their relatively high levels of identification conflict with them. By contrast to the 'Asian' adolescents they attribute many negative characteristics to their elders and, given that their most important positive reference models are individual friends of the same sex, it is apparent that they have a highly individualistic and antiauthority orientation to their social world. In practice, this probably amounts to a diffuse orientation accompanied, as we have seen, by generally high identity diffusion. 'West Indian' boys in Bristol differ from the girls in that indigenous whites feature rather more positively in their identifications than they do for girls. This, by no means wholly positive, orientation accounts for the salience of their previously noted identification conflicts with whites.

Table 16. 'Asian', 'West Indian' and English adolescents' ego-involvement with teachers, 'own' and 'other group' adults

Ego-involvement with (scale: 0.00 to 5.00 max)

	Teachers	'Own group' adults	'Other group' adults
'Asian' boys and girls	3.78*	3.38	3.31
'West Indian' boys and girls	2.93	3.21*	2.95
English boys and girls	3.20*	2.94	2.45

* Denotes with whom, out of teachers and adults labelled by ethnicity, the adolescents from the three ethnic groups are most highly ego-involved.

The school as a formal agency of socialization

In respect of the issue of relatively poorer attainment at school by 'West Indian' than 'Asian' adolescents (Little, 1975), the above analyses suggest why this is likely to be the case in Bristol. The 'West Indian' girls' individualistic and antiauthority orientation will tend to diminish the influence of the school as a formal *agency* of socialization in ways intended by the education system, whatever other important effects their time in school might have (schools which *fail* to gain their respect compound their lack of respect for authority in general). Whilst the 'West Indian' boys do not exhibit the strong generalized antiauthority tendencies of the girls, their greater ego-involvement with their parents, adults and peers of their own ethnic group puts these people ahead of teachers as their significant others, thus diminishing the potential influence of the school. By contrast, the 'Asian' adolescents are more favourably disposed towards, and more strongly ego-involved with, teachers than adults from their own ethnic groups, excepting their parents, implying a generally more positive orientation towards school (data concerning ego-involvement with teachers and adults labelled by ethnicity are summarized in Table 16).

3. PROCESSES OF RE-DEFINITION OF ETHNIC IDENTITY

Differences in identity development of adolescents from two minority ethnic groups in Bristol have been established and their practical importance illustrated in relation to their orientations towards schooling. Their resistance to self-devaluation in circumstances of discrimination, and other threats to identity development arising from conflicts in cultural values, has been explained, in part, in terms of their reference models, in which it is evident that these vary substantially according to ethnicity. But a further part of an explanation arises from their own *agency*. The final section of this chapter focusses attention on propositions concerning processes whereby individuals of minority ethnic parentage strive to redefine their identities, whilst retaining their ethnic distinctiveness.

Whilst their patterns of identification conflicts differ in important respects, 'West Indian' and 'Asian' adolescent boys and girls have in common pervasive conflicts in identification with people of their primary ethnic groups. With respect to their redefinitions of their own ethnicities, this commonality is especially significant.

As a result of the theoretical analysis of identity development given earlier in the chapter, two general postulates were stated:

> When one's identifications with others are conflicted, one attempts to resolve the conflicts, thereby inducing re-evaluations of self in relation to the others within the limitations of one's currently existing value system (resolution of conflicted identifications).
>
> When one forms further identifications with newly encountered individuals, one broadens one's value system and establishes a new context for one's self-definition, thereby initiating a reappraisal of self and others which is dependent on fundamental changes in one's value system (formation of new identifications).

Applying these theoretical postulates to the empirical results of the Bristol study, six propositions are derived which are specifically related to processes of ethnic redefinitions in adolescents of subordinate ethnic groups *vis à vis* indigenous people.

Six propositions concerning ethnicity and self-concept change

Proposition 1

Salience of ethnicity in self-concept change

> Insofar as there exists within ethnic minority adolescents a commonality of identification conflicts with their primary ethnic group, there will result a concern with redefinitions of their own self-concepts in which issues of ethnicity play a salient part.

A consequence of these conflicts in ethnic identification is an experience of the everyday importance of ethnic things, so that these adolescents are sensitively attuned to ethnic views on moral issues and dress, and to symbols of group belongingness (as we have seen, the empirical data indicate that 'West Indian' and 'Asian' boys and girls are more ego-involved in ethnically categorized adults and peers than are indigenous whites). It follows from the two theoretical postulates above that, since ethnic identification conflicts are pervasive in ethnic minority adolescents, their attempts to resolve them will result in redefinitions of themselves in which ethnically related issues predominate.

Proposition 2

Part identification with dominant cultural values

> The routes to ethnic redefinition include partial identifications with the values of the 'alien' dominant culture or subcultures (represented by the mass media, the school, the playground, the street and park cultures).

It has been argued that the conflicts in ethnic identification in these adolescents become established through their experience of dual socialization. The empirical evidence indicates substantial degrees of identification (both empathetic and role model) with representatives of the indigenous population. The proposition therefore follows from the fact that conflicts in ethnic identification are indicative of the incorporation of values from the indigenous community during 'secondary socialization'. It makes explicit the application of the second theoretical postulate above and emphasizes the fundamental changes in value systems to be expected.

Proposition 3

'Dialogue' of gender roles across ethnic boundaries

> The development of 'new' ethnic identities consists of processes of attempted resolutions of individual identity conflicts in which the constellation of primary ethnic gender roles and parental identifications conflict with powerful secondary identifications with other salient (i.e. indigenous) gender roles.

Moral issues concerning sex, 'love', marriage and family are central to these processes. This proposition follows directly from proposition 2 and gives due emphasis to the significance of gender roles and relationships between the sexes. Processes of redefinition of ethnic identity entail considerably more than the status of one ethnic group *vis à vis* another. The division of labour between the sexes, notions of femininity and masculinity, sexual mores, the subjugation of one sex by the other or the manipulation of the one by the other, are factors associated with identifications across ethnic boundaries. Redefinitions of gender roles are central to redefinitions of ethnic identity.

Proposition 4

Variable routes towards ethnic redefinition

> The specific nature of ethnic redefinitions depend on the avenues open to individuals, given their patterns of identification with significant others.

In working towards partial resolutions of their ethnic identification conflicts, modes open to some adolescents will be inappropriate for others. This is because their different patterns of identifications impose constraints on the adjustment of identifications with others entailed in processes of self-concept change. A discussion of possible routes towards ethnic redefinitions for the Bristol sample of 'Asian' adolescents and 'West Indian' boys and girls is given in Weinreich (1979b).

Proposition 5

New ethnic coherence

> New ethnic coherence between individuals is developed through establishing 'inner strength' or self-esteem based on competence judged according to newly shared and self-chosen values, when these arise through common elements in ethnic redefinitions.

This condition does not necessarily arise as when, for example, individuals find heterogenous solutions to their identification conflicts as it is argued to be the likely case for the Bristol 'West Indian' adolescents, given their spread of ethnic identification conflicts (Weinreich 1979b). If a new ethnic coherence is formed, then the judgements of competence by the ethnic group concerned (an example would be certain 'Asian' groups in Britain) challenge the rationale used by dominant groups to subjugate and discriminate against them.

Proposition 6

Reactive ethnicity in the dominant culture

> It follows by reaction to the challenge presented to the indigenous population that ethnicity becomes an issue for the indigenous or dominant group, leading to an upsurge in nationalism and national identity.

Reification of the concept 'ethnic identity'

It is intended that the spelling out of these propositions will guard against propensities to reify a concept of 'ethnic identity' which ignores the specific sociohistorical circumstances of different ethnic groups, the changing circumstances from generation to generation, and the gender differences at any moment in time in conceptions of ethnically appropriate behaviour.

It follows from these propositions that, whilst the impetus for redefinitions of ethnic identity resides in conflicts in ethnic identification, it is mistaken to view the formation of new ethnic awareness as an uniform process. 'Ethnic identity' is not an uniform concept that refers to the same constellation of meanings across different ethnic groups. Different reference groups and patterns of identifications conflicts are predicated on different primary cultural value systems. There is no reason, therefore, to expect uniform outcomes concerning self-concept development for different ethnic minority groups within the same dominant culture. Whilst it is permissable to generalize about the *importance* of ethnic awareness in these groups, the experience of that awareness, and the consequences for action, will differ from group to group.

Two studies of self-concept change and identity

Two case studies of changes in self-concept will illustrate the first four propositions above. One concerns a boy, the other a girl, from the 'West Indian' sample in the Bristol study. The empirical data were collected at two points in time, before and after leaving school, using the conceptualization outlined in this chapter. The analyses of self-concept change are based throughout on quantitative indices. Though neither case should be regarded as typical, both represent some common concerns and certain dilemmas of adolescents of 'West Indian' parentage attempting to negotiate threats to their identities in which both their gender roles and the value of their ethnicity are questioned.

The first case study is of Kevin, a black Jamaican boy (Weinreich, 1976a). On first meeting him, his strongest identification conflict was with 'black boys who steal'. He construed himself as feminine. Females dominated his current identifications, in particular, Jamaican girls. Females also featured strongly as his positive reference models, especially one white woman who led a West Indian drama group in which he was active.

The first theoretical postulate concerning self-concept change suggests that his current identity tasks would be to resolve his conflicted identification with black boys who steal and to redefine himself as masculine in accordance with his ideal self-image. Successful outcomes would be his reappraisal of 'black boys who steal' as more favourable than hithertofore, and a decreased identification with Jamaican girls by way of an increased identification with the machismo qualities of such boys. In fact, his behaviour during the eighteen months between meetings with him was commensurate with these tasks.

After leaving school he had been in and out of work. He had been in violent fights. As the result of one episode he had been convicted of Actual Bodily Harm and sent to a Detention Centre. A white girl with whom he had formed a steady relationship became pregnant by him. After his period in the Detention Centre, and just before the second meeting with him, he had attempted to rob a village post office. In this abortive attempt, during which he was caught by the police, he had been goaded on by a delinquent white boy whom he had met at the Detention Centre.

His redefinition of self conformed to the two general postulates concerning self-concept change. Though his self-evaluation had suffered considerably, he had achieved a conception of himself as masculine. He identified less with females and his highest current identifications now included several males. The extent of his decreased identification with Jamaican girls meant that he currently identified more strongly with Jamaican boys than girls. His achievement of masculinity had involved a readjustment of his perception of gender roles, which included an overt demonstration of his virility, especially through the relationship with the white girl and her consequent pregnancy. The fact that his most positive reference model was the white woman drama leader, together with his liaison with the white girl, indicate how that, in redefining himself as a masculine Jamaican boy, he was crossing ethnic boundaries and forging a gender role which enabled him to displace Jamaican girls in favour of Jamaican boys in his current identifications. His diminished self-evaluation was in accordance with the second postulate, in which his broadened value system led him to judge his behaviour, in being easily led and liable to further spells in Detention Centres, in derogatory terms.

The propositions concerning ethnicity and self-concept change received support as follows. For Proposition 1 (salience of ethnicity), we see that ethnicity was both salient in his self-concept and played a dominant role in his redefinition of himself in the interval between the two meetings with him. In support of Proposition 2 (dominant culture), the data clearly indicate that, in his redefinition of himself as a Jamaican boy, elements of identification with members of the indigenous population played a significant part. Proposition 3 (dialogue of gender roles) is demonstrated by his concern over masculinity, which involved gender definitions that were in part grounded in Jamaican cultural norms, but which were modified through his interaction with English people.

Proposition 4 draws attention to the varying routes to ethnic redefinition, which is well illustrated by the contrast between Kevin and the subject of the second case study, Paulette (Weinreich, 1976b). Paulette sequentially identified with specific groups of English girls in coming to a new appraisal of herself in terms of her own ethnicity. On first meeting her, she was in a state of identity crisis, that is, on quantitative criteria, she exhibited a high degree of identity diffusion and negative self-evaluation. Her past self-image indicated a former identification with 'English girls who go out with West Indian boys'. She was currently identifying in a conflicted manner with 'English girls in my class' at school. She construed the former group of girls as compliant (helpful, passive, etc.) and good, and the latter as aggressive and bad. After eighteen months, she had reduced her conflicted identifications with English girls in her class. She had done this by reorganizing her value system, so that instead of valuing compliance, she came to value assertive and independent behaviour. She remained in a demoralized state, with continuing high identity diffusion and low self-evaluation, but she had radically altered her self-concept. She had developed a robust ideal self-image, a consequence of which was her continuing low self-evaluation judged against tougher criteria.

Ethnicity played an important part in her redefinition of herself (Proposition 1: salience of ethnicity) which she used in ways that have not generally been anticipated (for example, in discussions of *black consciousness raising*). In successively identifying with different kinds of English girls, she turned to lifestyles and models beyond her own ethnic group and used them, in effect, as resources in her own self-development. By adopting their standards and their expression of a feminine gender role (Propositions 2 and 3: dominant culture and dialogue of gender roles), she was able to reappraise herself, free herself from her formerly passive role, and develop sufficient assertiveness to feel that she could, in her own words, 'control English girls'.

CONCLUSION

This chapter has been concerned with a number of objectives, which have entailed for their implementation a synthesis of concepts derived from the psychodynamic and Personal Construct Theory traditions. One objective has been to specify propositions about the general antecedent conditions for self-concept development and change. A second has been to define a number of analytic concepts, an objective necessitated by the need to clarify the meanings of such terms as *identity*, *identification*, identity and cultural *confiicts*, and others. A third has been to use the analytic power of the resultant theoretical conceptualization and empirical measuring procedures to determine common characteristics of people differentiated by societal criteria (in this case, ethnic group membership). A fourth has been to derive six propositions elucidating adolescents' redefinitions of their ethnic identities from the two theoretical postulates concerning processes of self-concept change. Their derivation was based in part on the empirical finding that, whatever the other major differences between them, Bristol boys and girls of 'West Indian' and 'Asian' parentage had in common heightened identification conflicts with their own ethnic groups, a phenomenon explained in terms of their dual socialization.

Continuity in identity development

Continuity in identity development has been stressed throughout. As Bannister and Agnew (1977) say 'We entertain the notion of our continuity over time, we possess our biography and live in relation to it'. The general propositions concerning the resolution of identification conflicts on the one hand, and the formation of new identifications on the other, have been applied to the case studies of Kevin and Paulette to make the specific nature of their continuities manifest.

Both adolescents are struggling to emerge from *threatened identities.* Both demonstrate considerable changes in self-concept, the continuities of which also illustrate four of the six derived propositions concerning adolescents' redefinitions of their ethnic identities: salience of ethnicity in self-concept change; part identification with dominant cultural values; dialogue of gender roles across ethnic boundaries; and variable routes towards ethnic redefinitions. The continuity between Kevin's current self-construal as something of a failure though *masculine* and his former construal of himself as *feminine* is found, in part, in the delinquent actions he undertook in order to resolve his earlier conflicted identifications with black boys who steal. Paulette's biographical continuity, whilst she herself is much changed in terms of her current value system, is manifested in her resolution of her earlier conflicted identifications with English girls in her class. She has reappraised them favourably in terms of a newly acquired value of *assertiveness* which she successfully pursues herself, and which is contrasted with her former high regard for *compliance* and identification with essentially compliant white girls who go out with 'West Indian' boys.[6]

Ethnicity and gender

Ethnicity and gender contribute in important ways to identity development and neither can be considered without the other. However, variations in identity development arising from gender roles are different in kind from those arising from membership of one ethnic group or another. Socialization into gender roles is in some ways more fundamental than socialization into an ethnic group, presumably because, though gender roles vary, sex categorization is universal. In other ways it is conditional on ethnicity, specifically, in terms of the ethnic variation in the definition of gender roles. Both features have been demonstrated in this chapter: self-concept development in Bristol adolescents varies according to ethnic by sex categories, but on certain criteria gender is the important variable and on other it is membership of a minority ethnic group. Irrespective of ethnicity, girls in Bristol have a more 'realistic' orientation to the social world than boys, but, irrespective of gender, minority adolescents have greater ego-involvenment in ethnically defined prople, whether their own or other group, than do their indigenous counterparts.

A particular instance of a fallacious argument using sex and ethnic group (or 'racial') membership as equivalent categories is the parallel that has been drawn between the supposed effects of discrimination on the grounds of sex and of 'race'. The Bristol study clearly shows that the parallel is false, and it also throws into doubt the proposition that, as a generalization, discrimination results in devalued self-images. The reasons for this are: first, that adolescent boys and girls tend to be ego-involved and to idealistically identify with role models beyond the dominant group; and second, that they actively strive to resolve identification conflicts that result from their partial identifications with selected representatives of the dominant group.

Ethnic minorities in British culture

Finally, Identity Structure Analysis (as the conceptual framework outlined here has become known) has clarified the way in which adolescents from ethnic minorities form part of British culture. Identification with various members of the indigenous population plays an important part in the identity development of 'West Indian' and 'Asian' adolescents in Bristol. Each is strongly affected by the values held by particular white peers and adults with whom they come into contact, even though their own ethnicity remains salient. Because their developing identities emerge within a context of relationships between themselves and native whites, their self-concepts inextricably bind together elements of these relationships. They might subscribe to a shorthand ethnic label as an identity marker (e.g. Jamaican), but in reality they are a complex amalgam of identification elements that cross ethnic boundaries. They perceive themselves like English adolescents in many respects. They value various English characteristics and wish to be identified as English in these respects. They are essentially British with a consciousness of their ethnic origins, expressed in distinctive life-styles, in which modes of dress, characteristic relationships between the sexes, preferences for work and play activities, are continuing to develop out of their redefinitions of ethnic identities. Their *Black* British or *Asian* British distinctiveness will continue to evolve through processes of further redefinitions, predicated on their attempts to resolve identification conflicts grounded in their primary ethnic identifications, but subsequently accociaed with people representing different cultural values. Whilst such ethnic distinctiveness is far removed from uniformity, each will nevertheless become a distinctively *British* subculture that diverges from current life-styles of people in Jamaica, Trinidad, Pakistan, India or wherever. Traditional identities, insofar as they remain static, are inevitably being continually 'threatened'. In emerging from 'threatened identities' and in evolving new conceptions of themselves, many adolescents will be vehicles of social change, but they will also transmit updated elements of the traditions of their respective subcultures.

NOTES

[1] The material reported in this chapter is drawn from a research programme within the SSRC Research Unit on Ethnic Relations when it was housed at the University of Bristol (now at the University of Aston). The research was led by P. Weinreich and the other members of the team were A. K. Brah, M. I. Fuller, D. Louden and R. Miles.

[2] 'West Indian' and 'Asian' are inaccurate terms. They serve only to locate the respective cultural milieux as being based initially in the Caribbean or the Indian subcontinent.

[3] Prevailing interpretations of data have led to a broad concensus that black people are fundamentally damaged. As victims of discrimination they are seen as devaluing their own people in line with the discriminators' view of them, and thence themselves. Self-hatred, self-rejection, and the 'mark of oppression' are said to be the outcomes (on children: Clark and Clark, 1947; Goodman, 1946; Horowitz, 1939; Lasker, 1929; Minard, 1931; Morland, 1963, 1966; Trager and Yarrow, 1952; on psychiatric patients: Grier and Cobbs, 1968; Kardiner and Ovessey, 1951; the concensus is repeated in: Banks, 1972; Isaacs, 1975; Poussaint and Atkinson, 1972; Stein, 1975).

[4] Sue and Sue (1971) describe the individual in culture conflict as someone who is heir to two different cultural traditions, who may have difficulty in reconciling their effects on his personality and find it difficult to decide which culture he owes primary loyalty. They state that such a person often experiences an identity crisis and feels isolated and alienated from both cultures. Sue (1973) focuses on the 'psychological costs of culture conflict'. Weiss (1970) finds many Chinese–American girls expect boys they date to behave boldly and aggressively in the traditional Western manner. He observes that 'the individual may develop a kind of racial self-hatred that leads to lowered self-esteem and intense conflicts'.

[5] The point which is being made here is that discrimination against blacks does not result in a general across-the-board self-devaluation of themselves. In individual cases, elements of self-rejection as a result of discrimination do occur, though even then this may not be global self-rejection (Weinreich, 1979a).

[6] There is both a determinism and an indeterminism about this continuity. The determinism is expressed in the proposition that the individual will attempt to resolve his identification conflicts. Given knowledge of the conflicts and with whom they exist, it is possible to predict how a person would *strive* to resolve them. The indeterminism arises from the possibility that all kinds of incidental events may deflect his efforts, including unforseen consequences of his actions in pursuit of them. Also, whilst it is possible, given knowledge of social transitions such as leaving school for college, to predict the kind of people with whom the person might form new identifications, the actual identifications possible will be constrained by who is actually available (see Weinreich, 1976c).

REFERENCES

Banks, J. A. (1972). Racial prejudice and the black self-concept. In: J. A. Banks, and J. D. Grambs (eds.). *Black Self-concept*. Maidenhead, McGraw Hill.

Bannister, D., and Agnew, J. (1977). The child's construing of self. In: *Nebraska Symposium on Motivation, 1976*. University of Nebraska Press.

Bannister, D., and Fransella, F. (1971). *Inquiring Man: the Theory of Personal Constructs*. Harmondsworth, Penguin.

Binder, J., Mayman, M., and Doehrman, (1974). Self-ideal-self discrepancy as a defensive style, *Comprehensive psychiatry*, **15**, 335–343.

Clark, K. B., and Clark, M. P. (1947). Racial identification and preference in Negro children. In: T. M. Newcomb, and E. L. Hartley, (eds.), *Readings in Social Psychology*, New York, Henry Holt.

Constantinople, A. (1969). An Eriksonian measure of personality development in college students, *Developmental Psychology*, **1**, 357–372.

Constantinople, A. (1970). Some correlates of average level of happiness among college students, *Developmental Psychology*, **2**, 447.

Erikson, E. H. (1958). In: J. M. Tanner, and Inhelder (eds.), *Discussions on Child Development*. (WHO study group on the psychobiological development of the child, Geneva, 1955.) London, Tavistock.

Erikson, E. H. (1965). *Childhood and Society* (Rev. ed.). Harmondsworth, Penguin.

Erikson, E. H. (1968). *Identity, Youth and Crisis*. New York, Norton.

Goodman, M. E. (1946). Evidence concerning the genesis of interracial attitudes, *American Anthropologist*, **48**, 624–630.

Grier, W. H., and Cobbs, P. M. (1968). *Black Rage*. New York, Basic Books.

Hauser, S. T. (1971). *Black and White Identity Formation*. New York, Wiley.

Hauser, S. T. (1972). Black and white identity development; aspects and perspectives, *Journal of Youth and Adolescence*, **1**, 113–130.

Hauser, S. T., and Shapiro, R. L. (1973). Differentiation of adolescent self-images, *Archives of General Psychiatry*, **29**, 63–68.

Horowitz, R. E. (1939). Racial aspects of self-identification in nursery school children, *Journal of Psychology*, **7–8**, 91–99.

Isaacs, H. R. (1975). Basic group identity. In: N. Glazer, and D. P. Moynihan (eds.) *Ethnicity*. Harvard University Press.

Kardiner, A., and Ovessey, L. (1951). *The Mark of Oppression*. New York, Norton.

Kelly, G. A. (1955). *The Psychology of Personal Constructs*. New York, Norton.

Laing, R. D. (1961). *The Self and Others*. London, Tavistock.

Lasker, B. (1929). *Race Attitudes in Children*. New York, Henry Holt.

Little, A. (1975). The educational achievement of ethnic minority children in London schools. In: G. K. Verma, and C. Bagley (eds.) *Race and Education Across Cultures*. London, Heinemann.

Marcia, J. E. (1966). Development and validation of ego identity status, *Journal of Personality and Social Psychology*, **3**, 551–558.

Marcia, J. E. (1967). Ego identity status: relationship to change in self-esteem, 'general adjustment', and authoritarianism, *Journal of Personality*, **35**, 118–133.

Marcia, J. E., and Friedman, M. L. (1970). Ego identity status in college women, *Journal of Personality*, **38**, 249–263.

Minard, R. D. (1931). Race attitudes of Iowa children, *Studies in Character*, **4** (2). University of Iowa.

Morland, J. K. (1963). Racial self-identification: a study of nursery school children, *The American Catholic Sociological Review*, **24**, 231–242.

Morland, J. K. (1966). A comparison of race awareness in Northern and Southern children, *American Journal of Orthopsychiatry*, **36**, 23–31.
Pouissant, A., and Atkinson, C. (1972). Black youth and motivation. In: J. A. Banks, and J. D. Grambs (eds.) *Black Self-concept*. Maidenhead, McGraw-Hill.
Rios-Garcia, L. R., and Cook, P. E. (1975). Self-derogation and defense style in college students, *Journal of Personality Assessment*, **39**, 272–281.
Silber, E., and Tippett, J. S. (1965). Self-esteem, clinical assessment and measurement validation, *Psychological Reports*, **16**, 1017–1071.
Stein, H. F. (1975). Ethnicity, identity and ideology, *School Review*, **83**, 273–300.
Sue, D. W. (1973). Ethnic identity: the impact of two cultures on the psychological development of Asians in America. In: S. Sue, and N. N. Wagner (eds.) *Asian-Americans: Psychological Perspectives*. Palo Alto, Science and Behavior Books.
Sue, S., and Sue, D. W. (1971). Chinese-American personality and mental health, *Amerasia Journal*, **1**, 36–49.
Trager, H., and Yarrow, M. R. (1952). *They Learn What They Live*. New York, Harper.
Waterman, A. S., Geary, P. S., and Waterman, C. K. (1974). 'A longitudinal study of changes in ego identity status from the freshman to the senior year at college, *Developmental Psychology*, **10**, 387–392.
Waterman, A. S., and Waterman, C. K. (1971). A longitudinal study of changes in ego identity status during the freshman year at college, *Developmental Psychology*, **5**, 167–173.
Weinreich, P. (1976a). Ethnic identification and masculine identity formation in a black adolescent boy. Mimeographed Report: SSRC Research Unit on Ethnic Relations at the University of Aston, Birmingham, England.
Weinreich, P. (1976b). A Jamaican girls identity crisis involving her strongly conflicted identifications with English girls. Mimeographed Report: SSRC Research Unit on Ethnic Relations at the University of Aston, Birmingham, England.
Weinreich, P. (1976c). Strong feminine sex-role identification in a West Indian girl for whom the school leaving transition results in a minor identity crisis. Mimeographed Report: SSRC Research Unit on Ethnic Relations at the University of Aston, Birmingham, England.
Weinreich, P. (1979a). Cross-ethnic identification and self-rejection in a black adolescent. In: G. K. Verma, and C. Bagley (eds.) *Race, Education and Identity*, London, Macmillan.
Weinreich, P. (1979b). Ethnicity and adolescent identity conflict. In: V. Saifullah Khan (ed.). *Minority Families in Britain*. London, Macmillan.
Weinreich, P. (1980). *A manual for identity exploration using personal constructs*, London, SSRC.
Weinreich,P., Carr, I., French, A., and Chivers, A. (1981). *IDEX: Identity Exploration computer program* (rev. ed.), Ulster Polytechnic, N. Ireland, and SSRC Research Unit on Ethnic Relations at the University of Aston, Birmingham, England.
Weiss, M. S. (1970). Selective acculturation and the dating process: the patterning of Chinese–Caucasian interracial dating, *Journal of Marriage and the Family*, **32**, 273–278.

Section C: Threats to the identity of groups

Threatened Identities
Edited by G. Breakwell

Identities and Conflicts

GLYNIS M. BREAKWELL

INTRODUCTION

This chapter will focus upon what happens to a group's identity when it is involved in intergroup conflict. What happens to a group which *already* has a threatened identity when it engages upon conflict will be explored. Most particularly, the object here is to show how the conflict in these situations is pursued and how the group's identity predicates the form of the conflict. As part and parcel of this task it is vital to show how the group's identity can be remoulded within a conflict.

These processes were studied with real groups engaged in a real conflict rather than with artifical groups created by experimental manipulation because it was felt that too little is known about the course of real world conflicts as yet and so only fragments of them can be modelled in experiments. This means that this chapter entails telling the story of a real group and a real conflict and neither can be explained without some outline knowledge of their history. Social workers are the group concerned and the conflict is the social work strike which took place between August, 1978 and June, 1979.

A BRIEF HISTORY OF SOCIAL WORK IN BRITAIN

It would be naive to claim that social workers are a homogeneous group. Social workers have never been a homogeneous group as the history of social work shows clearly. McCarthy (1980) described the growth of social work and most of the following very brief description of its background is dependent upon his work. Social work started as an occupation with the recruitment of full-time workers concerned with the moral welfare of 'fallen women' by the Church of England in the 1850s. By 1869 the Charity Organization Society had been founded to coordinate the effort and establish scientific methods in the provision of charity. Workers were introduced to hospitals in 1895 to identify the deserving poor and arrange free treatment for them together with a follow-up service on leaving hospital. Such workers remained to become the first hospital almoners. By this time, the probationary service had already been initiated and vested with statutory responsibilities under the Probation of First Offenders Act 1887 and became a national service in 1926 when the Criminal Justice Act was introduced. During the same period the impact of psychoanalysis created the psychiatric social worker. So, already by the end of the 1920s, several social work specialisms had been established.

Most of these early social work groups were independent of State control because they were organized by voluntary agencies. But the 1930 Poor Law Reform Act introduced statutory duties and state funded posts. State control increased with the 1948 National Assistance Act which gave Local Authorities responsibility for the care of the aged and children. The Children Act of the same year set up a new local department in each area and there were the origin of self-management for social workers.

It should not be thought that by this stage there was a group of people who could be labelled 'social workers'. With such diverse backgrounds and methods of control, the specialisms within social work found unification to be a problem. Certainly, the establishment of any comprehensive professional organization was hard work. In 1936, the British Federation of Social Workers brought together 12 different bodies representing social work specialisms including almoners, probation officers, family caseworkers, moral welfare officers and psychiatric social workers. But the BFSW ran on a federal system—each member group remained independent. Later, the constitution was amended to allow individual membership to qualified social workers and the increasing number of such qualified social workers ultimately led to the formation of the Association of Social Workers in 1951. The aims of ASW were to unify the social work profession by encouraging generic training and the ideology of casework. In fact, the government intervened to rationalize the provision of the personal social services in the sixties. In 1965, Seebohm led a review of the services and reported in 1968 that a generic social work service should be established under local authority social services departments. These recommendations were incorporated into the Local Authority Social Services Act of 1970 and when taken together with the 1974 Local Government Reorganization Act left all but the probation officers under the direction of the local authority social services. This reorganization encouraged professional unification and the British Association of Social Workers was formed in 1970. Nevertheless, BASW did not include probation officers or residential social workers (these formed the RCA). BASW was essentially an organ representing a small section of qualified fieldworkers in local authority social services.

ASCRIBED AND ACKNOWLEDGED IDENTITIES

So, over one hundred years after their conception, social workers remain a heterogeneous group. Lines of differentiation criss cross the profession:

fieldworkers are distinct from residential workers; local authority workers are distinct from voluntary sector workers; and qualified are distinct from unqualified workers. For those inside the profession, if such it can be called, these distinctions are of paramount importance. For those outside the profession they are meaningless or even invisible. Those who are not social workers tend to attribute characteristics to *all* social workers without pause for subtle subdivisions. The media, the general public and, indeed, other professions *ascribe an identity to social workers as a whole*. This ascribed identity is what social work is—for those outside of it.

Not all outsiders ascribe the same identity to social workers of course. But at any one time there is a dominant ascription—one to which the majority adhere. All groups are targets for ascribed identities: images of themselves pinned upon them by others. The number of different ascribed identities attributed to any group is a function of that group's social role and social power. The less power a group has and the greater the uncertainty as to its social role, the greater the room for a multiplicity of ascribed identities. The process of stereotyping is an integral part of the ascription of identity, serving the needs of groups to differentiate themselves from one another.

The ascribed identity, tacked upon a group from outside, coexists with the acknowledged identity. The acknowledged identity is that image which a group holds of itself. Outsiders may have strong ideas about what social workers as a group are and do but social workers themselves may have equally strong notions about what they are and do. The point of vital importance here is that ascribed and acknowledged identities are not necessarily compatible. Outsiders may have one image of social workers and this may be partially or even totally at variance with how they view themselves. Frequently groups find that they have an image of themselves which is at variance with the image that others have of them. When this happens, it is like looking into a mirror expecting to see a blonde, blue-eyed beauty and suddenly finding that the creature staring back has hair the colour of a raven and features to match. In such cases, self-conception is not matched by social reflection. The identity ascribed is not that acknowledged.

When this happens, there is ambiguity as to the identity of the group. Such ambiguity threatens the efficient functioning of the group and its membership. A group without clearcut parameters of identity lacks lucid guidelines for the behaviour of its membership, since group norms are immutably tied to group identity. It is therefore vital for the continuance of the group for the ambiguity to be nullified if not erased.

Excision of ambiguity may take many forms. Yet all comprise some sort of change in the parameters of self-definition. Either the group changes the way it thinks of itself or manoeuvres others so that they change the way they think of it. Whatever route is chosen, the object is the same: to bring ascribed and acknowledged identity into alignment. As long as they remain out of phase, ambiguity surrounds the group's identity and the group is at risk: its identity is certainly threatened and so may be its very existence.

THE STRUCTURE OF THREATS TO IDENTITY

Threats to a group's identity come in all shapes and sizes—there are as many ways of threatening an identity as there are ways of redefining it. A threat cannot be defined in terms of what it is, only in terms of what it does. Abstract definitions of the content of a threat is pointless but definitions of the structure of a threat can be useful.

Something of the structure of the mismatches which occur between ascribed and acknowledged identities can be described. Differences between them can be on one or both of two dimensions: the dimension of content and the dimension of evaluation. The content dimension entails what image is built of the group—the traits attributed to it. For instance, a group might be said to be rich, powerful and secure or poor, powerless and insecure. The content dimension has attached to it a parallel evaluative dimension: wealth is good; poverty is bad or the converse, wealth is bad, poverty good. Ascribed and acknowledged identities may be mismatched on one or both of these dimensions. So, outsiders may say of a group that it is rich, powerful and secure while members of that group claim that it is poor, powerless and insecure. This would be a clash upon the dimension of content. Similarly, outsiders may consider it good to be rich, powerful and secure while group members consider these characteristics to be bad or undesirable. This, obviously, would be a clash upon the evaluative dimension.

In terms of the content dimension, probably the worst thing that could happen is for outsiders to ascribe an identity to a number of people which denied their claims to membership of a group by denying the very existence of the group. This is not inconceivable since other groups may seek to break down boundaries which act to articulate the substance of the group by engulfing it within another superordinate group.

A mismatch of the evaluative dimension could be equally damaging to the group. Ascribed and acknowledged identities may concur on the attributes of the identity but the ascribed identity may be based upon an antithetical value system. Thus, the group is permitted all the characteristics it claims for itself but is told just how little value they have. The group which thinks itself to be powerless, poor and insecure is told 'yes, you are all of those things and how terrible it is'.

THE THREAT TO SOCIAL WORK IDENTITY

Social workers might be considered a classic case of a group with a threatened identity. As was said earlier, social work was built on the back of casework ideology derived from psychoanalysis. It constituted a federation of different specialisms but there was a continuity of ideology and approach across specialisms. The ideology was built on notions of vocational caring, allied to voluntary organizations. Most of its early assumptions were based on a medical model of care and a compatible conservativism of aim—saving the poor and dissolute from themselves. The acknowledged identity of social work revolved around these ideological and methodological assumptions.

With the reorganization of social work after the Seebohm Report in the 1970s, many of these assumptions were challenged. Old specialisms were replaced by generic training, integrated methods and systems analysis surplanted casework, and doubts about the value systems appropriate to social work were voiced. Some began to ask, should social workers be helping the clients to cope with their position in the world as it stands or should they seek to militate to change that world. Others queried whether social work is necessary at all, they put it to social workers that their clients were misfits and scroungers who should not be represented by public servants at the taxpayers' expense. Whenever their overall value system was not under attack, social workers found themselves criticized and abused for failing in their vital functions. They were said to have failed in cases of child-battering, tug-of-loves, and hyperthermia. In terms of both content and evaluative dimensions of identity, social workers found themselves under attack.

Throughout the years since reorganization this paradoxical series of attacks has continued. They have had an impact of the way social workers see their role and construe their professional identity even though the legitimacy of the attacks has been challenged. Social workers have responded with attempts to define their task, values and methods (see all BASW and CCETSW literature). But they have failed. The attacks continue and the defences are of no avail. Maybe this is because social workers have no social power—whether economic or political—or perhaps it was because they have no central philosophy to unite them or, alternatively, it may be the result of having no easily identifiable symbol or tool of their trade. Whatever the reason, their efforts to redefine their character have had little effect. The result of all this definitional activity has been a kind of identity flux; unconvinced of their own definitional propaganda they no longer appear to have an acknowledged identity. They do not know themselves. It would be going out on a limb to say that there has been a dissolution of the old identity and yet the ascribed identity is so paradox-ridden that it has failed to act as a substitute.

Some of the failure can obviously be put at the door of fragmentation: BASW, RCA and POA. BASW represents the fieldworkers who are the prime focus of this study but it only represented the qualified social workers (at the start of the period studied) and only 30 per cent of them were members. Moreover, it had no control over training, recruitment or entry to the profession; these were controlled by CCETSW under the DHSS Secretary of State. Control of such things is rather important for a professional association wishing to create and mould the identity of a profession. Moreover, it did not have control of pay negotiations or conditions of service. The majority of social workers in local government belonged to the largest white collar union NALGO. Negotiations for pay were conducted through NALGO on the National Joint Council which established the pay scales of all local government officers. BASW had no representation on the NJC. It was represented on NALGO's Joint Consulative Committee—the union's main organ of policy development—only on sufferance and could find itself evicted at any time (and, in fact, was evicted during the period studied). In short, BASW was in no position to protect the identity of social work. Neither was anyone else. In fact, the status of BASW both reflected the difficult position of the profession and aggravated it.

All of this goes to show that the identity of social workers as a professional group was threatened in the period leading up to the conflict. If this account is not totally persuasive the reader need only ask a social worker, those who find their way into print certainly support the view that the threat was real and was perceived widely. In purely concrete terms, the effects of these threats can be seen in the high rates of staff turnover and in social service provision cutbacks.

THE CONFLICT

The prime purpose here, however, is not to show that the identity of social workers was threatened. It is to show what occurred when social workers took their threatened identity into conflict. In August, 1978, social workers started their first-ever indefinite industrial action.

Trouble had been brewing for over a year. It stemmed from the nature of the salary negotiating system. Social work pay was based on a national scale like all local government officers. Changes in the scale had to be made through the NJC on which both NALGO and the local authority employers have representatives. Local authorities could not negotiate locally for changes in pay or conditions of service. In June, 1977, NALGO passed a resolution making it policy to abolish all national prescriptive gradings. This opened the door for social workers to pursue local pay and regrading claims. The push was started in November, 1977 by Lambeth social workers with the threat of a strike. This strike was averted when NALGO negotiated a compromise adjustment in scales with the local council. When Southwark social workers laid similar claims to their local authority in

April, 1978, NALGO refused to replicate the Lambeth compromise. Newcastle, Tower Hamlets and Liverpool social workers voted to follow Southwark in calling for an indefinite strike in pursuit of their claims.

The interesting thing here is that the NJC employers were willing to consider national regrading of scales since the social workers had a good case for their claims as their jobs had changed considerably since the last grading in 1971. Social workers were recognized to have taken on greater responsibilities due to legislative changes.

However, the NJC employers were unwilling to allow local negotiations to breach national scales. Their fear was that NALGO would use this as a precedent for all other local government workers. They consequently urged local authorities to stand firm against the claims. The local authorities stood firm and the social workers came out on strike.

Newcastle was first out on 14th August, 1978 with Southwark. They were followed by Tower Hamlets. Between then and October there was little action by employers or NALGO. In October, Lewisham and Liverpool joined the strike. By this stage, the strikers were already frightened that NALGO would betray them. This fear originated in the fact that NALGO compromised over the claims made by Brent social workers against the wishes of the local social workers. This fear welled up in a mass demonstration on 25th October outside the NJC meeting where NALGO were talking to the employers. At this meeting, a working party was set up to discuss a plan for local negotiations within a national framework. The national officers of NALGO emerged from this meeting to assure the strikers that they had not changed their policy.

While the working party held talks, Gateshead, Greenwich, Knowsley, Leeds and Sheffield joined the strike. By the end of November, the working party had a set of recommendations which both sides agreed. But NALGO had to put the recommendations to the strikers and they rejected them in their local branches. NALGO was obliged to send the proposals back to the NJC where the employers side accepted them. But they could not be instituted until accepted by NALGO and NALGO would not go against the overwhelming sentiments of the strikers at this point.

December saw little change in the situation except that Islington and Cheshire came out on strike and BASW made an abortive call for an independent inquiry into pay. By January, fourteen areas were on strike, including the new additions of Manchester and Rochdale. As the working party discussions resumed, NJC employers told local authorities to stand firm. On 26th January, NALGO finally accepted the working party's offer (one which was not substantially different from the November offer) but advised areas to return to work only after 'meaningful progress' had been made in local bargaining. This advice was taken seriously by the strikers and many places had no intention of returning to work until a full local settlement was agreed. Eleven areas were still on strike in mid-March (remember the agreement had been accepted by the union at the end of January). At this juncture, NALGO made the strike unofficial and stopped paying strike pay which had been running at 55 per cent of the strikers' normal gross pay. When the final area to return to work, Tower Hamlets, did so on 11th June, 1979, only one-quarter of the local authorities in England and Wales had implemented the social workers complex pay deal. Where agreement had been reached, social workers were not satisfied and many felt betrayed by NALGO.

To put it in a nutshell: social workers got more money out of the strike but they did not win the concession which they were fighting for—local negotiations.

Rhetoric of conflict

These are merely the moves in the social work conflict. The facts underplay what was really happening during this time. Conflict between groups normally takes place on two planes: the physical and the symbolic. The physical plane involves acts of physical aggression. The symbolic plane entails the aggressive arguments and posturing involved in the conflict. Most industrial conflicts entail minimal physical hostility and maximal symbolic hostility. This is merely to say that nowadays, once labour is withdrawn, much of the conflict revolves around argument and negotiation processes. Labour and management do not cudgel one another with sticks—they do it with words. Of course, the real power lies in the withdrawal of labour or the control of employment but the arguments lubricate the realization of this power and may constrain its use.

In the case of the social-work strike, conflict on the physical plane was fairly static in form. The social workers withdrew their labour and picketed social services departments, often disrupting the machinery of the Local Council in doing so. While their industrial actions were reasonably static, the arguments which raged around the dispute were dynamic. These arguments can be called the *rhetorics of conflict*.

The proposition is that these rhetorics are used by groups in a conflict to manipulate their position and that of other groups. Rhetorics rarely entail a single argumentative proposition. They are more like a mosaic of arguments. Each of the arguments is akin to an attitude having a cognitive and evaluative component. The argument proposes that a thing is true and then shows how that thing should be valued. The rhetoric can be like a fine tapestry woven of may threads of argument. The rhetoric is never balanced, it is always biased—serving the interests of the group which creates it.

In order to serve group interests, it may evolve and change in the course of the conflict. In its responsiveness to the demands of the conflict rhetoric shows another aspect of its functioning: it is tailored both to influence members of the group which produce it and to influence members of other groups. Rhetoric is a two-edged sword—its effects on both sorts of audience interact. This multiplier effect means that the consequences of rhetoric cannot always be anticipated. Rhetoric designed to serve one purpose may become the slave of another.

Insofar as rhetorics are tailored to group interests and objectives they are a function of the group ideology. In many, they are ideology in action; they encapsulate beliefs and objectives and actively seek to inculcate them in others. Of course, rhetorics are consequently context specific in a way that ideologies are not expected to be. Rhetorics are only efficient in achieving their objective if they take advantage of things of the moment: rhetorics are opportunist.

Rhetorics tend to have a structure characterized by inconsistency in the content of arguments but consistency in the objective of argument. The structure encompasses illogical shifts of argument but these arguments are invariably emotive and they are subject to stereotyping.

Moreover, rhetoric feeds off itself. Once the ball is rolling, the arguments gather their own momentum and ferocity of attacks on the target of the rhetoric builds. Rhetorics, while mouthing adherence to moral codes, are the very means of their destruction. Rhetoric enters the ring and the referee is blinded as a precursor to the real business.

The rhetorics used in the socialwork strike are interesting because they show how a group identity can be attacked in a conflict. They also show how rhetoric is a powerful shaper of group identity. In fact, the rhetoric of the strike shows how ascribed identities determine and are determined by rhetoric. Certainly the rhetoric of the social-work strike was founded on the ascribed identity of social work and was instrumental in revising that identity. To the extent that the rhetorics aggravated the disparity between the ascribed and the acknowledged identity of social work, they formed a threat to socialwork identity.

Problems of studying rhetoric

There are, however, problems when trying to study rhetoric. For one thing, there is the problem of access. Much rhetoric must go on behind closed doors where an individual representing one group meets an individual representing another group. However, this is not most influential rhetoric in terms of identity formation because the rhetoric needs to be fairly well known to have the requisite impact on the perceived ascribed identity.

In the case of studying the social work strike, access to dominant rhetorics was eased by the presence of social work media which reported the arguments of the relevant groups with considerable detail. Since these were the channels through which most social workers would learn of the arguments, I feel that rhetorics used in them are the most vital ones for study.

But there is a second problem in studying rhetoric: it does not occur in discrete simple packages. Rhetoric evolves over time and has to be studied over time. Moreover, any attempt to impose a fragmented classification system such as would be dictated by standard forms of content analysis might aid quantification of the arguments but it would be spurious. Rhetoric works as a complex network and should be investigated in its entirety not by breaking it up to look at its innards—at least not initially.

So the process I adopted in looking at the rhetorics of the socialwork strike was a relatively simple, if time-consuming, one. The steps in what will be called 'rhetorical analysis' were as follows:

1. Four journals which had involvement with social work were chosen: *New Society; Health and Social Services Journal; Social Work Today*; and *Community Care*. In fact coverage of the strikes was only really prevalent in the latter two. So *SWT* and *Community Care* were taken as the source of the rhetorics. These are weekly magazines both supposedly independent in management. Though it should be stressed that *SWT* is published by *BASW*. Of course, other organs of the Press did print stories about the strike. These were not used for several reasons: they were spasmodic in coverage; they did not represent the views of the major protagonists; and most merely reported the strike through the misted glass of very strong editorial lines. In fact, this is a point that should be emphasized: the media (including TV and radio) entered the conflict with quite strong rhetorics of their own. The impact of these rhetorics on the strike should not be underestimated but they will not be the central focus here.

   It is necessary to outline the editorial rhetoric of the two magazines used in the rhetorical analysis of course since this may have influenced the reportage of other groups. However, it seems unlikely that these biases were very great since the two magazines had different editorial lines and yet the rhetorical analysis showed them to be producing similar outlines of the rhetoric used by other groups.
2. Each edition of both magazines between January, 1978 and August, 1979 were collected and read and all mentions of social workers' industrial action and any comments on it noted verbatim.
3. The main groups in the socialwork strike were identified. From the

notes that had been made the rhetoric used by each group during the entire eighteen month period was established.

4. The line of rhetoric for each group was then examined to see the way in which the layers of argument built up over time. The interest was to see how old arguments were dropped and new ones picked up and how this process related to the rhetorics of other groups.
5. It was only at this stage that categories of argument were superimposed on the lines of rhetoric in an attempt to show how the groups differed in the profiles of their arguments across time. The profiles can also be seen as an attempt to examine how rhetorics interact with each other and with events.

The groups in the conflict

On an *a priori* basis, it was thought that nine groups had been involved in the dispute: the employers (which is to say the local authorities represented by NJC and Councillors); the socialwork strikers (there were of course the nonstrikers but these were not included in the analysis); the unions (NALGO, NUPE and BUSW—the latter being established during the strike); the government (since it had involved itself in virtually every other industrial dispute in the 1978 'winter of discountent'); BASW; the Social Services Directors (these are distinct from the employers, they are managers of social services and often ex-social workers themselves); and last, but not least, the clients (those from whom social work provision was withdrawn).

In fact, NUPE and BUSW did not evolve rhetorics during the strike. More importantly, neither did the clients. This latter was interesting because the absence of a voice from the clients became a central part in the rhetorics of some of the other groups. Perhaps the absence of a rhetoric from the clients should not be regarded with too much surprise. They are not a group in the sense of a corporate entity with representatives to voice its views. The clients are an amorphous mass—separated by time and space. In fact, if they have a voice at any time it tends to be that provided by social workers who represent them—deprived of that voice, they had no means of expressing how much they needed it or what they thought of the strike. The nearest we can get to clients' attitudes come from the ways in which other groups portray the clients' responses in their own rhetoric and this portrayal can hardly be considered objective.

In describing the results of the rhetorical analysis on these groups firstly it is necessary to describe briefly the rhetorics used by each group and how they built up in layers over time. Secondly, it is useful to show how the arguments in the rhetorics can be categorized and how groups moved from one sort of argument to another over time.

1. *The government*

During the period of the strike there was a change of government. David Ennals was succeeded by Patrick Jenkin as Secretary of State for Social Services in the May changeover. Ennals, in December, 1978, made his one and only reported pronouncement on the strike. It had two lines of argument:

(a) Social workers are playing into the hands of their critics by striking—the victims of the strike were the clients whose distress was hidden from sight. He predicted that there would be countless cases of irreparable damage done by the decision of social workers to leave their clients, stranded and in the lurch, unaided. It would destroy the social worker–client relationship.
(b) Social work is the second victim of the strike since they are contradicting their own value system. He argued that they 'might find their present actions merely served the interests of greed, selfishness and ruthless individualism which they normally opposed'.

The second line of argument is a beautiful example of ascribing an identity to the group and then arguing that they are not living up to it.

Having stated his opposition to the strike (in terms that make it sound as though his only interest is for the social workers and their future), Ennals refused to enter actively into the negotiations. The government played no further part in the genesis of rhetorics about the strike. Not, at least until the Conservatives took office when Jenkin stated that social work had got nothing but grief from the strike and set up an inquiry into the effects of the strike.

So, the government thought it was a bad idea to go out on strike (not surprisingly) but were extraordinarily quiet about it (especially given its interventions in other strikes at this time).

2. *The employers*

The employers, that is the local authorities and their representatives on the NJC, had a much more complicated set of arguments in their rhetoric. Moreover, it is dependent on the stage at which they were in the negotiation process.

1978 July: NALGO is not interested in improved pay, they only want to break the national negotiating machinery.

August: NALGO irresponsible to strike before all other channels have been exhausted.

NALGO is using the social workers to fight its battles Local negotiation will cause leapfrogging and will be unfair.

The National agreement will not be broken.
Strike will cause hardship and inconvenience.

Sept.: Public will not understand rejection of negotiation through proper machinery.
Social workers are using the vulnerable.
Strike will breach social worker–client relationship.
National agreement will not be broken.

Oct.: Anxious to talk.

Dec.: Industrial action should end during talks since it is not conducive to discussion.

1979 Jan.: Strike undermines all social services progress—fuels the views of those who think that social work is unnecessary. In future new appointments will be carefully scrutinized.

April: Councils are in no mood to settle.

Aug.: Priorities will change—no longer 100 percent qualified the aim.
Re-evaluation of social work methods necessary.
Industrial action is intolerable.

The one thing that is immediately noticeable is that the employers move from a position founded on arguments that the strike itself is illegitimate to the position that the strike should cease because of its potential consequences for social work and its clients. The rhetoric at the start appeals to the strikers sense of fair play and by the end is appealing to their self-interest. But the appeals to self-interest are couched in terms of the social workers' fears about their identity.

The other thing which is blatantly obvious is that there is a break in aggressive rhetoric issuing from the employers during the period of negotiations that produced the proposals that were finally accepted by NALGO. It is as if the employers were observing a ceasefire as they might in physical hostilities during discussions that prepare the way for peace. The interesting thing is that the rhetorical onslaught resumes once the settlement has been negotiated.

3. *The directors*

The directors of Social Service Departments are the managers of social work. They have their own professional body—the Association of Directors of Social Services—which promoted the rhetoric which the directors used. However, it should be emphasized, many of the arguments used by the directors came from a small number of the directors; notably those nearest the action—directors of Southwark, Tower Hamlets, Newcastle and the Chairman of ADSS at the time (Ted Brown).

1978 July: Support regrading of social workers on basis of changed responsibilities.
Not an argument about pay but about breaking down national and provincial negotiating machinery.

Aug.: Strike will damage clients and impair service.
Local negotiations will result in differential service across areas.
Residential staff review also important.
Review should be at a national not a local level.
Strike action is not popular with Councils or public.
Effects of strike will never be known.
Damage the public image of social work.
Main sufferers will be the clients.
Long term effects will be very serious.
Deplore NALGO's methods and action.
Dispute not about money.

Sept.: Strike is not to do with pay and conditions but the 'destruction of the system'—wrong issue, wrong time.
No way to measure the harm being done.
The serious effects on the community will not be recognized by councillors or public at large.
Strike is immoral.
Predict unemployment for social workers.

Oct.: Local negotiations would be bad—cause discontent and a high rate of mobility.
Irreparable damage to public image.
Cutbacks can be expected.
Strikers were misled and badly advised by the union.
Incalculable damage to clients and social workers.
Residential staff case is stronger.
People are seriously questioning the need for social work.
'Someone has probably died as a result of the strike'.

Nov.: Only those not aware of the social work role think the strike shows that social work is unnecessary.

1979 Jan.: Residential workers are the unsung heroes who do not strike.
Strike has put the profession back a number of years.
There will be strife between strikers and nonstrikers.

Feb.: Settlement is difficult to interpret and time-consuming.

Aug.: Public now question the efficiency of social work.
Strike caused the Councils and public to doubt value of social work.
Forfeited the idea that they are dedicated people and must be measured in work like others 'we must see that there are real rules for social workers'.

The directors' rhetoric shows the paradoxical nature of arguments in rhetoric. They tell social workers that they are needed (they cause deaths by removing labour) and in the same breath deny that they are needed. They claim the effects of the strike cannot be known and say that people do not recognize the serious effects of the strike and yet they then state that incalculable damage is known to have been done by the strike.

The other characteristic of this rhetoric is that it highlights the potential for strife within the social work group: between the residential and fieldworkers. The residential workers were also fighting for a pay increase at this time but refused to take industrial action to pursue it. The other schism that the directors play on is that between the strikers and those who were refusing to come out on strike in fieldwork departments. The directors were not only telling the social workers that they were damaging their public image and credibility, they were also predicting that the unity within social work professional groups which had been fought for and was only recently in any way apparent was likely to be destroyed.

Also, underlying all of this, there is the emphasis on the fact that NALGO is misleading and using the social workers for its own ends. This theme was present in the rhetoric of the employers too and its impact on the strikers is clearly evident in their rhetoric.

4. *The strikers*

The strikers, it should be said immediately, did not get their views very well represented in the journals. Individuals were interviewed on the picket lines and asked questions about their morale and so on but there was no centralized voice for the strikers. However, during the course of the strike, the need for such a voice and source of rhetoric became recognized and a group did come to represent the strikers. This was the All London Social Work Action Group (ALSWAG). ALSWAG co-ordinated much of the national action of the strikers such as rallies and demonstrations. The lines of rhetoric below are taken mainly from their statements, since strikers interviewed on the picket lines were not making self-conscious appeals to an audience but more frequently just answering questions about how they felt. ALSWAG comments are supplemented by comments made by Shop Steward Strike Committees.

1978 July: ALSWAG: it would be foolish to break with NALGO.
Aug.: No alternative but to strike.
Risks are overestimated.
Not guilty for effects of strike—councils that brought us to it are responsible for suffering—cynically indifferent.
Better salaries for social workers will mean a better service.
Morale is good.

Emotional blackmail results in 'carers' being low paid—determined to get justice.

Sept.: Morale good.

Oct.: Angry at establishment of working party.

Nov.: ALSWAG: NALGO obsessed with settlement—sell out feared.
Angry that views are not published.

1979 Jan.: Threat to reduce strike pay is blackmail.
Wish offer to be rejected.
Lack of public concern confirms that the public do not understand the social work task.

Feb.: Proposals are divisive.
ALSWAG: calls the new national scale a straight jacket.
Managers are politically paranoid.

March: NALGO indecent in haste to settle, typical of strike mismanagement.

The major thing noticeable in the reported strikers' rhetoric is the fact that most of it is not self-justificatory or defensive. It does not even attack the opponents in the dispute. Instead, it is levelled at the strikers' own union. While the employers and the directors claim that the union is using the strikers to its own ends; the strikers claim that they want the ends specified by the union and fear that the union will 'chicken out' before they are attained. From their perspective their own ends and those of the union are identical, the social workers simply thought that they were willing to go further to get them.

5. *The Union*

It is appropriate here to consider what NALGO was saying.

1978 April: Time for local authorities to meet responsibilities to their employees.
The idea of BASW setting up a union is a crazy idea.

Aug.: Local negotiations are necessary—faceless men from Whitehall do not understand local conditions.
Improving conditions of staff will improve the service.
Public support strong.
Suffering of clients will be avoided by emergency cover arrangements.

Sept.: Claims are justified—changed responsibilities.
Action 100 per cent—solidarity across Local Authorities.
Emotional blackmail has been used against social workers to keep pay down.

Improve conditions of service will improve service itself.
Public support—even press sympathetic now.
Claims have been ignored.
Not responsible for hardship of clients.

Oct.: Willing to talk.

1979 Jan.: A major step forward toward free local negotiations.

Feb.: A good agreement.

April: Attack on BUSW.

June: Adamant on expulsion of BASW from JCC.
Social workers pay deal is one of the best ever negotiated by NALGO.

The main themes in the rhetoric of NALGO are clear: the strike is justified primarily because clients will benefit in the longrun; there is considerable support for the strike both from social workers and the public; and damage to clients will be minimized. They steer clear of any comment on the need for social work—they justify the strike, *not* the profession. This is very important, since the employers and directors were not simply attacking the strike they were also attacking the profession. Neither strikers nor the union seek to defend the profession. The only group left to do this are BASW.

Before going on to BASW's role in this, it is important to point to the curious 'ceasefire' effect in NALGO's rhetoric during the negotiation period. It echoes that of the employers except when the ceasefire ends NALGO devotes its rhetoric to support of the settlement. The employers resume their attack on the profession but NALGO, even at this stage, does not offer a rejoinder. It is simply concerned with gaining support for the settlement from the social workers who feel it is a betrayal. In fact, the greater betrayal might well be the absence of any supportative rhetoric for the profession.

6. *BASW*

That leaves BASW. The rhetoric of BASW is strangely ambiguous.

1978 Aug.: Endorse the right to strike but only after all other machinery is exhausted and then only if the strike can be justified in terms of the ultimate good of the client.
Emergency protection of vulnerable is always necessary.
Supports national minimum scale and regional negotiations to meet local conditions (this approximates to the compromise which was eventually agreed).

Sept.: Case for pay is good.
No public sympathy.
Moral blackmail to use clients.

Have to pay for higher standards.
Again the code of strikes—no strike unless ultimate value to client and then emergency cover must be provided (BASW opened membership to the unqualified and created a union).
The value of social work is no longer accepted—accused of eroding self-sufficiency and personal responsibility.
No solidarity with strikers.

Oct.: Debate the pros and cons of the strike.
No pronouncement from central BASW.

Nov.: Code for strikes again.
Local negotiations do not merit strike action.

Dec.: Proposals ill-thought out and divisive.
Call for government inquiry.
Condemn lack of urgency in negotiations.
Clients bear the brunt.
Little public awareness.
Angry at talks breakdown.
Local negotiation goal is not justification for strike in the eyes of most social workers—local negotiations are a sacred cow—the money for increased pay is there but being refused by NALGO since they want the local negotiations more than the money.
BASW stated its stand:
(a) Regrading claim is justified;
(b) Local negotiations would be a free-for-all disaster;
(c) Need a career grade (something NALGO refuses to get);
(d) Local negotiations do not justify strikes;
(e) Money on the table so there is no need for spread of strikes.

1979 Jan.: NJC inappropriate for social work.
No social worker had been directly involved in negotiations at NJC.
Strong case for separate machinery.
Attack NALGO—wrong battle fought in the wrong way.
Settlement will be slow to implement.

The strange mixture of condemnation for the strike and support for the claims for greater pay that BASW produced makes confusing reading. It is clear that their arguments are sometimes drawn from those of the strikers and sometimes from those of the employers. They sit uneasily between the two major groups. They are certainly not providing a defence of the profession, except insofar as they are suggesting that in future, strike action should be controlled by a strike code. This serves to highlight how negative their attitude to the existing strike was. They are acknowledging that the strike is unprofessional and is damaging to the image of social work. In many ways they bolster the identity-attack embedded in the rhetoric of the employers and managers.

Profiles of rhetoric

Profiles of rhetoric allow comparison between groups and across time.

The first step in compiling the profiles is to establish what arguments were used. In fact, 34 different argument lines were used. These could be collaposed into 13 categories of arguments. Unfortunately, these 13 were quite distinct and further collapsing of cells would have been unrealistic. Table 1 shows how many different lines of argument were used by each group in each of the 12 months covered.

From an examination of Table 1 and from the sorts of arguments used it was decided that there is a break in the rhetorics used. During the period of the initial working party on settlement, the groups damped down their rhetorics; it was also suspected that the very nature of the rhetoric changed in the case of some groups between pre- and post-proposal periods. So the profiles represent both sorts of argument line—each group has two profiles: Profile 1 for the period August–October, 1978 (before the settlement proposals) and Profile 2 for the period December, 1978–August, 1979 (after these proposals). These are summarized in Table 2.

A series of brief comments can be made on these rhetoric profiles. The dominant finding is that there is indeed a marked discontinuity of argument usage over time—there is a change in the rhetoric of most groups between the pre- and post-proposal phases. Not surprisingly, there is a move from evaluating the strike to evaluating the settlement proposals. But the interesting thing is that in this post-proposal phase the employers and directors argue that damage has been done to social work as a profession. The other interesting thing about the profiles is the similarity between arguments used

Table 1. Number of lines of argument used by each Group over time

	1978					1979							
	Aug.	Sept.	Oct.	Nov.	Dec.	Jan.	Feb.	Mar.	Apr.	May	June	July	Aug.
Employers	3	2				3							2
Strikers	10	1	1	1		2	1	1					
Directors	15	6	8			3	1						1
NALGO	4	6				1	1						
BASW	3	5			9	2							
Government					2								

Table 2. Profiles of Rhetoric

Category of arguments	Govt.		Employers		Directors		Strikers		NALGO		BASW	
	P1	P2	P1	P2	P1	P2	P1	P2	P1	P2	P1	P2
Damaging to clients		√	√		√							√
Damaging to social work		√		√	√	√					√	
NALGO Irresponsible			√		√							√
Wrong issue for strike			√		√							√
Strike justified					√		√		√		√	√
Strikers not responsible for damage to clients							√		√		√	
Support for strike strong							√		√			
Social work needs re-evaluation				√		√						
Strike code needed											√	√
NALGO sell-out							√	√				
Proposals bad						√		√				
Agreement good										√		
Residential better claim					√	√						

A tick indicates the presence of that line of argument in a group's rhetoric.

by the employers and the directors. They say that killer whales go around in kinship groups called pods. The way in which the pod keeps its members together and can differentiate them from other killer whales is through song patterns. Each pod has a unique song pattern that enables them to keep together and exclude strangers—rhetoric can act in the same way. Groups using similar rhetorics come into alignment and simultaneously express that alignment.

In terms of alignment, BASW's rhetoric profile is particularly interesting. BASW have their own rhetoric of the strike code which is not adopted by others but they are influenced by the rhetoric of the others. Their second profile echoes the first profile of the directors and employers. They are acting as an echo of the song—a sort of sad refrain. BASW seems to change sides or be caught in the middle: pre-proposals echoing the strikers; post-proposals echoing the employers–directors. The nature of the profiles shows the ambiguous position of BASW in these dealings.

The most interesting aspect from the point of view of the present argument however was the emphasis on the employers and directors' side of the attack on the profession. If one was to look at the frequency of usage of each category of argument, it becomes clear that employers and directors use the 'damaging to social work' and 'damaging to the client' categories most frequently. The social workers were being told that what they were doing was unethical, dangerous and irresponsible *and* that they were at risk of losing all public belief in their value. They were told no one understood what their role was and no one felt they were necessary. They were told that they could no longer be considered a 'caring' profession. Their value and their values were therefore simultaneously attacked. The very root of their acknowledged identity was being dug up, pulled away from sustenance and incinerated. The ascribed identity for social work evolved in the rhetoric was such that social workers might feel their entire future threatened.

In such a situation, the threatened group should act to protect itself. Yet the strikers and NALGO did not protect themselves. Their rhetorics were addressed to legitimating the strike not the profession yet the attacks wove the strike around the profession and threatened both simultaneously. The social workers were attacked with their defences down. The vital feature from the present point of view is what consequences this had for identity.

The effects of the rhetorics

There are a series of ways to estimate the effects of rhetorics used in the conflict. The one chosen will depend upon which group is the focus of concern. One could look at the responses of the general public, of the professional bodies or of policy makers. The fact that rhetorics can potentially influence several sorts of groups highlights the fact that rhetorics may serve different ends. They can consolidate support of the membership of the group producing them. They can seek support from noncombatants. They can work to confuse, defy or compromise the opponents. Looked at in this light, it can be seen that the strikers and the employers were using rhetorics aimed at different ends and to some extent different audiences. The employers aimed to compromise the strikers and dissuade them from their course of action while encouraging the public to disapprove of the strike. The strikers were trying to consolidate their own group—particularly in its alliance with the union.

The fact that the union settled against the strikers wishes shows that the strikers' rhetoric was ineffective; their failure to have any impact on the management and employers' stance is equally indicative of their failure to put their own house in order.

The rhetoric of the management and employers was not only more complex and elaborated, it was tailor-male to influence the strikers. The rhetorics of the employers had barbed shafts that sank deep into the wounds of the strikers' already threatened identity. The rhetorics took each weakness of the profession, highlighted it, and showed that the strike was making other people realize these weaknesses existed. The message was clear—through all the paradox and inconsistency of argument—the employers and directors were saying something akin to: don't be silly and call people's attention to the fact that you are worthless and unethical; people won't realize that you are an unnecessary occupational group if you only return to work.

Of course, the employers' rhetoric did not persuade the strikers to return to work. The effects of the rhetoric can be seen in other directions however. Firstly, in the changing self-perception and acknowledged identity of social workers since the strike. Secondly, in the means chosen to evaluate the effects of the strike and in the way in which report of these effects has been received. They will be dealt with briefly in turn.

Researchers working at Liverpool Polytechnic under the direction of Pat Clayton have investigated the course and consequence of the strike for social workers in Liverpool. One of their findings is that social workers are reporting a changed self-perception since the strike. Social workers interviewed in Liverpool see themselves as 'workers' not professionals with a caring vocation. They believe that they have thrown off the shroud of emotional blackmail associated with professionalism. They have moved closer to other unionized labour during the dispute and now experience solidarity with them—especially since they feel rejected by other professionals. It seems that the rhetoric which questioned the professionalism of social workers mediated the effect of the strike which was to transform the 'professional' identity of social work. Told that they were not valued as a profession, social workers have begun to translate their self-image. Unionism replaces professionalism as an ideal—at least in the aftermath of the strike. The ascribed and the acknowledged identities begin to move into phase again. Social workers failed to repel the ascribed identity and are changing their acknowledged identity. Even BASW, that bastion of professionalism, has opened its membership to the unqualified and has set up a parrallel union (BUSW). Of course, the Liverpool sample may not be representative of the rest of British social workers. The majority may not have resolved the threat so easily and obviously the strike rhetorics are not the sole cause of the changes. The rhetorics were shaped by the context of their introduction, they merely encapsulate and accelerate a process which has resulted in identity changes for social work.

The second type of consequence of the rhetoric can be seen in the DHSS report on the effects of the strike. The effects of the strike were evaluated by DHSS researchers on the instruction of the then Secretary of State, Patrick Jenkin. They investigated the effects of the strike in Tower Hamlets, a London borough which had been on strike for one of the longest periods and had a reputation as an area with extreme social problems (housing, unemployment, racial conflict). The interesting aspect of this investigation from our point of view is that all of the questions asked were predicated on the rhetorics of the conflict. The point is that the rhetorics of the strike establish the milieu in which its consequences will be evaluated and in this case the rhetorics can be seen to be simply reiterated in the report: in the questions asked and in the answers given. One dominant rhetoric of the strike had been that the effects of the strike would be unmeasurable. The investigators failed to establish any criteria on which the effects of deprivation of social work during the strike could be measured. They merely reported the opinions of relevant groups: there had been irreparable but invisible damage; there was a loss of confidence in social workers, their public image was spoiled; contacts with clients had been ruined and association with other professions broken. Yet none of these things was measured, the data—if it existed—was not presented. The important thing here is that this report was a report to the Secretary of State that would presumably influence DHSS policy and yet for all one knows it may have been based on speculation, surmise and anecdote. Much of what was said is predictable on the basis of the rhetoric of the strike and the question must be 'how much of the report itself remains rhetoric?' One hopes that understanding something of what rhetorics are about will forestall a repetition of this investigative approach. Incidentally, the dynamics of rhetoric would also predict the reception of such a report. To put it mildly, it was greeted with mixed feelings. *Social Work Today* said that it showed the importance of social work. *Community Care* said that it showed the importance of social workers but that the voluntary sector had managed to step into the breech and they were not so much missed. *New Society* indicated that it showed that home helps and the like were much more important than the social workers who had hardly been missed. *The Spectator* ran an article by June Lait which said the report not only showed how pointless social workers are but also how pointless DHSS researchers are. The report becomes another cudgel on the back of the social work profession in the hands of the majority. The threatened identity is one step nearer dissolution under attack—the absence of social workers really wasn't so traumatic, we can do without you is the main message. Again, the case of the social workers is not presented in the report—their perspective on the effects of the strike is the only one missing and yet in most situations they are the only ones with information on exactly what had not happened that should have happened during the period of the strike. They lie like the ghost at the feast—one can almost imagine them walking the streets of Southwark or Tower Hamlets with head under arm. The consequences of their absence is reported without reference to themselves or how they evaluate the consequences. But then you would hardly expect the executioner to put his head on the block and the chopper in the hands of the accused. Social workers were being afforded no weapon. The terms of reference lay in the rhetorics of other groups—after all the social workers had evolved no protective rhetoric during the conflict.

CONCLUSION

The analysis presented above was not meant to say much about social work *per se*. It was meant to say something about what happens when a group with a threatened identity goes into conflict. If a group with a threatened identity goes into conflict, it should expect to be attacked in ways which focus upon the very places where the identity is most in doubt. Moreover, this is true even when such foci of attack are irrelevant to the real issues involved in the conflict. After all, the fundamental value of social work had no real relevance to the issue on which the strike was launched. Rhetorics which are used in such conflicts work best if they can tap the weaknesses in the identity of the group under attack. Any weakness in identity structure is grist to the mill of rhetoric. However, the circularity of this process should never be overlooked: rhetoric feeds off threatened identities but it in turn breeds them. Rhetoric can actually be the origin of a threatened identity for a group because it establishes an ascribed identity for the group which is at variance with the identity its members would acknowledge.

Whether rhetorics are really only prevalent in industrial conflict is hard to say. Certainly, there are similarities in the structure of the rhetoric across strikes. Strikes, which followed that of the social workers, which involved large sections of the steel industry and the motor manufacturers saw the use of rhetoric. Steelworkers and car workers were treated to the same paradoxical message that they were unnecessary since their industries are in decline and yet they were destroying the economy through their actions. Also, in an era of strikes, it is interesting to consider how a 'rhetorical climate' may evolve—where styles of rhetoric are transplanted from one strike to the next: the same lines being adopted with different workers. Certainly, there is some evidence for this.

The next step must be to understand more about the structure of rhetoric—how it responds to changing circumstances, how it is formulated, and how it is connected to other strategies in a conflict. More than this, it is necessary to establish what effects it can have not only on the identity of a group but also upon the identity of individuals who are members of that group.

REFERENCES

McCarthy, P. (1980). *Professionalism and Unionism in Social Work*. Unpublished. M.Sc. Thesis, University of Oxford.

Threatened Identities
Edited by G. Breakwell

Environmental Change and Community Identity

JUDITH A. MATTHEWS

The definition of the term 'community' has long been a subject of debate in the social sciences; Hillery (1955, 1968), for example, identified 94 different definitions of the term in the sociological literature. In this Chapter, an 'ecological' definition (Hunter, 1974) will be adopted, so the term will be used to refer to a spatially contingent group of people whose interactions are mediated through the spatial and physical environment. The purpose of the research which will be reported was to investigate how the definitions of that group as used by its members, and by those concerned with planning for it, interact to produce the form in which the physical and social environment of the community is cognized by its members. It will be argued that 'the community' as a group of people living in a given area is threatened by the proposal that some part of its physical surrounding be altered. Public responses to planning are therefore interpreted as the response of a threatened group.

The person's 'knowing' of the local environment has a degree of consistency over time, but is, nevertheless, a dynamic process. The physical form of the person's surroundings changes with the weather, with the passage of the seasons, and the passing of time, irrespective of human intervention. Being used by people, it is subject to the changes which they bring about. Accepting this continual change, an image of the physical environment is still developed by the person which has a certain persistence, and which is therefore capable of directing the person's behaviour in that environment. Such consistency of image has been used to explain how suboptimal routes between places come to be regularly followed even when the person may have very comprehensive knowledge of the area of the route (Lynch, 1960). The consistency has value in so far as it reduces the necessity to be continually making decisions about the path to be taken. It has disadvantages where the image which is developed is highly inaccurate. Lynch argues that one of the bases for inaccuracy may lie in the complexity of the shape of the urban environment. He proposes that the earliest stage in the learning of an area is the recognition of the relative positions of prominent landmarks, followed by the discovery of routes between them, and lastly by a more finely discriminated image of the areas between. If landmarks are not easily identified, or the paths between them are undistinguished or confusing, an inaccurate image will come to be accepted as the basis for route finding. Other sources of inaccuracy may be the adoption of the first route found as the only possible one, or constraints imposed upon exploration, for example, by traffic management. Whatever the sources of inaccuracy, the consistent image which develops may overide temporary changes brought about by the weather or the seasons, and may lead to a failure to incorporate more permanent changes, such as a shortening of the route, made possible by demolition. The consistency of the image does not, however, mean that it remains static. The person must adjust to immediate conditions, even at the apparently trivial level of detouring to avoid roadworks or using alternative pathways during heavy snow. Such small scale changes alert the person to the total environment, and thus give rise to adjustments in what is known about that environment. The environment that is known to a person is, then a representation, continually being adjusted, of the 'world as it is', outside the person. In understanding the person's behaviour, interest must be focused on the form of the internal representation, since it is this which directs behaviour.

The construction of this representation of the external world may be modelled as shown in Figure 1.

The environment constitutes a set of physical elements, and a set of people whom the observer of the environment associates with various social groups. These two sets can be called the Physical Environment and the Social Environment, respectively. The observer has a set of predispositions which are derived from past experience, from membership in groups, and from current interests. These dictate the ways in which the social and physical

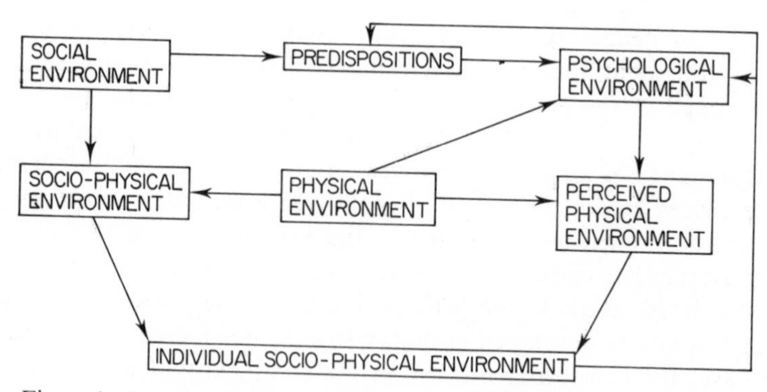

Figure 1. Processes in the cognition of the socio-physical environment

elements are cognized. The results of predispositions and of the cognition of the Physical and Social Environments can be said to constitute the Psychological Environment of the individual. Since social and physical elements in the person's surroundings are not cognized in isolation from one another, the environment which the person cognizes is always a Socio-Physical Environment, and any description of the world around is always a description of a Perceived Environment. The interaction between Individual Socio-Physical Environments creates the Socio-Physical Environment in which people live. Since perceptions relate in part to group attitudes and stereotypes, this Socio-Physical Environment is always a product of intergroup processes as well as of physical elements.

When the Socio-Physical Environment of interest is that in which the person lives, the whole system of social and physical elements and their relationships can be said to constitute 'the community' for that person. It is within this framework that relevant groups are identified, and significant physical features selected to form the Perceived Physical Environment.

The residents of an area may vary considerably in the extent to which they consider themselves to be members of a local community, and the size of the area which they see as being the preserve of their own community may also vary (Lee, 1968). Webber (1964, 1968) argued that the ties people have with their local communities are diminishing in an age of rapid communication over long distances, and that this is particularly the case for members of the higher socioeconomic groups, with their greater degree of mobility, both in residential and occupational terms. Residents also vary in terms of the spatial scale at which they assess the importance of the community. Differences in this respect will depend upon the purpose of the community definition and upon the attributes of the assessor. A question concerning health care, for example, may be considered to have significance for a community defined in city wide terms if hospitals are at issue, and in terms of a smaller, more locally based community when the question relates to general practitioner services. Variations between residents on this latter issue may relate to a larger area perceived to constitute one community by a resident who has access to private transport, as compared with a limited area, served by a single doctor's practice available to the resident whose mobility is restricted.

The importance of these variations in definition lies less in the precise nature of the variations than in the fact that 'the community' represents a meaningful concept for people. However it is defined, it constitutes a reference group, having both social and physical connotations. Treated in this way, the community as a group must be incorporated into models of the development of social identity, where such identity is held to be a product of interactions between the various group memberships and nonmemberships which have significance to the person. Social identity, then, is seen to develop out of membership of at least one group—the community—whose dimensions are construed not only in terms of social elements, but also of the physical components and spatial location of the group's position. Social identity develops in *response* to spatial and physical environments experienced by the individual, and not merely *within* those environments. Consequently, positive and negative statements about physical elements or characteristics of the environment are likely to be understood as statements about the groups who believe themselves to be identified with those elements. Equally, positive evaluation of a group may lead to detailed knowledge of, and deep affection for, a place with which that group is associated; many of the 'special places' remembered from childhood have the characteristic of having been associated with valued groups.

It can, therefore, be argued that the implications of group membership for individual social identity also have significance for the way in which physical environments and the communities within them are perceived. An example of this is to be found in the way in which positive and negative evaluations of the physical environment of particular parts of a city are readily believed by residents in those areas to be assessments of themselves. The response of residents to negative evaluation of their area is frequently one which asks the evaluator to reassess the environment in new terms—'it may not be much to look at, but it's ever so friendly'. The response is reminiscent of that shown by the boys in Lemaine's (1974) experiment who had been set an impossible task in a competition. Two groups of boys were set the task of building a hut. One group was supplied with tools and materials adequate to the task, the other group was insufficiently provided with the necessary equipment. Both groups built their hut. That built by the second group was inevitably a poor structure—but they surrounded it with a garden. When judging began, this group argued for a change in the criteria of evaluation to be used by the competition judges, arguing that the quality of the garden should also be considered. Residents in a rundown 'inner city' area are similarly faced with a situation in which the inferiority of their group on a given dimension—in this case, that of the aesthetic qualities of the built environment—cannot be disputed. The appeal to other aspects of the setting suggests that evaluations of the area are treated by its residents in terms of their affiliation to the group which is defined by local residence.

By delimiting a particular area as a zone for planning action, environmental planners can be said to define an 'ingroup' within the zone of action, and an 'outgroup' beyond that zone. Discussions about effects on the local community are then structured in terms of these groups. The planners' delimitation of the zone and its associated community is often different from that which the residents would propose as the appropriate spatial boundaries of the community. In such a situation the 'ingroup' established by the planners conflicts with existing notions of the resident 'ingroup'. Each is claimed to represent *the* community, and for those within the disputed zone marked conflict is induced. Residents' affiliation to the group they know as 'the community' comes under threat. The planners' designation of the area which contains the community confronts residents whose concept of their community is different with two choices. They can either accept the planners' definition, in which case they will abandon membership of a valued group, i.e. 'the community' in their own definition, or, alternatively, they can reject the planners' definition, and continue to claim membership in that group which the residents themselves perceive as being the local community. In this latter case, the continued affiliation of residents to a group which is not recognized by the planners may demand that they overcome barriers, both physical and conceptual, which declare their claims to membership in the community to be illegitimate. Whether or not the planners' definition of the community is accepted, a tension is induced between residents' and planners' estimations of the appropriate criteria by which membership in the community is to be determined.

Breakwell (1978) has described the operation of tensions similar to those described above between residents and planners in terms of conflict between 'internal' and 'external' criteria of membership. She has shown how disparities between the person's own, internal, evaluation of the validity of their membership, and those which are imposed by external agencies, give rise to conditions of 'threatened identity', and lead to the adoption of strategies designed to resolve the conflict induced by the disparity. The power of planners to determine the external criteria of membership in communities is of the utmost importance for the way in which strategies are evolved to deal with the threat posed by planning activity for individual identity and for the identity of the community as a group.

This chapter is concerned with the way in which the community *as a group* responds to the effects of environmental planning. Since the definition of the community that has been adopted is dependent upon the identification of the physical boundaries within which a group of people lives, interest is focused on the ways in which such boundaries are recognized by people living within them, and on the effects of imposed changes which alter the boundaries. In a case where the definition of a zone of action by planners excludes areas whose residents are generally felt to be legitimately part of the community, the identification of these residents with members of the officially designated 'ingroup'—the area declared by the plan to be the home of the community affected by the plan—may be expected to be endorsed by those residents who have been officially recognized as 'community members', and whose sense of group membership is therefore not threatened. On the other hand, in the case where the official designation of an area includes people who were not previously accepted as part of the community, their identification with the group may be rejected by established members. Both situations are likely to lead to conflict with the planners, but the second situation is also likely to produce conflict *within* the community.

The community is therefore envisaged as a group which is the product of the relationships between social groups within given spatial and physical boundaries. It is a creation of the way in which individuals cognize their surroundings. The responses to the threat posed by planning, outlined above, envisage the results which will ensue when the parties to the discussion of community definitions are constrained to accept participation in the process, either through inability to remove themselves physically from the area, or through the generality of the effects of the particular planning decision. When noninvolvement is a realistic option, the form taken by the opposition between the groups becomes more complicated, at the very least in so far as the option of noninvolvement introduces a new dimension to the intergroup setting. The terms in which the response to the new situation is couched will refer to characteristics of the groups which evolve. Since they develop with reference to events in the Physical Environment, it can be expected that the criteria of membership in the new groups will incorporate attitudes toward this environment.

Such attitudes are not only evoked under conditions of environmental change, however. Community membership always partakes of the nature of the Physical Environment. In that the social idenity of the individual incorporates notions of community membership, then, this identity itself has a physical environmental component. The community as a group may therefore be incorporated into the model of environment cognition proposed earlier as shown in Figure 2.

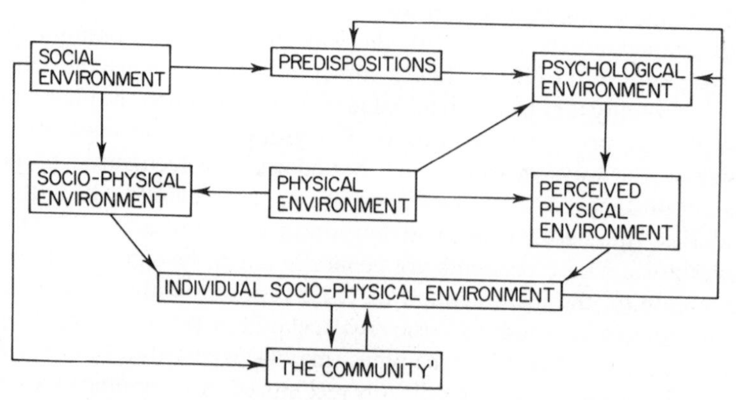

Figure 2. Processes in the cognition of the local community

THE OBJECTIVES OF THE RESEARCH

The research which is to be reported was carried out in a newly declared Housing Action Area, and focused on the ways in which those involved in a long term series of planned environmental changes structured their perceptions of the changes. A Housing Action Area was chosen because the policy which Housing Action Areas (HAAs) represent is one which addresses itself to both physical and social conditions. HAAs generally have easily identifiable boundaries, major roads or railway lines for example. This has two implications for the research described here; first, it allow residents to identify the 'ingroup' of those living in the HAA, and the 'outgroup' of those not included; secondly, this clearly defined group offers itself for ready designation by planners as 'the community'.

The 1974 Housing Act envisages that a Local Authority will receive reports.

'Having regard to
(a) the physical state of the housing accommodation in the area as a whole, and
(b) social conditions in the area,' (Housing Act 1974. Part 4, Section 36).

and that if, on the basis of such reports it is satisfied that within five years improvements can be made to housing, the well being of residents currently in the area, and the management and use of accommodation, the Local Authority 'may declare the area to be a Housing Action Area.' After declaration, householders are eligible to receive larger improvement grants than are normally available, the Local Authority has additional powers to enforce the improvement of tenanted property, and external environmental improvement, through traffic management, the provision of public open space, and the painting and restoration of fences etc. becomes a priority. Considerable emphasis is placed on the intention that the HAA should benefit the present residents, rather than leading to their displacement by new migrants, so, in many cities, a householder may be required to pay back any grant given for a house which is sold within five years of the improvement work being carried out. The effects of declaration are therefore considerable. They are likely to affect residents directly, in their own homes. The policy is oriented toward physical and social objectives, and is explicit about its emphasis upon improvement for the benefit of the existing 'community' of the area.

In the city where this research was conducted, the goal of public participation in the decision making process, which receives prominent attention in the Act, was pursued through the establishment of Liaison Groups in each HAA. These were regular meetings between the officers of the Local Authority who were to be primarily responsible for the area, and residents or representatives of the residents. In these meetings the varying definitions of 'the community' amongst residents and planners were most apparent. By analysing the content of discussions in one Liaison Group during the early stages of HAA status, it was possible to identify the groups which were perceived by residents and by planners as constituting the Social Environment of the area. The attitudes expressed by representatives of these groups indicated the predispositions that influenced Psychological Environments for the participants, and hence their Individual Socio-Physical Environments. By tracing the ways in which the various groups responded to the area, defined its problems, and evaluated proposed changes, the intention was to examine the processes by which environmental change comes to be incorporated into cognition of the local environment, and to identify the way in which varying definitions of the community affect these processes. The discussions which are analysed are those which took place in one Liaison Group during the first six months of the existence of the HAA, which is referred to in the rest of this chapter as The Area.

RESEARCH METHOD

I attended the first five meetings of the Liaison Group and took notes of everything that was said. The method of note taking was used in preference to tape recording the proceedings, since it was felt that the latter method would be intrusive in a situation which was new to the majority of the participants and hence, of itself, somewhat threatening, and where the issues discussed were likely to be sensitive ones. The proceedings were minuted by an official of the Local Authority and sometimes by a member of the Community Association in the area, so the presence of a third notebook seemed less likely to influence expression of opinions. Residents and officials of the Local Authority at the meetings knew of the research and of its broad aim of studying the effect of the HAA on local residents. Although it is possible that some comments were not noted due to momentary lapses of attention, meetings generally lasted little more than two hours, and it is not felt that fatigue effects are significant for the accuracy of the notes made.

At the end of the first year of the HAA, copies of the Formal Minutes of the meetings were obtained. These had been compiled for the information of residents, Local Authority Departments, and Councillors by the Liaison Officer, who was a member of the Housing Department of the Local Authority. It was his responsibility to deal with enquiries about the HAA from residents, and to coordinate the work of the various Local Authority Departments concerned with HAAs in the city. The Liaison Officer had been responsible for convening the meetings of the Liaison Group, and the minutes he compiled can therefore be seen as the means whereby he 'interpreted' the work of the Local Authority for interested parties. Two analyses were performed, one of my own 'Verbatim' account of proceedings at the meetings, the other of the Formal Minutes produced by the Liaison Officer. The two analyses were compared to assess whether the Liaison Officer's representation of the discussions indicated any bias, and if so, the implications of such bias.

The analyses consisted of seven stages, and resulted in the production of temporal 'profiles' of the progress of discussions over the period. The stages of the analysis were as follows.

Stage 1. The Minutes and Verbatim Record were read and the interest groups which emerged during the course of the discussions were identified. There were eight such groups. Five groups represented the professional distinctions amongst the officers, for example, between Housing and Environmental Health Department officials. Amongst the residents, the general group of all HAA residents, referred to in the rest of this Chapter as the 'Local' residents, contained two subdivisions, which were not necessarily exclusive. The first of these groups will be referred to as the 'Informed' residents, and consisted of those residents who were also members of the local Community Association. The second grouping varied in its constitution according to the changes taking place within the HAA. This group, the 'Affected' residents, consisted of those people who were immediately affected by some specific result of the HAA, such as building or demolition.

Stage 2. Statements made at the meetings were classified according to the group membership of the person making the statement, and the content of statements by each group for the whole period was recorded.

Stage 3. From interviews conducted with officers and Community Association leaders before the Liaison meetings began, concerning the functions of the proposed Liaison Group, a categorization of statement types was constructed. The use of statements within these categories then acted as a measure of the operation of the perceived functions of the Liaison Group. Six categories were defined, ranging from the prescriptive 'Request for Action' to the relatively passive 'Comment'. The categories are shown in Figure 3.

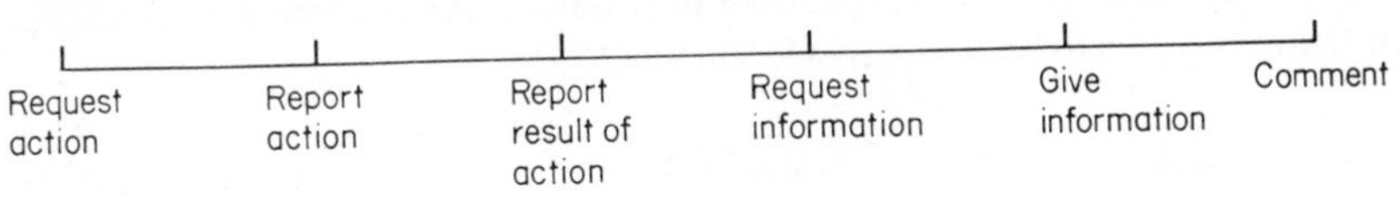

Figure 3. Categorization of types of statements made during Liaison Group discussions

Each statement was scored on a five-point scale between the poles, as stated below, of dimensions to which the statement was judged to apply.

DIMENSIONS

Dimension number			
1.	Issue is physical	– – – – –	Issue is social
2.	Effect of issue is physical	– – – – –	Effect of issue is social
3.	Issue assessed positively	– – – – –	Issue assessed negatively
4.	Issue affects everyone in area	– – – – –	Issue affects particular groups in area
5.	Groups stereotyped	– – – – –	Groups not stereotyped
6.	Officers stereotyped, positively	– – – – –	Officers stereotyped negatively
7.	Residents stereotyped positively	– – – – –	Residents stereotyped, negatively
8.	Nonstereotyped group, praised	– – – – –	Nonstereotyped group, blamed
9.	Officers judged powerful	– – – – –	Officers judged powerless
10.	Liaison Group judged powerful	– – – – –	Liaison Group judged powerless
11.	Issues judged negotiable	– – – – –	Issues judged non-negotiable
12.	Own group has knowledge	– – – – –	Own group has no knowledge

Figure 4. Dimensions for evaluation of statements made at Liaison Group meetings, used in the analysis of the Verbatim Record and Formal Minutes

Stage 4. Twelve bipolar 'Dimensions' for the evaluation of statements were established as a means for testing hypothesized relationships between statements made by the various subgroups within the Liaison Group. The dimensions expressed the polarities which were expected to occur between the groups on the series of issues which were central to the operation of the Housing Action Area. Three dimensions were concerned with the nature of the issues, the hypothesis being that officers would be inclined to see issues in terms of their physical implications, while residents would be concerned with their social effects. Five Dimensions dealt with the perception of social groups within the area, the first of these (Dimension 4) being designed to test the extent to which groups within the area were recognized as such. Four Dimensions were addressed to questions of power within the area (Dimensions 9–12). The remainder of this chapter will discuss only four of these Dimensions, but the full list is shown in Figure 4. An extended discussion of all Dimensions is to be found in Matthews (1981).

Stage 5. Each statement was assigned to one of the six categories outlined above (Stage 3), and to such Dimensions as were appropriate. For each such Dimension, the statement was scored on a five-point scale between the poles;

thus a statement such as 'Mrs A asked when the trees were to be felled' would be scored at the 'Physical' end of the scale on Dimension 1, while 'Mr B complained that children's noise in the play area was causing a nuisance' would be scored at the 'Social' end of Dimensions 1 and 2, toward the 'Negative' pole of Dimension 3, and toward the 'Blame' pole of Dimension 8.

Stage 6. When all statements had been recorded in this way for all meetings, the median position for each group on each Dimension was plotted by recording the position which marked the mid point of the number of statements made by each group on each Dimension. By plotting this median position for each Dimension over the entire series of meetings for which the records were analysed, a 'Profile' was constructed showing movements in the position taken by each group over period.

Stage 7. After I had scored all statements for the two sets of records of the meetings, two independent judges were asked to perform the same task for a 25 percent sample of the Formal Minutes and Verbatim Record. Each judge worked independently according to the same printed 'protocol', and was unaware of the experimental hypotheses. Agreement between the judges' scores and my own was very close (Matthews, 1981), my own scoring being, if anything, more conservative in terms of the hypotheses than were those of the judges. In view of this, my own scoring for the full set of the Formal Minutes and Verbatim Record is used throughout the report which follows.

PERCEPTIONS OF THE COMMUNITY AND COMMUNITY INTEREST—RESULTS FROM THE ANALYSES OF LIAISON GROUP DISCUSSIONS

From the categorization of statement types, it was apparent that there was general agreement on the information giving and receiving role of the discussions, and on their function of allowing residents to request action and receive reports of action in relation to the work of the Local Authority. It was also apparent that the meetings were a forum for comment on the progress of the HAA.

The 'comments' and 'requests for action' formed the principal context within which residents and officers evolved their declared perceptions of area, and of the community it contained. In one sense, discussions in the Liaison Group may be said to involve only these two groups—the Local Residents and the Officers. This distinction, indeed, formed the basis of stereotyping by each group of the other. The residents saw the officers as 'the planners', a stereotype vehemently rejected as such by a representative of the Planning Department (a 'real' Planner) in a letter to the local press. The letter complained about an account of events relating to the proposed demolition of houses in the area:

> 'It really is about time reporters realised that town 'planners' cannot be used for any old town hall official. The pulling down of houses. . . has nothing to do with planners. It is mainly the concern of health officers and their committee.'

Evidence that the officers perceived the residents as a unitary group is afforded by the establishment of the '*Residents*' Liaison Group', which gave rise to the first indication that HAA declaration might constitute a threat to group identity in the area. The form of this threat related to the role of the Community Association within the Liaison Group.

The Community Association had existed in the area for four years at the time of HAA declaration. The Association drew its membership from an area which included three 'high-rise' residential developments and the old houses which eventually formed the HAA. The Community Association had campaigned vigorously for declaration of the Housing Action Area, against an apparent unwillingness of the Local Authority to make such declaration. The main thrust of the Association's campaign had been the conduct of a detailed survey of conditions in the older houses, leading to the preparation of a report which was submitted to the Local Authority under the provisions of the Housing Act, 1974.

When the HAA was eventually declared, it covered an area considerably smaller than that proposed by the Community Association. Following declaration, the Association's requests that it be included in discussions with officers about the Area were repeatedly turned down, and at the establishment of the Liaison Group it was declared that while members of the Association who were resident in the Area were welcome to attend the Liaison Group meetings, the Community Association as a group would not be formally invited to attend. A senior officer (who did not come to subsequent meetings) said at the inaugural meeting that the Area was one in which various 'factions' were to be found, the Community Association was one such, of which the residents 'might' have heard. In the light of the Community Association's claim to have contacted most households in the area during their survey, this statement can be seen as the embodiment of a considerable threat to the identity of Community Association members who were also residents in the HAA. They were, in effect, being told that their Community Association membership did not exist for the purposes of Liaison Group discussion, and that its existence was in any case fairly doubtful as far as the majority of residents were concerned. The group as a whole was threatened by the establishment of an alternative 'representative' body to which residents were encouraged to declare allegiance, particularly since the Liaison Group had 'official' recognition. The establishment of the Liaison Group therefore threatened the community in the area at two levels, firstly, in so far as it imposed a marked spatial limitation upon the area officially recognized as encompassing 'the community', and secondly, in its denial of the claims of a major group within the area to represent 'the community'.

The response to this threat can be seen from a comparison between the profiles for Officers and Informed Residents (the members of the Community Association who attended Laison Group meetings) on Dimension 4. The poles of this Dimension specify alternative perceptions of the impact of HAA policy. At one extreme is the view that the effects of the policy will be general—the HAA is for 'the well being of residents presently in the area'—at the other extreme is the opinion that effects will vary as between different groups of residents. Figure 5 shows the profiles for Officers and Informed residents, as derived from the Verbatim record of the first five meetings, and clearly demonstrates the way in which the Community Association members argued that their knowledge about 'the community' gave them the competence to assess variations within it. The officers moved from an initial position in which they tended to recognize the possibility that the actions might affect groups within the area differently, toward the argument that there was one 'community' in the area, all of which would be affected by the HAA.

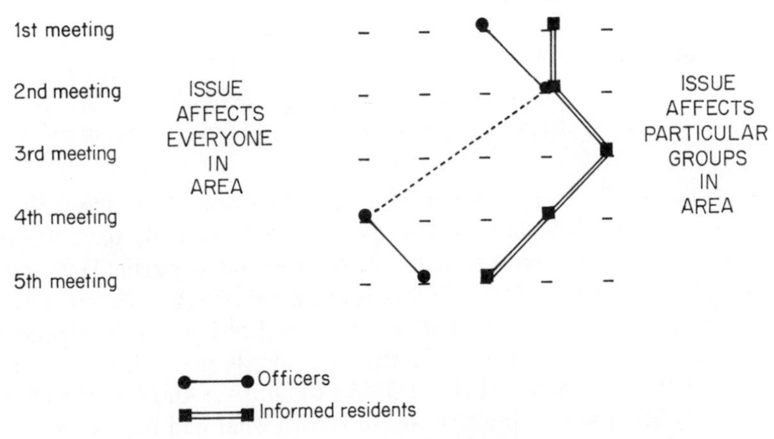

Figure 5. Profile for Dimension between 'Issue affects everyone in area' and 'Issue affects particular groups in Area' (Dimension 4). From Verbatim Record

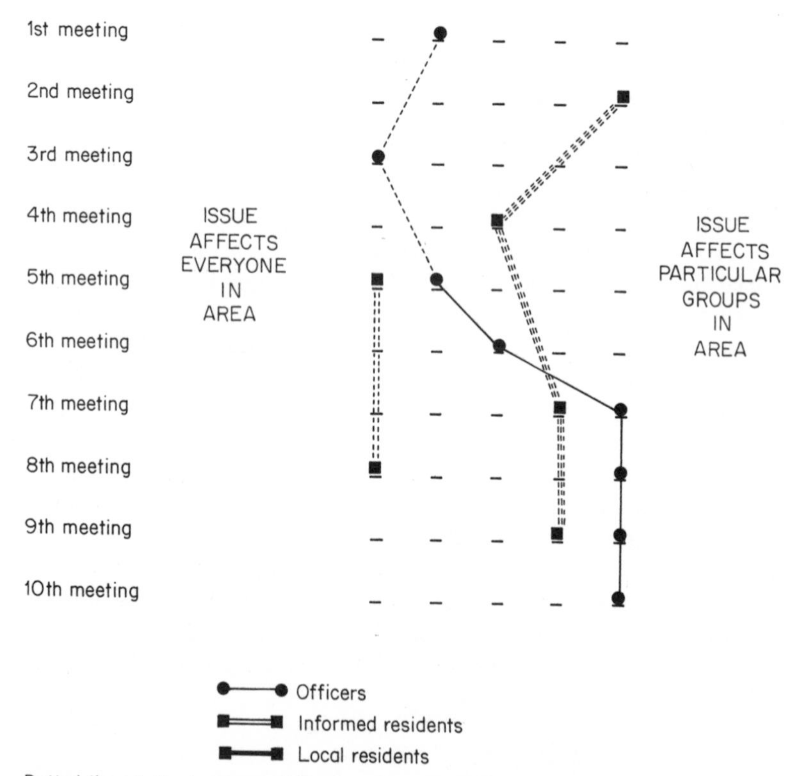

Figure 6. Profile for dimension between 'Issue affects everyone in area' and 'Issue affects particular groups in area' (Dimension 4). From Formal Minutes

The profile for Dimension 4 as drawn from the Formal Minutes is shown in Figure 6. It was difficult to assess the positions taken by the Informed Residents group from analysis of the Formal Minutes, particularly in the early meetings, since in order to do this, it was necessary that the name of the speaker be given. In compiling the minutes, the Liaison Officer frequently used the impersonal 'residents said that . . . ' or 'it was asked . . . '. This resulted partly from the fact that the Officer did not yet know all the names, and partially because his objective was to record what had been said, rather than who had said it, particularly since the expressed purpose of the meetings was to discuss matters with 'the residents' in general. In order to account for all statements which were made by the Informed Residents, therefore, Figure 6 shows the profiles for the Informed Residents, where this could be established, and also for the Local Residents (i.e. those statements attributed impersonally to 'the residents')

Two interesting features may be noted about these profiles. Firstly, it can be seen that many of the statements made about the general or group-specific impacts of the policy, identifiable in the Verbatim Record, do not appear in the Formal Minutes. Secondly, the apparent trend in statements made by the residents during the first five meetings is toward agreement with the Officers that the effects of the HAA are general to 'everyone in the Area', and not restricted to particular groups. This is in direct contrast to the trend shown in the Verbatim Record. However, during the meetings in the second half of the year (meetings 6–10), Officers and Local Residents appear to agree that the issues affect particular groups, while the Informed Residents stress the generality of effects.

In view of the apparent differences between Residents and Officers in their definitions of the social impact of the HAA, and of the apparent tendency of the writer of the Formal Minutes to emphasize agreement between the Local Residents and the Officers, it is of interest to compare the Profiles for the two groups between the two accounts, 'Verbatim' and 'Formal', of the meetings, for the area of discussion where the differences between the groups might be expected to be greatest. The Officers' task in the HAA was to effect a series of changes in the built environment which would lead to better living conditions for the residents. It could be predicted, therefore, that their concern in discussions with the residents would be to discuss the practicalities of such changes, while residents might be expected to be more concerned with the ways in which such changes would affect the immediate conduct of their lives. Dimension 1 was designed to investigate such differences. Figure 7 shows the profiles for Dimension 1 from the Ver-

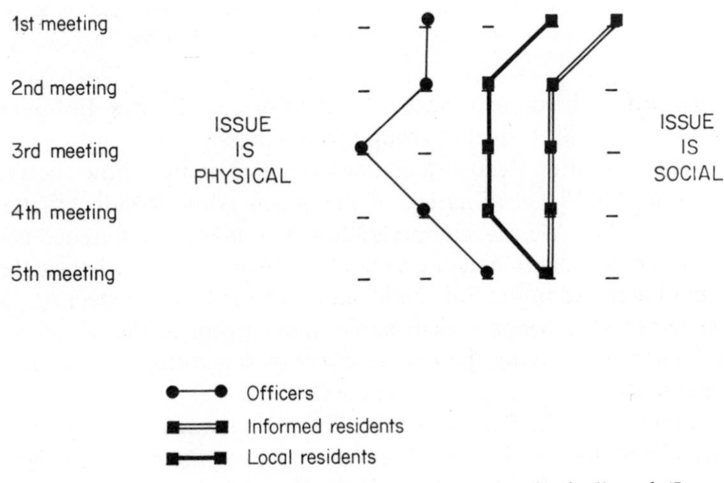

Figure 7. Profile for dimension between 'Issue is physical' and 'Issue is social' (Dimension 1). From Verbatim Record

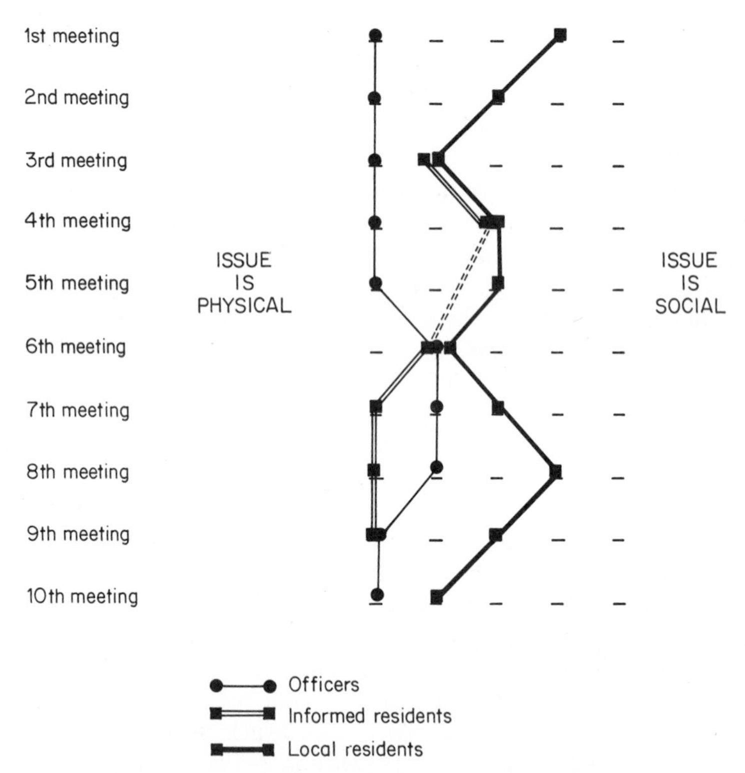

Figure 8. Profile for dimension between 'Issue is physical' and 'Issue is social' (Dimension 1). From Formal Minutes

batim Record, and Figure 8 those from the Formal Minutes. In both cases, Informed and Local Residents group profiles are shown.

Both the Verbatim Record and the Formal Minutes show the Officers emphasizing the 'Physical' nature of the issues, while Residents' attention is devoted to their 'Social' characteristics. The marked difference between the Informed Residents and the Officers, shown in the Verbatim Record, is all but obliterated in the Formal Minutes for the first five meetings. When their statements do become identifiable, they appear at the 'Physical' pole of the Dimension, having the overall effect of suggesting broad agreement between the Residents in general and the Officers.

The attention of the Officers to the Physical characteristics of the issues discussed is, on the whole, a predictable one, given the nature of their task. However, in view of the way in which the Housing Act interprets the inten-

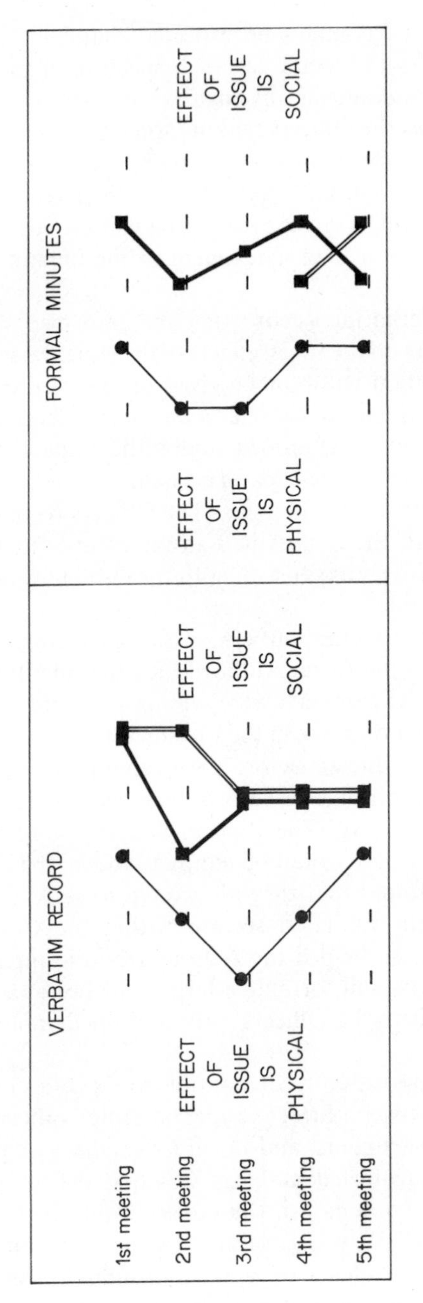

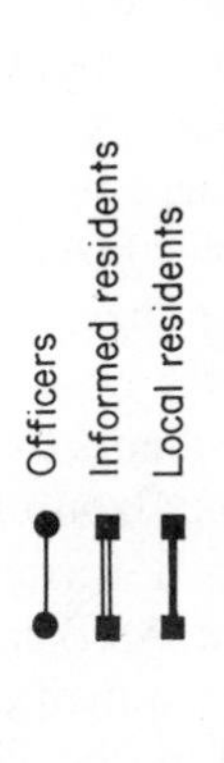

Figure 9. Profiles from Verbatim Record and Formal Minutes of first five meetings, for the dimension between 'Effect of issue is physical' and 'Effect of issue is social' (Dimension 2)

tion of Housing Action Areas, it might be expected that Officers would express the *effects* of the issues in 'Social' terms. Inspection of the Profiles for Dimension 2 in Figure 9 disconfirms any such expectation.

The Verbatim Record shows the Officers making some reference to Social effects, but on the whole they focus on the direct Physical manifestations of their actions. In the Formal Minutes, the extent of their recognition of social effects is diminished, leading to an apparent broadening of the disparity between Officers and Residents in their assessment of the impact of HAA policy.

It is apparent from the Verbatim Record that the Informed Residents were vociferous in commenting on the social effects of the issues raised during the early meetings. A description will now be given of one of these issues, since it illustrate the way in which this emphasis on social effects was used in the generation of community definitions under the impact of issues perceived as a threat to groups in the area. The issue was a proposal to demolish some houses in one street in the Area. The Officers recommended demolition because, they said, the houses had so far deteriorated that to repair them would be prohibitively expensive, both for residents and for the Local Authority.

Residents, supported by the Community Association, formed a Street Action Group, and petitioned the Local Authority for the retention of the houses on the grounds that the residents were willing to spend money on repairs. A series of arguments took place in the Liaison Group as to whether adequate surveys had been conducted before the proposal for demolition was made, and over the question of whether residents wanted to stay and improve their houses or move way. The Liaison Officer found from his discussions with residents that they would be happy to move, the chairman of the Street Action Group found that they all wanted to stay. The Street Action Group was a formally affiliated section within the Community Association, and the Association helped the Action Group in interviewing residents, lobbying Councillors, and forming a large audience at a meeting of the Council Committee where the Officers' proposal for demolition was put forward.

One of the results of the opposition to demolition was a series of special meetings which took place between Street residents, senior officers of the relevant Local Authority Departments, and Local Councillors. A principal constituent of the argument against demolition was that the Street had a 'real and lively community'. To demolish the houses would be to destroy this community. Considerable heat was generated by the assertion of some residents that the proposal was evidence of racial discrimination against the ethnic minority which had members resident in the Street. Maps were produced showing the ethnic composition of the population, suggesting that the houses of the minority groups were the ones under threat, and photograph of members of this group headed a front page report in an 'Independent' newspaper sold throughout the city, which set out the discrimination allegations. Although the chairman of the Street Action Group told the Liaison Group meeting that the Action Group as a whole did not see the issue in racial terms, it seems likely that this line of argument was of considerable importance in prompting the decision in the Council to defer decision, and ultimately to turn down the demolition proposal.

The proposal to demolish homes was clearly a threat to those who lived in the affected houses. In their response can be seen the manipulation of the concept of 'community' as a weapon in the conflict. To demolish the Street would be to destroy a multiethnic community—to do this would be for the Local Authority to appear racially prejudiced. The Community Association, already threatened by the establishment of the Liaison Group, evolved an approach to issues which emphasized their difference from the Officers, and which claimed for them an ability to represent the local community. This claim was emphasized by their organization of the impressive attendance at the Council Committee meeting.

The conflict between the Informed Residents and the Officers developed as a consequence of the power of the Local Authority, and was a response, on the part of the Community Association members, to a challenge to the power of their group. Because the declaration of the HAA was seen by the

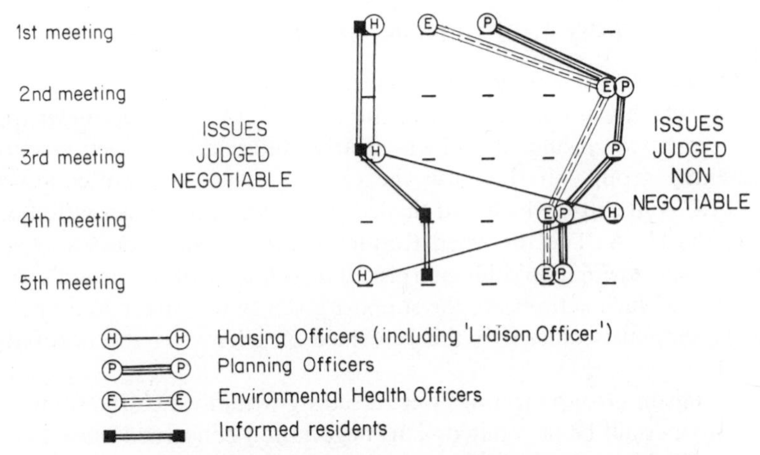

Figure 10. Profile for dimension between 'Issues judged negotiable' and 'Issues judged non-negotiable' (Dimension 11) for three 'Officer' groups and Informed Residents. From Verbatim Record

Association as a result of its actions, acceptance of the Liaison Group as an aspect of the HAA was inevitable, whatever form the Group took. Having accepted its existence, the Informed Residents interpreted the role of the Liaison meetings in the light of Community Association views on public participation in local decision making. They saw the Liaison Group as being powerful, and all issues affecting the HAA as subject to negotiation. For the Officers, such a perspective threatened to limit their power to carry out their professional activities, particularly for those Officers whose principal concern was with the execution of physical changes. This is clearly shown by the Profiles in Figure 10, where decisions which often had not yet been officially approved, are presented by the Planning and Environmental Health Officers as incapable of further negotiation. The Informed Residents, on the other hand, show a firm determination that these same issues can, and should, be discussed.

The 'Liaison' function of the Housing Officers is clearly shown by their concurrence with the Residents at all meetings except the fourth, during which Officers were heavily criticized over the demolition proposals discussed above, and at which a petition was presented which criticized the Local Authority's lack of control over the building operations on one of its own residential developments in the Area. On both these issues the Officers argued unanimously that matters were 'under control' and that no action by the Liaison Group was necessary.

INTERPRETATION OF THE RESULTS

The Informed Residents group behaved, in the Liaison Group meetings, in a way which was consonant with the behaviour of a group under threat. They presented arguments which clearly differentiated them from the threatening group—in this case the Officers, seen as representatives of the Local Authority, which had denied the Community Association a role within the HAA. The Informed Residents also pursued courses of action which, if successful, could be interpreted as evidence of the group's power. Examples of such actions are the support given to the Street Action Group and the emphasis placed by the Informed Residents on the negotiability of issues.

The Liaison Group meetings were a setting within which the future form of the area could be negotiated. This negotiation concerned more than the relatively minor physical changes that would take place. It was also concerned with the form of the Social Environment of the Area. It was a negotiation of the form of the community. In declaring the HAA, the Local Authority presented residents with a set of spatial boundaries within which they would find people who shared common experiences in respect of their homes and physical surroundings. At the Liaison Group meetings, the way in which these common experiences were to be understood by residents within the defined Area could be developed through discussion. Thus, the meetings offered the opportunity for residents to revise their Individual Socio-Physical Environments in the light of new information about the Physical Environment and about the way this Environment was preceived by members of the newly identified group.

In the Liaison Group discussion, definitions of the community played an important part. The early attention of the Local Residents to 'particular groups in the Area' who would be affected by issues (Dimension 4) appears from the Formal Minutes to have given way to a perspective which interpreted issues in terms of their effects on 'everyone in the area', or, in other words, on the 'community as a whole'. In the discussions about the proposal to demolish houses, the Street Action Group pressed its claims by means of an appeal to respect for a 'lively community', and strongly advocated that other residents should recognize the cause of the Street as one affecting the whole of the Area, not just those who were immediately affected. The pre-existing community in the vicinity was threatened by the declaration of the HAA in three main ways; firstly, through the imposition of new spatial boundaries; secondly, through proposals for physical change, which would mean that the physical forms with which the community identified itself would be changed; and thirdly, through a challenge to the existing framework of group memberships in the area. The Community Association, as the group most seriously challenged in its self-conception, spearheaded the response to this third form of threat to the community.

The environmental changes proposed were threatening because their proposer, the Local Authority, was powerful, a fact emphasized by the stress placed by some Officers on the non-negotiability of issues in the Area. Further evidence is afforded by the way in which the Formal Minutes muted the differences between Officers and Residents on some issues (e.g. Dimension 1), and emphasised the differences on others (e.g. Dimention 2). Because the Formal Minutes were the means by which those who did not attend Liaison Group meetings obtained information about the progress of the HAA, the effect of the interpretation they afforded was to emphasise the Officers' view of the community and the issues, and to restrict the effectiveness of the Residents, and particularly of the Informed Residents, in presenting alternative perspectives.

CONCLUSION

Both residents and officers are taken to have been acting in good faith with respect to the HAA. The research did not set out to discover whether the officers were 'really' the 'Running Dogs of Capitalism' that some members of the Community Association apparently believed them to be, nor were the 'Subversive Revolutionary' tendencies of the Community Association as apparently perceived by some Councillors investigated. Neither extreme was particularly apparent in the generally good natured discussion of the Liaison Group, even at its most heated.

What the research does show is that planned environmental change has the capacity to threaten the identity of a community. This occurs in two ways, firstly through its imposition of a new physical form for the area in which the community is located, and secondly, through its ability to change intergroup relationships in the area. Changes in the relations between groups determines the nature of issues over which conflict is likely to occur. Those issues most closely associated with the stated interests of the groups are likely to be the 'flash point' for conflict. In the HAA described above, the Community Association had a history of successful 'pressure group' activity; this led to a prominent part being played by the Informed Residents in the discussions about the proposed demolition of houses in one street.

The kinds of argument used in discussions are determined only partially by the nature of the issues themselves. More important in determining the way issues are approached are the processes of differentiation between groups, which can lead to the adoption of extreme perspectives in reaction to those displayed by other groups. If the processes which challenge the community are those of planned change in the physical environment, then the discussion which occurs between the groups also represents the process by which the community and its area is known. It is, truly, the process of 're-presentation'.

Physical changes have consequences for the Social Environment, in the sense that they give rise to discussion between groups. At the same time, discussion between the groups has consequences for the Physical Environment, either directly, through their ability to bring about decisions on action, or indirectly, through their moulding of people's cognition of, and therefore behaviour in, the Physical Environment. Community identity is established through the interaction of the community's members with and about its Physical Environment. It is therefore threatened by changes in that Environment.

REFERENCES

Breakwell, G. M. (1978). Some effects of marginal social identity. In: H. Tajfel (ed.) *Differentiation between Social Groups*, London, Academic Press.

Hillery, G. A. Jr. (1955). Definitions of community: areas of agreement, *Rural Sociology*, **20**, 111–123.

Hillery, G. A. Jr. (1968). *Communal Organizations: a Study of Local Societies*. Chicago, University of Chicago Press.

Hunter, A. (1974). *Symbolic Communities*. Chicago, University of Chicago Press.

Lee, T. (1968). Urban neighbourhood as a socio-spatial schema, *Human Relations*, **21**, 241–267.

Lemaine, G. (1974). Social differentiation and social originality, *European Journal of Social Psychology*, **4**, 17–52.

Lynch. K. (1960). *The Image of the City*. Cambridge, M.I.T. Press. Mass.

Matthews, J. A. (1981). *Social Identity and Cognition of the Environment*. (Unpublished PhD. Thesis). University of Sheffield.

Webber, M. (1964). Culture, territoriality and the elastic mile, *Papers of the Regional Science Association*, **11**, 59–69.

Threatened Identities
Edited by G. Breakwell

Arson, Nudity and Bombs among the Canadian Doukhobors: A Question of Identity

SHIRLEY ARDENER

This paper is concerned with the *internal* and *external* threats to the identity of the Doukhobors, a religious sect of Russian origin.[1] Apart from those members living in Russia itself, émigrés have settled outside this homeland, and it is a large group of Canadian Doukhobors which concerns us here. Estimating their numbers is difficult for reasons which will become apparent, but in 1970 there were about 20,000 in Canada. They have an interesting history which includes dramatic, and at times heart-rending, episodes of mass protest, which are surprisingly little known outside Canada. Although only a minority of all Doukhobors were involved, nevertheless in 1932, for instance, roughly 600 men and women were in detention for participating in nude demonstrations (Hawthorn, 1955:284). In 1950, more than 400 were in Jail (Hawthorn, 1955:3). Other forms of direct action were also initiated, and by 1953 about 600 known instances of arson and dynamiting by Doukhobors had been reported, the majority of incidents involving their own property.[2] By 1964, their depredations had cost Canada over $20 million (Holt, 1964:8), and 20 lives. In 1979 minor incidents still occurred.

What led up to these extraordinary events? What did they oppose? And in particular, why was their protest presented in the form of nude exhibitions? Are there parallels elsewhere which taken in this context raise general implications? Let us try to deal with the questions in the order in which they are posed. First we will turn briefly to the emergence in history of this sect.

RUSSIAN ORIGINS

Aylmer Maude, a Quaker who became personally involved with the Doukhobors, and who wrote a book about them in 1904 called *A Peculiar People*, considered them to be 'spiritual descendants' of various Russian sects dating back to the end of the fifteenth century, or even further back to the seventh and subsequent centuries. It is, however, probably more useful to place the origins of the Doukhobors in the middle of the seventeenth century when there were many revisions in the Russian Orthodox Church. These changes spawned a large number of splinter groups and sects, which continued to divide and re-form from then onwards. Sylvan Kolesnikoff (who was active from the middle of the eighteenth century) has been singled out by some as the first Doukhobor leader. An important turning point came when, in 1801, Alexander I allowed some of the Doukhobors to congregate at a place called Milky Waters, where they became not merely a scattered religious sect but an industrial and economic community, whence came the bulk of the Canadian Doukhobor settlers (Maude, 1904; Tarasoff, 1969).

The sect was anti-institutional and in many ways resembled other such movements: for example, those of the Anabaptists, Mennonites, and Quakers, which have been said to have influenced Doukhobor thinking. Conflict with authority, amounting at times to official persecution, forced the Doukhobors to become accustomed to repeated migration within Russia; indeed, it was Maude's opinion in 1904 that the branch of the Doukhobors in Canada had 'during the nineteenth century, probably migrated more than any other sect in the world' (Maude, 1904:176). Following a particularly troubled period in the last quarter of the century, when opposition focused especially on the refusal of Doukhobors to undertake military service, their leader of the day, Peter Verigin,[3] who was influenced by Tolstoy's pacifist writings, applied through the Czarina for permission for the Doukhobors to emigrate from Russia altogether. This request was eventually granted,[4] and on application the Canadian authorities agreed to admit them.

SETTLEMENT IN CANADA

The main party of Doukhobor immigrants (7,427—somewhat less than half of the then Doukhobor population) arrived in Canada in 1899; a few more followed later. Today, as already stated, Canadian Doukhobors number around 20,000.[5] In Canada, they maintained a separate identity, retaining their Russian language, dress and other customs. They settled first in Saskatchewan, on about 600 square miles of land provided for homesteading by the Canadian authorities. The negotiations for the settlement had been undertaken on behalf of the Doukhobors by Aylmer Maude. He had been accompanied by a Russian sympathizer, Prince Hilkoff, and by two Doukhobor men and their families. Maude tells how he found it very difficult to get the two Doukhobors to take any responsibility for decisions on the terms of settlement, and it is possible, therefore, that the final agreement did not have their full support, even though Maude says that the details were made absolutely clear to them. The Doukhobors were admitted as immigrants, subject to Canadian law, with the special privilege that they and their heirs should be exempt from compulsory military service for ever.[6]

From early days, there was friction with the Canadian authorities. As soon as the Doukhobors were settled on their homesteads in Saskatchewan, the government required each to register their titles to the land which had been allocated to them, in accordance with standard Canadian practice. This was, by and large, rejected since the practice did not conform with the religious beliefs of the sect. Neither would they all register their marriages, births and deaths. Later on, many resisted the implementation of compulsory education for their children. This defiance of Canadian law, which at times lead the authorities to discriminate against them[7], drew its strength from Doukhobor theology, and a brief diversion into this subject must be made here in order to understand the violence of the group which lead the resistence.

DOUKHOBOR BELIEFS

Although there has been a very strong sense of Doukhobor self-consciousness and group loyalty when in opposition to the non-Doukhobor world, there have been many internal divisions, which have continued the Russian nonconformist tradition of fision and fusion already referred to above. Many of the factions have been given names: The Christian Community of Universal Brotherhood, Orthodox or Community Doukhobors, Independent Doukhobors, Named Doukhobors, Sons of Freedom, and so on. Membership of these subsects appears to have been somewhat fluid, with individuals of one group sometimes having sympathy with the distinctive positions held by other groups, and Doukhobors have moved from one subsect to another. This internal differentiation makes it difficult to characterize Doukhobor theology substantively, but the following dogmatic generalizations will suffice for our purposes: Basic is the idea that each man or woman is the image of God on earth. Pacifism is enjoined. The Perfect Life is attainable on earth, but only through the rejection of materialism. Luxury in food and dress is condemned because, '*luxury indulging the flesh, strengthens it to stifle the inward light coming from above*'.[8] Each Doukhobor has direct communication with God and listens above all to the 'voice within'. Strictly, since '*by nature all men are akin and equals of one another*' (Maude, p. 15, from Novitsky, 1832), there is no recognized human authority structure. Only God's laws are acknowledged, and as a result Doukhobors have been opposed to State legislation of any kind, as well as to organized Christian Church law. They have particularly abhorred oath taking.

In this philosophically and economically egalitarian system, the problem of community decision-making is partly resolved by what we may call 'consensus politics' operating through the 'sobranya' or community meeting. But of importance is the fact that although Doukhobors are, in a sense, all equally divine, one, the spiritual leader, seems to be diviner than others and therefore can offer guidance or claim implicit obedience.[9] 'If', writes Maude, 'one rejects the evidence pointing to the Doukhobor belief in the divinity of their Leaders and to the evil this occasioned, the most remarkable occurrences in Doukhobor history become absolutely unintelligible, whereas, when once this key to the situation is grasped, all that happened at the Milky Waters, in the Caucasus, and finally in Canada, becomes quite intelligible' (Maude: 145). According to Maude, it was under the domination of Kapoustin, who became leader of the Milky Waters group, that the Doukhobors 'lost the freedom of thought that had been characteristic of the sect, and became a clan yielding blind obedience to hereditary leaders' (Maude: 127–8). Kapoustin 'established himself as absolute ruler, and instilled into the people habits of secrecy with reference to all that concerned the sect, and of implicit obedience to himself' (Maude: 129). Sometimes miraculous powers have been attributed to a spiritual leader (Maude: 132). We cannot discuss the interesting but complicated history of the various Doukhobor leaders here. Some of them have been accused of following 'controversial' life-styles, which have been described in some detail by Simma Holt. We can note that spiritual leadership is typically hereditary.[10]

We have stated that each Doukhobor listens to his own internal voices. Nevertheless, the voices of others—particularly of course that of the spiritual leader—are, as indicated, also important. Such voices are often expressed in a special code or symbolic form. We learn from Maude (p. 170n) that Doukhobors are 'remarkably found of catchwords', and Herbison tells us that 'The people will always be watching those who are influential looking for some sly indication, a subtle hint, unwilling to believe that anything is said without a double meaning (Herbison, 1955: 170).' When a Doukhobor witness, Kolesnikoff, was asked in Court (in 1950) whether members of the extremist group known as the Sons of Freedom looked for signs given by the leaders, he replied, 'Well, naturally they pay attention to all the movements, yes.' He agreed that Doukhobors would look for a sign in any movement that a leader would make (Holt: 126). In her testimony, Annie Koftinoff explained 'We are spiritual people and we joined the Spiritual Community, therefore we never understand everything direct.'

Bible texts are often quoted—not, according to Maude, because such texts are authoritative to the Doukhobors, but because they are a safe way for persecuted groups to express their decisions (Maude: 132; for 'hidden meanings' cf. Wright, 1939:61)—and Doukhobors believe that these texts must also '*be understood symbolically to represent things that are inward and spiritual. It must all be understood to relate in a mystical manner to the Christ within*' (Maude: 16, from Novitsky, 1832). The Quaker, Hugh Herbison, in his discussion of Doukhobor religion, notes that such mysticism is invulnerable. 'The intensity of conviction engendered by mysticism needs no external confirmation.' Its danger is, he thinks, that it has led to a certain self-righteousness and smugness (Herbison: 163). When Annie was asked about her understanding of certain speeches and talks given by Michael 'Archangel' Verigin, she replied: 'I didn't enter his mind. I did as I understood. Some people understood one way, another understood another way, as we are all spiritual community people.'[11]

Not surprisingly, contradictory statements as to what various spiritual leaders and other have said, or meant, abound. This tendency was even mentioned long ago by Maude, but conflicting statements have not all necessarily been a result of differing interpretation on the part of auditors. Maude distinguished two different notes in statements of Doukhobor belief: the one calm, moderate, and sometimes mystical; the other clear, resolute, radical and intolerant. As well, no doubt, as reflecting two different views, the difference, Maude thought, may 'have corresponded on the one side, to what they dared to say, and on the other, to what they wished to say' (Maude: 13–14). It certainly seems probable, on the modern evidence, that contradictory public statements by spiritual leaders have sometimes been formulated to suit the audience. It was a practice which could sow the seeds of confusion. Maude (1904) noted that 'whenever people use the same word for two different things . . . they are in danger of not quite knowing what they mean themselves'. Whether or not this habit leads to self-confusion, there is no doubt that it may easily confuse others unless established conventions are rigorously followed.

DOUKHOBOR ATTITUDES AND CHARACTERISTICS

Students of the Doukhobor sect have drawn attention to a number of general characteristics, which may not be unconnected with their religious doctrines, and their methods of expressing them. These have a bearing upon our understanding of the recourse by some to nudity. The psychologist, Alfred Shulman, detects certain problems which Doukhobors have regarding their perception of their experience of the world (which may be associated with their imprecise mode of language decoding). He notes that the 'need to arrive at some explanations, however ill-defined, of events not fully comprehended encourages [Doukhobors], in dealing with experience, to use certain techniques that cause further difficulties. In concocting explanations to fit situations that are not fully understood, they must necessarily have recourse to a private, highly personal way of thinking exclusive of reality and of the ideas of other people.' Shulman states that this sort of thinking, which he calls 'autism', 'creates considerable problems in the way of communication of goals'.[12] He goes on to suggest that the tendency of the Doukhobors in a crisis is to have recourse to behaviour which is quite inappropriate to the ends which they wish to achieve, and as an example, he cites the use of nudity (Shulman. 1955: 131–132).

The doctrinal stress on individuality is, paradoxically, accompanied by an emphasis on social conformity and restraint, especially in the formative childhood years. Claudia Lewis draws attention to the stern, even harsh discipline meted out by adults to children, by smacking, fierce scolding, 'bending the ears back', and the like (Lewis, 1955: 106). According to Alfred Shulman, 'The most desirable child is one that is passive, obedient and placid; noisy impulsive behaviour is frowned upon' (Shulman: 127). Deferential behaviour is also admired. As early as the eighteenth century, Kolesnikoff had adjured: 'Let us bow to the God in one another, for we are the image of God on earth.' 'To this day', wrote Holt in 1964, 'Doukhobors rarely meet without bowing to each other and they still, as then, kneel and touch their heads to the ground before their leader.'[13] As an adult, observes Shulman, generally 'the Doukhobor is noteworthy because of his quiet passivity, his lack of what we would call normal aggression and self-assertion' (Shulman: 128). This, he thinks, results 'in the inability of the passive Doukhobor to take any responsibility or to assume the duties of leadership' (Shulman: 130). We may note in passing Maude's complaint that the Doukhobor 'delegates' to the resettlement talks would not accept any responsibility for decision-making.

Bodily appetites are a source of danger, and a puritan approach is encouraged. In 1832, Novitsky noted the belief that '*Desires reaching man through his senses of hearing, seeing, smelling, tasting, or touching, including sexual desire, sow the seeds of future torment*' (Maude, p. 15, from Novitsky, 1832). In the sixties according to Lewis (p. 106), 'Ignorance, silence, shame, avoidance and guilt are the ingredients of the sex tabu as it operates in everyday life.' Sexual curiosity in children is thus considered shameful; modesty is required. Lewis cites examples of behaviour which she thinks indicate this. When a two-year-old baby boy accidentally exposed his genitals, 'Mrs. H. happened to glance around and see him standing there looking at us, all exposed in this way.' We read that: 'She let out a little exclamation of horror, and lost no time jumping up to pull up his pants.' On another occasion, when he idly began to finger himself, a neighbour, 'her eyes popping with horror', 'let out an "Ooh", and then jumped up and smartly slapped the little boy's hand, while she covered him up again' (Lewis: 276). After a nine-year-old girl, to the surprise of the investigator, was seen scrubbing the back of a six-year-old boy while he was in the bath, the little boy emerged from the tub wearing his swimming trunks. Another little girl about seven came in one day wearing a bathing suit. 'She got into her blouse and skirt right there in our presence, but managing very modestly', writes Lewis (p. 273). These examples were provided by Lewis to indicate Doukhobor attitudes, but they could possibly be interpreted as evidence of respect for *her* supposed modesty. Other evidence which will be presented later confirms, however, that exposure of the body has not always come easily to all Doukhobors.

The relationship between men and women in Doukhobor society is interesting but cannot be dealt with fully here. A Doukhobor, Fred Davidoff, explained: 'The women have a strong influence in our group because we practice to have all the same level both men and women' (Holt: 229). To some observers, Doukhobor men are seen as being particularly docile, while the women are noted for their relative assertiveness. Maude considered the women to be the main preservers of Doukhobor unity. Many of the men, at the beginning of the century when he wrote, would have been inclined to break out from what he called the 'enchanted circle', were it not that the women held them back. The women, he thought, were the chief repositories of the corpus of belief, the unwritten so-called 'Living Book' that enshrined the traditions of the sect, and they were exceedingly conservative.[14] Ever since the arrival in Canada, the active male population has tended to obtain work some distance from home, and the consequent disproportionate daily presence of women in the community has given them relatively great prominence. Often they have been left to manage affairs for long periods while their husbands have been in prison. 'Because the women have fewer outside contacts than do the men,' explains Hawthorn, 'they get to know fewer non-Doukhobors as individuals and are less able to soften their judgements by their knowledge of the individual exceptions. For these and other reasons as well,' he explains, 'it is usual to find the women more assertive and aggressive, more hostile to other Canadians and condemnatory in their judgements, and more stubbornly conservative in their opposition to the changes which nevertheless continue to affect their lives.'[15] Woodcock and Avakumovic (1968: 236) attribute what they call 'The persistence of conservative attitudes among the Doukhobors' to the fact that 'in Canada it has always been the women, living in far greater isolation from the outside world than the men, who have played the dominant role in shaping the attitudes of the children at a formative age'. Holt (p. 205) also notes that women are 'always the major force and influence in this society'. It is particularly interesting that Shulman, after characterizing the men as unusually passive, notes: 'In a somewhat oversimplified fashion we might say that the women resemble the more aggressive Doukhobor men.' Some women 'can express their hostility in an even more direct fashion than the aggressive men. In this connection,' he says, 'we might mention their proclivity to tear the clothes from the back of anyone who annoys them. It seems that their anger is directed not only at outsiders, but also at the men of the community, whom they attempt to depreciate. Yet all these satisfactions,' he goes on, 'do not seem to solve their problem; frequently the women are tense, obsessive and perfectionistic and suffer from headaches and like ailments.' (Shulman: 150)

THE PROTEST MOVEMENT TAKES OFF

When the Canadian authorities demanded that the Doukhobors, on their arrival in Canada at the turn of the century, should register their lands, this was generally rejected, since it would have meant recognizing an earthly authority. The majority of Doukhobors were, in any case, against the individual ownership of land. Many of them shared community houses and farms. There were technical difficulties to land registration therefore, as well as theological ones. A year after their arrival, the Doukhobors officially notified the Government that not only would they not record their homesteads in their individual names, neither would they register their marriages, births and deaths.[16] The Government saw this policy as a repudiation of the terms of the immigration agreement. At that time, when the initial resistance began, the spiritual leader of the sect, Peter Verigin, was still in Russia. He was in communication with the immigrants, however, and under his inspiration some Doukhobors further resolved not to till the soil if they could eat fruit, not to use metal which had supposedly been smelted by their enslaved brothers, to liberate their beats of burden, and to dispose of their material possessions.[17]

Partly because a warmer climate would make it easier to put into practice this philosophy and to achieve the simple life desired, in 1902, nineteen Doukhobors decided to set off in search of new lands. As they marched they collected followers, until 2000 has joined the trek which aimed towards the American border. They carried no provisions and ate very little, and they threw away their belongings. They attracted official attention, and the police diary for 30th October, 1902 recorded that

> 'the Doukhobors discarded a good deal of their clothing between here and Rokely, so sent officers out this p.m. to gather up same. They returned with two waggon loads of rubber boots, socks, shirts, doffed by the roadway.' (Quoted in Holt, 1964)

The rubber boots had been used to replace those made of animal products which were no longer permitted, but they were found to be unsuitable for marching. The *Manitoba Free Press* noted that

> 'the trail over which those thousand feet have travelled is worn as level as the floor of a dancing pavilion. Their tired feet are cut and bruised, some of them bleeding.' (Maude, 1904: 236–39; Holt, 1964: 34)

A contemporary sympathizer, H. P. Archer, noted that the Doukhobors held what became a very characteristic hope: that such marching would 'so inconvenience the Government that it would concede their demands as to the land question and registration ... or would at once take means to transport them to a warm climate'.[18] Eventually, half starved, they were forcibly turned back by the police, who were aided by the prevailing icy weather conditions (Maude, 1904: 216ff; Holt, 1964: 35).

Peter Verigin arrived from Russia at the end of 1902. He began to tour the Doukhobor communities, with a choir of virgins. In public he advocated compliance with Canadian laws, but it seems to have been believed by many Doukhobors that he was merely doing so to protect himself, and that at the same time he was intending the people to continue their resistance. He had advocated the simple migrant life in his letters from Russia: 'Take up thy cross and follow me and to follow Christ—we must live as he lived, and we see that Christ did no physical work, nor did the Apostles .... That the Apostles and Christ wore clothes and ate bread was natural, for there were plenty of clothes and bread, and (one must add) even Christ and the Apostles were not able, all at once, to go naked' (Maude: 225). It was a critical time for the Doukhobors: the pattern of their life in Canada had to be determined, and there were among them many who were attracted by the prospect of individual ownership of homesteads, and by the material rewards which hard work could bring. Many, eventually most, of them, did break away on their own (e.g. the Independent Doukhobors), and the bitterness which this aroused in those who lived the communal life, and the actual hostility engendered, has continued for over 70 years. Intolerance towards deviationists is longstanding.[19] As part of his antimaterialism campaign, Peter Verigin stressed the temporary nature of their Canadian possessions. 'We will leave some day. We must leave our houses so they are clean, swept, and even our tables set, so that those who come in after and take over know that people lived here' (Holt, 1964: 40). This so-called 'prophesy' was repeated in various forms through the years, and much subsequent militant action was seen as a means of forcing the Canadian authorities either to waive the various registration requirements for Doukhobors, or to exile them. In 1962, Simma Holt asked Davidoff why the Doukhobors did not migrate through ordinary channels, individually.

'We cannot migrate through ordinary channels because we are not tourists,' he replied. 'We will remain in Canada until Canada exiles us' (Holt: 238). Pete Zarubin confirmed in Court his belief in the prophesy 'that from Canada our people will migrate through the prisons,'—a common Doukhobor phrase (Holt, 1964: 245).

In the spring of 1903, when the deadline for homestead registration was reached, Peter Verigin's words were enacted. Another trek began, and this time the discarding of material possessions was taken further to include all clothing. 'After the twelfth of May', wrote Alexey Makhortov in a letter published later that year,

> 'we [20 men and 17 women] went in the manner of the first man Adam and Eve, to show nature to humanity, how man should return into his fatherland and return the ripened fruit and its seed.
>
> We began to go naked from the villages of Efremovka and finished at the village of Nadezhda. We went through sixteen villages in all. When we were stopped naked, we were much beaten with twigs [by other Doukhobors] all in blood, so that it was terrible to see us. . . . And night came on; the weather was bad, rain and snow and wind. Then we clustered into one heap, and lay on the ground one on another. . . . We remained naked; and really it was wonderful to us ourselves that in such a wind we were not frozen.'[20]

The North West Mounted Policeman who went to investigate reported that shortly after his arrival in one village, Wasyl Conkin appeared on the street divested of his clothing.

> 'I stopped him and ordered him to put on his clothing, but he went past me laughing and shaking his head. After a half hour afterwards I visited the house he had come from and found a meeting going on, the room being crowded with Doukhobor men and women singing and praying. Two were totally divest of their clothing. They appeared quite pleased at having the chance to parade in front of us, especially a policeman, and wanted us to come in and sit down. . . .
>
> In the street later we found twenty or more men and women stripped of their clothing and forming up to march down the street, which they did.
>
> It appeared to us that they did this last act simply in defiance of the police. The whole proceeding was thoroughly disgusting although as far as could be ascertained, there was not much immoral in their action outside of the fact of their being naked.'[21]

The group moved on, eating grass and leaves, until at Yorkton they were met by Mounted Police. 'We stopped, undressed and advanced,' wrote Makhortov. They were directed by the police into the immigration shed. Still they refused to dress. At night the police kept the doors open and hung lamps to attract swarms of mosquitoes, which tormented the nudists, a technique which proved effective since they finally resorted to their clothes. The 28 men were arrested, charged with nudism, and sentenced to three months in prison. The women went home.[22] So ended the first nude demonstration.

At this stage, the nudity might well have been mainly the symbol of 'unwordliness' that has often been claimed for it by Doukhobors. Schulman states that 'Nudity among the Doukhobors in Russia had little of the emotional loading that it has for non-Doukhobors in [Canada]. It must have been with some astonishment', he thought, 'that the Doukhobors discovered the shocked horror with which people here responded to the sight of a completely nude body.'[23] But, *pace* Shulman, not all Doukhobors undressed, only a large minority, and those who did so for the first time were often reluctant: 'Oh, it was awful the first time we took our clothes off, wit all those people looking,' reported one woman. 'Something just made us do it' (quoted by Herbison, 1955: 167). In one critical Doukhobor document, preparations by Michael Verigin (born Orekoff) for the mass nudity of 1932 were described as follows:

> 'He commandeered into partnership community members from your own midst, forced them to imbibe liquor and after nightfall went to this out-of-way place where neither the authorities nor any outsiders set foot. And there he conducted nudist manoeuvres, himself playing the role of comic-artist and stage manager. He shed tears and beseeched them to disrobe; he threatened them, cursed, and predicted terrible judgement for them. He prophesied terrible prophecies and mysteries stressing that all this is essential for the salvation of Doukhoborism and the Freedomites themselves. The parents wept, reluctant to bare themselves in the presence of their sons and daughters, but the stern leader had the upper hand and compelled the execution of his commands.'

The same document reports that the young people held out longer,

> 'being more ashamed of denuding themselves in the congregation. . . . During the meeting the leader fondled the breasts of the younger women standing there in the nude, and the one who cringed . . . he rudely castigated by telling her that she wasn't eligible for the Kingdom of God on earth. . . . "You are still filled with apprehension because of the presence of your husband!" In conclusion he ordered everyone to go to bed, wives and husbands in mixed order. As to the leader himself, he made a couple of teenage girls accompany him to his own quarters to enjoy the "Kingdom of God" he had just created.'[24]

In 1932, not long after the series of nude parades (420 nude marchers on May 5th, 133 on May 13th for instance, and 725 subsequent arrests), a statement was put out in the name of Michael 'the Archangel'. Verigin, entitled 'Nudism and the Destruction of the Altar of Satan'. It too stresses the sense of shame which was associated with the nude body and which must be overcome. It read in part:

'The body of man is the temple of the living god but we have made of it a "den of thieves". We call certain parts of the body—and their creative powers—as shameful and obscene; while at the same time almost everyone daily use these parts for purposes of uncleanliness, self-gratification and corruption. They are even commercialized–through various devised forms of temptation and carnalism. Clothing with people has ceased to serve its true, original purpose as essential protection against the elements, cold, heat, etc. . . . but has become an indispensable idolic object for concealment of that which is called "shame" . . . . ' (Holt, 1964: 102).

By 1932, the sense of shame might, of course, have been introduced as a result of, or have been strengthened by, the sojourn in Canada. We have no way of judging the situation outside the Canadian context since nudity had not been part of the Doukhobor pattern of life before the sect reached Canada.[25] We might note that at the first nude episode, it was the *display* of nudity before the police which was particularly sought. The evidence does, therefore, seem to suggest that nudity was not merely a simple unselfconscious absence of clothes, carrying no great emotional load. The modesty enjoined upon young children, referred to above, also seems to confirm this.

Anyway, whether or not the original nude parades were undertaken entirely as symbols of 'unwordliness', the nudists must indeed, as Shulman writes, have very quickly become aware of their effect on witnesses, including other Doukhobors. In the fall of 1907, 78 Doukhobors went east to Fort William. On new year's day, 18 of these went out in the snow 'as Christ was born—naked'. They burned their clothing; people came from miles around to see the strange people. Parades continued in various places. The prisons would not accept those convicted of nudity. In Yorktown, 70 nudists were detained in the Agricultural Hall. 'It was bedlam there. The Doukhobors constantly trying to break loose to show their nakedness to the citizens outside and screaming insults at the police' (Holt: 51). The police had a difficult time: 'Rounding up the naked pilgrims, retrieving clothes they had cast aside, protecting them from angry settlers, shielding them from prurient publicity, calming their frenzy and shepherding them back to their homes, constituted duties as distasteful as any the police have had to perform in all the Forces history,' a Mounty was later to write (Featherstone, R. C., 1938, *Royal Canadian Mounted Police*, pp. 151–54, quoted in Holt, 1964). On one occasion 'two policemen were sat on by naked women as a group of Sons of Freedom laughed at the lost dignity of these symbols of government'. (Holt, 1964: 166–67).

That Doukhobors used nudity for political ends can be documented by a paragraph taken from the statement on nudism just referred to, which purports to repudiate the continuation of this technique of confrontation.

'It has been unanimously resolved [by the elders] that nudism amongst us, the members of the Spiritual Community of Christ shall not be further effected towards the outside world but only as a method of revivication of the free Spirit of Christ within—as a means for the conquest of the spirit over flesh and the extirpation of the principle of private ownership.'[26]

Shulman seems to be correct therefore in seeing Doukhobor nudism in terms of hostility. To him, however, it primarily results from the repression of natural aggression which erupts in this disguised form. Nevertheless, he did admit that: 'Removing one's clothes is a remarkably effective device for making other people uncomfortable and angry; such behaviour can be easily rationalized and made to appear something other than the hostile act it actually is.'[27] 'Nudism is the more favoured weapon of the extremists Sons of Freedom; arson and dynamiting, with their obvious hostile implications, are disturbing to a considerable portion of them,' he writes (Shulman, p. 145). Lewis, (p. 110) confirms that: 'When the older women approach in a nude parade, surround one, question, demand, affirm their beliefs, with mounting excitement, it is easy to detect the presence of a hard, unbending hostility in some of the faces (others, to be sure, reflect merely the enjoyment of a ceremony).' Nudity has also been used to add emphasis to the logic of an argument. When one side appears to be loosing out, resort is often taken to stripping. Shulman cites this kind of behaviour as an example of Doukhobor 'autism': 'Nudism ... is generally a hostile manoeuvre; however, at times it has been used for other purposes, for example, as an expression of a wish for the success of a meeting of the Consultative Committee. But disrobing [he thinks] in no way ensures the successful outcome of a meeting and is, at best, irrelevant to the job' (Shulman: 132). Helen Derhousoff explained in Court in 1950, that whenever there were visitors of any kind—'we often had them like Quakers and other ideal-minded men—well, the Krestova people would always undress right in the building when the person was trying to conduct a speech or something, right in the building they would undress and everything was disorganized and the person wasn't able to say anything. There was always confusion' (Holt: 131). In this way, some Doukhobors continue to disrupt court proceedings and embarass visitors today, as we shall see.

Shulman thinks that: 'The Sons of Freedom women use their nude bodies as desexualized objects to browbeat others. This custom of desexualized nudity, with its implications of complete indifference to the feelings of the men' further diminishes the security of women 'in their sexual role' (Shulman: 129). Notwithstanding his earlier remarks as to its inappropriateness, Shulman does see that, as a weapon, nudity has a number of advantages:

(1) In its use there is little danger of releasing disruptive forces within the group.
(2) They need have no fear of retaliation in kind—no non-Doukhobor is ever going to take his clothes off in order to annoy a Doukhobor, and even if he did the effect would be simply ludicrous.
(3) This hostile manoeuvre is also useful because of its extreme simplicity. We have commented on the lack of a well-developed social organization among the Doukhobors; as a result of this deficiency, organized, planned group behaviour of a complex sort is impossible. Nudism is different; no detailed plans need be made, no capable leader nor structured social organization is required; it is applicable to all situations and can be resorted to without any difficulty. One has only to take off a few clothes and the enemy is demoralized, if not routed. As a hostile device it is simple and very effective.
(4) Most important, however, is the fact that this way of acting out hostility enables them to maintain the fiction that they are neither hostile nor aggressive. Since to them, as to others, destructiveness is only destructiveness when it finds expression in physical or verbal abuse, they can deceive themselves as to what their true motives are and thus avoid guilt.' (Shulman, 1955: 145–146).

I will return to this topic later.

FIRE FOR SUPPER

Although the harming of human life is obnoxious to Doukhobors, in situations of conflict they have frequently, as already noted, resorted to arson. The symbolic role of fire was noted by Novitsky in 1832: '*The fire of abuse and contempt will burn and torment those who have striven for honours; the fire of aversion, shame, and loathing will be the consequence of impure love, and the flames of fury, emnity, revenge, rancour, and implacability will punish anger.*' (Maude: 15). As Fred Davidoff explained in the autobiography he wrote and submitted to Simma Holt while he was in jail in 1962:

> 'The act to burn is three hundred years old. First it was the ikons, what we call "the breakfast", then the burning of the arms, "the lunch", and now material possessions, the last act called "supper", instilled in us by Peter Chistiakoff [the former spiritual leader].'[28]

The breakfast and the lunch had both been eaten in Russia. The supper began in 1923, when a school was burned down.[29] (This temporarily solved the problem of the abhorred compulsory education for the community concerned.) Incendiarism continued for 5 years, and then dynamiting was added to the armoury of hostile tactics. 'If we bomb, burn, fill the jails, the Government will be so anxious to get rid of us that they will not only provide transportation for us and our baggage, they will even unload our outhouses for us' (Holt, 1964: 67). Eventually a fireproof prison was built especially for housing convicted Doukhobors.

Only a relatively few Doukhobors, mostly of the more extreme Sons of Freedom sect, were involved in the bombing of non-Doukhobor (mostly but not exclusively Government) property.[30] Hundreds, however, joined in the arson of homesteads, their own as well as those of other Doukhobors.[31] Simma Holt presents a poignant account given to her by a 23-year-old Doukhobor woman:

> 'My home was new. They call where we live Hollywood, because we have nicer homes. . . . I kept thinking maybe something would happen so I shouldn't have to do it. But it was the same then. I knew I had to do it, just like my mother did for me when I was a kid like my son Peter. I did like my mother did . . . I took nothing out. After the fire, I took off everything and I stood naked—like my mother. Peter cried. I told him not to be afraid, that it was right what I did. I told him it would bring daddy home to us from prison. So the kid laughed when our house burned down and he asked: "Will I see Daddy today?"' (Holt, 1964: 290).

Shulman would probably have interpreted her action as a means not suited to achieve its ends ('autistic' in his terms). He has also suggested that much Doukhobor behaviour is masochistic, and represents an anticipation of what is feared,

> 'as if by practising chastising one's self one can avoid the pain that otherwise would be suffered in the inevitable beating that is to come . . . possibly it hurts less to burn down one's house than to wait for someone else to do it.' (Shulman ,1955: 148)

He also draws attention to the 'see what you've made me do' approach to self-abuse. The Doukhobors certainly believed themselves to be persecuted, and their own depredations threw fuel on the fire, metaphorically as well as factually. Their fireraising not only gave them moral self-satisfaction and status in the eyes of their fellows: their consequential destitution offered vivid evidence to others of the existence of the often claimed 'Doukhobor problem' which Canada was expected to solve. According to Novitsky (1832), to the Doukhobors, '*Jesus Christ . . . is born, preaches, suffers, dies, and rises again spiritually in the heart of each believer*' (Maude: 14). Arson was one means of ensuring suffering, thereby living as Christ did.

CONFRONTATIONS, CONFESSIONS AND CONVICTIONS

The extraordinary chain of events in Canada cannot be set out in detail here, but to assuage curiosity mention will be made of certain salient features. Despite the foregoing account of the impoverishment of the Doukhobors, many groups and many individuals have prospered—at least at times. Peter Verigin, 'the Lordly', clearly had a talent for organization and a communal settlement which he founded on land purchased in British

Columbia through the help of a benefactor was remarkably successful. By 1924, it was capitalized at $1 million, with assets valued at $6 million.[32] After his death—he was assasinated by dynamite [33]—difficulties arose and mortgage commitments were entered into which could not in the end be fulfilled. To forestall closure and thus help the Doukhobors, the Canadian Government intervened.The mortgages and the Canadian government became increasingly the target of opposition. A Royal Commission in 1947 recommended that the law of Canada be enforced. In June 1950, as part of this policy, the trial of Michael 'Archangel' Verigin, and of one other, began (details of this and subsequent trials are given in Holt, 1964). Witnesses were questioned as to Verigin's attitude to nudity. Evidence was sought relating to arson. Maude noted in 1904 that 'the same type of mind that objects to definiteness and explicitness in property relations, often objects to definiteness and explicitness in marital relations also,' and he reports Doukhobor attempts while in Russia to introduce the 'community of women'. This was also tried in Canada for a while and was the subject of discussion in Court in the form of questions about 'wife swapping'. The witnesses were clearly perplexed: if marriage was not recognized how could wife-swapping have taken place? Some of the statements made at the trial have already been cited above. The two accused were eventually found guilty, but subsequently a retrial was ordered on technical grounds. Before this could take place Verigin died; the case against the other accused was not proceeded with. The Government set up a Doukhobor Consultative Committee. Compliance with the law was gradually enforced. From 1947, many Doukhobors, even those of the extremist groups, had in any case begun to register for social security benefits. Children were usually registered (as illegitimate) so that the mothers could claim children's allowances.[34] Even Canadian citizenship was redefined (to take account of Doukhobor religious sentiments) as 'Canadian, subject to the law of God and Jesus Christ'.

But—despite all these efforts of the Government—nudity, arson and bombing continued. Evidence of the breaking of the law by the display of nudity had, by the public nature of the offence, always been easy to establish. But, because of the very strong group loyalty, proof of implication in secret acts of arson and bombing had been impossible to obtain. The Mounties found it necessary, therefore, to set up a special 'D' squad to investigate these outrages. Gradually, by painstaking observations, they built up enough evidence for an indictment. Simma Holt describes these investigations, which make quite a gripping tale. Meanwhile, a Doukhobor youth had succeeded in blowing himself up. This death so shocked a respected elder that he called for a rejection of violence and of lying. At first there was no response, but suddenly confessing to such offences became popular. Alfred Shulman characterizes the Doukhobor propensity to 'repenting' (probably he is thinking of such confessions) as 'itself a highly autistic manoevre. It is as if by saying one is sorry, all the evil is erased, the harmful effects undone and forgiveness necessarily follows'. (Shulman: 132). The confessions spared no-one and Doukhobors did not hesitate to implicate their friends in their accounts of fireraising and dynamiting. The policemen who were sought out by the confessors were by now well known and they were almost treated as celebrities in the villages. Many Doukhobors were sentenced to terms of imprisonment. In 1962, nearly all the members of the 'Fraternal Council' of Doukhobors who were supposed to be behind much of the illegality and who were headed by Sorokin (who claimed the spiritual leadership though he was by now living in South America), were indicted, along with many others. Forty-eight confessions were eagerly spilled to the police. Various attempts by other Doukhobors to get these confessions retracted failed—until the mysterious arrival in the prison of 'spiritual cookies' containing matches.[35] Within six weeks 275 houses were destroyed by fire. The confessions were withdrawn, and since they were crucial to the prosecution's case the charges were dismissed.[36]

Those Doukhobors who had already been convicted, and who were imprisoned in the special fireproof jail, were uncooperative; they stripped themselves naked and went on hunger strike. In sympathy, a column of 750 Doukhobors set out on September 2nd, 1962, on a trek towards the prison. Two weeks later it had gathered 1200 people. Simma Holt states that the marchers expected to be turned back: they were not even dressed for a hike, some women were wearing quite unsuitable high-heeled shoes. But the authorities let them pass. At the end of September they continued their journey by bus, right into the heart of Vancouver where they settled in Victory Square and its neighbourhood. The authorities and the Press almost ignored them, much to their frustration. Eventually they moved on to the prison. In jail, the hunger strike went so far that forced feeding was resorted to and even then one young man died from starvation. When Simma Holt wrote in 1964, 74 women had just been released from jail but 90 Doukhobors were still in prison (Holt, 1964: 9). When Woodcock and Avakumovic visited the prison in March 1967, more than 400 sympathetic Doukhobors were still encamped in tents and huts outside the prison, giving witness of support for those incarcerated. Woodcock and Avakumovic saw the Great March as the end of an era for the Sons of Freedom. 'Since then', they wrote in 1968, 'there have been no mass nude parades, no house burnings, no dynamitings ... Krestova, so long a place of violence, has now become one of the most peaceful villages in western Canada ... Contrary to all expectations, the Sons of Freedom have recently decided to buy back the land at Krestova, and among the charred, grass grown ruins on the plateau, new houses are being built, solid structures with none of the air of deliberate impermanence of the old tarpaper shacks . . . Assimilation started late with the Sons of Freedom, but once begun it has been extraodinarily rapid. It is perhaps too early to prophesy that there will be no regressions into violence, but at the time of writing they seem unlikely.'[37]

Woodcock and Avakumovic were a little too optimistic, however. In December 1968 there was a boycott of the school at Agassiz, where the prison was located, and also at Krestova. At the same time there was agitation by some for the return from Uruguay of Sorokin, who did (in 1969) get permission to return (*The Globe and Mail*, 8th February, 1969). In August 1971, Mrs. Chernoff was sentenced to six years in prison for a fire at the home of Sorokin, and three months later Mrs. Astaforoff was found guilty of destroying J. J. Verigin's house. Three others were also in prison. The detained women 'went on a rampage in which they set fire to their room, smashed windows, barricaded themselves in and forcibly attempted to undress a famale nursing supervisor'. They went on hunger strike and were forcibly fed. Released on bail in May 1972, they broke this by participating in further demonstrations and were returned to prison where they stripped and for a while fasted again. Mrs. Chernoff claimed she had returned to prison to clear her name. 'I don't want the stigma on myself, on my children, that their grandmother or mother is something to be ashamed of . . . You put it to the public that it wasn't arson.' She thought that 'Arson is somebody who will go and burn something to get something out of it'. She claimed that, in contrast, *they* were protesting for their faith and religion. She had sacrificed everything she had built for something she believed in (*Globe and Mail*, 13th June, 1973).

In 1976, a teacher, Silver D. Cameron, sought out several of her former Doukhobor pupils who had once been taken away from their homes by the authorities for compulsory education. Nick, for instance, she found now had five children of his own. He and his wife had been among those who, years after leaving school, had been on the Vancouver trek. He referred to the old days: 'And then there was this prophecy that we'd return to Mother Russia that we'd emigrate through the jails. Well, how are you going to make this prophecy come true? You've got to get into jail. So all kinds of people pleaded guilty to things they had nothing to do with, and people would testify against them just to get them into jail. Joe Maloff spent five years in Agassiz [prison]—he burned down some old shack somewhere to do his part. But now we call ourselves the Community of Reformed Doukhobors, and we've put out a statement that anyone who has anything to do with bombs, burning, guns or violence is automatically excluded from membership. We've been manipulated by the left and jailed by the right, but basically we have nothing to do with politics. We're Doukhobors. Right? It's between us and Mother Earth, and that's it.' Nick took Cameron to a Sunday Meeting (*sobranya*) in Krestova. 'Don't be surprised if a few old girls take their clothes off, because there's an outsider there', he warned. During the magnificent singing which was 'enough to make you shiver with its passion and steady faith' four of five elderly women did strip discretely at the back of the hall. All bowed deeply to each other 'the one truly ceremonial act in the faith: the recognition of the spark of God which is in every human being' (Cameron, 1976).

Cameron described the village of Krestova as peaceful and as a model from which other Canadians could learn, yet only two years before her visit there was a report that there had been an unfulfilled plot to burn down 40 houses there. More surprising, perhaps, was the arrest two years later of J. J. Verigin and two others for arson. The case arose following four fires which included the attack on both Sorokin's house and Verigin's USCC community centre. Five women were arrested and tried in December 1978. The defendants, and some of the 100 audience in the public gallery, stripped. The sheriff's officers 'threw a cloth coat around [Stouchinoff's] bare shoulders, picked her up in her chair and carried her, along with four co-defendants, through the snow of a subzero British Columbia night to begin serving nine-month sentences'; one, in fact, got two years less a day. Olga Hoodichoff claimed that Verigin, respected winner in 1976 of the Order of Canada, had himself sent instructions for the arson—on pain of a seven-generation curse should they refuse. This was taken by the judge as a mitigating factor in their case. Verigin was arrested. Preliminary hearings took place in January, 1979 (Hopkins, 1979). He was eventually acquited.

So the old divisions between the different factions continue. In 1976, when Cameron visited Krestova, there was a sign on the wall of the meeting house: 'NO OTHER RELIGIOUS ORGANIZATION HAS ITS OWN POLICE FORCE, WHY MUST WE?' The RCMP special 'D' (for Doukhobot) Squad still existed in Nelson.

CONCLUSION

What implications relevant to the theme of this book do we draw from this material? We have considered a group of people who, at various periods, have felt their identity to be threatened. Their history up to the 1960's was characterized by *external conflicts* with the non-Doukhobor communities within which they lived, and by *internal conflicts* within the sect, which I suggest derived both from their religious ideology and from social precepts which embodied contradictory, paradoxical, or incompatible elements. The threats, and the responses generated to resolve them, became themselves *incorporated* within the self-definitions of the Doukhobors.

The first paradox we might note is the 'militancy' of their pacifism. No meek acceptance, no turning of the cheek for them. At the crucial periods any demands made by the larger communities in which they were embedded were likely to be rejected, resulting in conflict with the latter, because the hard-line Doukhobors never recognized the authority of any worldly State over them. Yet in Canada, at least, the Doukhobors did not entirely shun the wider community, for the majority of their men sought work within its economy. In due course more and more Doukhobors came to accept the benefits which full interaction with the State could provide. Where this happened, it was often seen by some as a danger to the cohesion of, and it produced friction within, the Doukhobor community itself.[38]

One problem for the Doukhobor purists was that the ideal of the humble, impoverished, Christ-like life-style, on the one hand, and the advocacy of self-discipline and hard-work on the other, were to some extent irreconcilable in Canada, where there was fertile land and wide economic opportunity. The rewards for the advocated diligence for some (but not all) were a continual threat to the simple egalitarian way of life that was prescribed. The more some worked and eschewed luxury and frivolity paradoxically the more prosperous they could become.[39] The pooling of wealth in the Community centre, and the like, did not altogether solve the problem because of the disputes which arose (as they had in Russia) over these assets. Such communal wealth was no more immune to destruction than private property.

A clear contradiction within Doukhobor dogma was the attitude towards the leadership. This was in practice, hereditary, often charismatic, sometimes exercising almost 'seigneurial rights', and sometimes accumulating great wealth—despite the tenet that Doukhobors, being equally identified with Christ, were themselves all equal.

Some contradictions derived from language usage. When a leader delivered an utterance, it was open to each Doukhobor to interpret this in a different way. It has been suggested that the words of the leader were often taken to mean the *opposite* of what would seem to be their commonday grammatical and syntactial meaning. Parables, religious texts, and various symbols, were used frequently, and these were particularly open to varying interpretations. There was, therefore, an imprecision, a lack of a standard one-to-one correspondence between utterance and import, such that incompatible meanings could be attributed to the same statement.

The contradictions which were generated by the self-definitions of the Doukohobors were resolved by three forms of action, each of which could fulfil more than one purpose, or carry more than one message:

1. *Migration*—Migration had been enforced upon the Doukhobors in Russia, as they tried to escape government edicts, or were sent into exile.[40]

It was one way of resolving conflict. But for the Doukhobors it became an end in itself. It provided certain benefits: it inhibited the accumulation of capital, which threatened antimaterialism and the internal egalitarian harmony of the community. Migration might also have been in the interests of the leaders, who could play a special part in organizing any population movements. Perhaps as important as all this, at the ideological level migration identified the Doukhobors with the homeless figure of Christ. As one man noted, they had no intention of being immigrants in Canada, only exiles.

2. *Arson* also had several positive features. Fire was seen as a purifying agent. Used in Russia to destroy ikons and arms, its revival in Canada was directed first against institutions which seemed to threaten the independence of the Doukhobors from the State. Then it was turned inwards upon the community itself. It too prevented the accumulation of capital goods and the development of inequality. It ensured personal and communal privation. Through the attitude of 'look what you've made me do' responsibility could be transferred onto the Canadian authorities, thus maintaining the external boundary of the community, and its solidarity in the face of supposedly threatening forces.

3. *Nudity* was employed as the third mode of resolving the contradictions which threatened the identity of the group. This technique was singularly effective for dealing both with internal and external conflicts. The Canadians had provided land and had generally welcomed the Doukhobors, and could not, therefore, easily be treated as hostile persons, especially by those claiming to be pacifist. Doukhobors of an integrationist tendency, or who welcomed higher living standards, or who were attracted to individualism, could not easily be harmed. More than this, convention demanded that these threatening elements, and in particular fellow Doukhobors, be accorded traditional tokens of respect. The militant Doukhobors turned to the language of deference and found a nonviolent yet coercive weapon in the form of an *inversion* of the traditional tokens of respect, which included public modesty. They adopted the nude parade.

The wearing of clothes is a supremely social act. It is part of a communication system. By disrobing, the Doukhobors withdrew recognition from, excommunicating, the witnesses; they set them outside the universe of discourse. At the same time, the nudity became a social artefact for identifying the group. It was both hostile to those against whom it was directed, and a badge for those who indulged in it. In itself it said something, and those who would not communicate through it were seen to be outside the group. It was a 'language' which was accessible to all who wished to use it. It had many other advantages, some of which have been set out above.

As I have shown elsewhere,[41] nudity has often been employed as a hostile gesture by a variety of persons and groups in many parts of the world and at different epochs. Sometimes its use has been an apparently *ad hoc* reaction of fleeting duration, but sometimes it is institutionalized. The Doukhobors made more of it than most because it slotted so well into their explicit rule of nonviolence. Shulman thought the nudism demonstrated behaviour quite opposed to the end wished to be achieved. On the contrary, it fitted the purpose admirably.

We should stress here that the Doukhobor protesters were never much concerned with their material 'rights' as conventionally understood. They were, instead, preoccupied with their 'liberty' to maintain their separate identity, to live like Doukhobors, to *be* Doukhobors. Deprivation, suffering, poverty had became part of their self-definition, which was reinforced by their identification with their great religious martyr, Christ himself. One gets the impression that it was their suffering itself which some extremists came to try to preserve. From being threatened by external forces, they became threatened by their own comfort and material success.

A word might be said about martyrs and the symbolic weight given to them. They are often revered for the morality of their teachings, and for their willingness to lay down their lives for them. But could it be that martyrs are also attractive because they are in some respects failures? Although the Jewish establishment may well have seen Christ's power as a threat, in his lifetime his followers were a fairly small band. The mass of the population stonily allowed him to be put to death. Was not his very inability to survive a sort of failure? The story of Che Guevara's exploits on the mainland of South America, and his ultimate death there, was surely a tale of tragic failure. Wrongly convinced that there would be a popular uprising, he and his few friends tracked backwards and forwards in discomfort and isolation until the dismal end. James Dean became more famous after his reckless driving led to his death. Bobby Sands challenged the prison authorities and lost (his life). It is often failure and not success, however, which makes folk heroes. The unproductiveness of the suffering is the important thing. In their lifetimes they are often each only one among a number of living heroes. What sets some apart in history may be their final fatal impotence, which attracts the public in retrospect, and paradoxically gives them their additional power as models.

The Doukhobors are not the only group which has tried to express symbolically, by self-inflicted wounds, their feelings of grievance and rejection. The suffragettes chained themselves to railings. Many different political prisoners have engaged in hunger strikes. Perhaps the disrobing and the 'dirty' campaign of the IRA were steps taken to dismay the humane instincts of the authorities and of the wider world looking on, while reinforcing the image of themselves as victims. They do not seem less adept in gaining publicity than the Doukhobors, who actively sought press coverage for their Vancouver trek, and who were reported to have been disappointed by the lack of attention they received. I have shown elsewhere how other groups (of women and young persons) have inverted the common conventions of courtesy, applying nudity and vulgarity in defence of their honour or to express their hostility. It has been suggested that such displays are often adopted by so-called 'muted groups' who eschew violence or who do not have fluency in or access to the dominant modes of communication by which to express their grievances, and redress their perceived wrongs (Ardener, S., 1973, 1975).

The Doukhobors are not the only group who have been threatened by their own success. Once an identity has become defined in terms of, say, underdevelopment, or pastoralism, for instance, then economic success, urbanization, and industrialization challenge the basic identification. I once heard a Canadian deplore the 'modernization' of the Eskimo, for an Eskimo who received social security, or one who drove a tractor and lived on rice and pork was not perceived to be an Eskimo. Bakweri of Cameroon who left their villages and permanently dwelt in towns were often felt not to be quite 'true Bakweri' by those Bakweri who stayed in the villages. The Scottish Gaeltachd is imbued with rural values (see, for example, Chapman, 1978). Development is both sought and dreaded by some who have the preservation of Gaelic culture at heart.[42] Even the identity of the Trades Unions may be thought by some to be in jeopardy from the very material success which is their purported aim. Changes, even for the better, may require the often painful experience of finding new definitions of identity. Perhaps, for this reason, certain inflexible elements sometimes prefer the perpetuation of the original definitions. But within the communities and groups mentioned, the rigid extremists are usually a small minority. Most human beings are open to redefinition of themselves and their environments. Real grievances once removed may soon be forgotten, and new images invoked. New events occur, and times change. It was the adoption by a minority of direct violence, resulting in the death of a young member of the sect, which led ultimately to greater integration and cooperation between the two communities.[43] Most Doukhobors embraced success and most have abandoned their impulse for migration. Today there are not many places to go. But, as Edwin Ardener has shown, templates for thought and action can often be realized in new and unpredictable forms.

As images change from one of deprivation to one of success, from rejection to one of participation, and as new markers of identity are adopted, the importance of the destructive rearguards, if they fail in their objective to preserve an outworn element in an identity, may dwindle away. The story of the Doukhobors inspires us with their moral values, their self-discipline, and their history which has had its heroes, heroines and heroic moments as well as its many victims. We see them fighting to retain their sense of community and identity. We admire their egalitarian philosophy. Their history is unique to them. Nevertheless, we can see parallels elsewhere, we see other groups whose identities may be felt to be threatened both from without and from within, from their successes as much as their failures. We may see Doukhobor history in this wider context, while we draw what lessons from it that we can.

NOTES

[1] I became interested in the Doukhobors in the context of a wider piece of research on modes of protest (still in progress), which includes the use of nudity, and began to look for comparative material in the literature to supplement my own fieldwork in Africa (Ardener, 1973, 1974). Coincidentally, I happen to have a special interest in Canada having lived there some years when young, although before I was mature enough to engage in research. I have not had an opportunity to return recently, but the written sources available to me are rich in detail. For the earlier period Alymer Maude's account, published in 1904, has been very useful. Wright's *Salva Bohu* (1940) is full of anecdotal material and reported oral history. In 1950, the Attorney General of British Columbia invited a number of scholars from the University of B.C. to undertake a special study which was published in book form in 1955. The contributions to this volume by the editor, H. B. Hawthorn, by C. Lewis, A. Shulman and H. Herbison and the separate, richly descriptive, book of Simma Holt have all been particularly useful. The University of British Columbia Library has issued some excellent bibliographies, annotated by Maria Horvath (Krisztinkovich). G. Woodcock and I. Avakumovic (1968), and other important studies, are also cited in the text and notes. I have had the advantage, also, at an early stage of my research, of being able to consult at Oxford, two Doukhobors trained in social anthropology, Claire Newell and Terrell Popoff, who were able to direct my attention to some of the literature. The work of another social anthropologist and Doukhobor K. J. Tarasoff was helpful. My debt to the research of all these is very great, and I commend their original studies to you. I take responsibility for my selection from their work and the interpretations which I put upon it.

[2] Hawthorn (1955) gives the 'number of depredations' by Doukhobors by the year from 1923–1955: (1) Burning or bombing of schools, 84. (2) Doukhobor owned or occupied property, 390. (3) Other government or non-Doukhobor property, 124. Total: 598. Depredations continued over the years, with fluctuating severity, certainly until 1979.

[3] For Peter Vasilivich Verigin's designation as leader by Loukeria Kalmikova (his second wife) and subsequent transportation in exile around Russia (see, for example, Wright, 1940: 52ff).

[4] For Tolstoy's influence on Peter V. Verigin and through him, on the Doukhobors generally, and for the active support which he and his followers (among them his son) gave to the Doukhobors in their efforts to emigrate, see Maude and Wright. Some Doukhobors were temporarily placed on Cyprus before joining their fellows in Canada (Wright, 1940: 108–9).

[5] Although there was a sudden drop in the official figures after 1970, which suggests

that either they were avoiding registration or they were unwilling to be identified as of Doukhobor origin. However, registration, as indicated in the text, has always been a problem and the figures cannot be assumed to reflect population changes due to genetic factors or migration, although they are of interest.

[6] The details of the negotiations are in Maude (1904), Wright (1940), and elsewhere.

[7] In 1912, an order in Council was passed forbidding the further entry of Doukhobors, Hutterites and Mennonites into Canada. In 1919, the ban was lifted, *except for Doukhobors.* (Horvath, 1970: 15). In 1926, the Minister from B. C. (Mr. King) invited more Doukhobors to enter Canada (ibid.). From 1934–1956 Doukhobors in British Columbia were disenfranchized (Tarasoff, 1969: 24).

[8] Maude (1904), who gives the belief system as it existed when he wrote soon after the Doukhobor immigration to Canada, bases much of his study on earlier Russian publications, particularly Oreste Novitsky's 1832 work which was said by Wright (1940) to have been accepted by the Doukhobors as authoritative. When I have quoted Maude's summaries of Novitsky's statements directly I have retained Maude's italics. I have not consulted the Russian original which was published in Kiev. Vegetarianism is said by Wright to date from 4th November, 1894 (Greg. Cal.) and like many other rules (e.g. refusal to take oaths) to have been introduced by P. V. Verigin (Wright: 67ff). Holt (1964), the contributors to Hawthorn (1955), and Tarasoff (1969), present material on current Doukhobor beliefs.

[9] Jesus Christ '*is the Son of God, but in the same sense in which we also are Sons of God. Our elders know even more than Christ did: go and hear them*' was the injunction noted by Novitsky in 1832 (Maude, 1904: 15).

[10] The succession to J. J. Verigin, who in 1939 was elected General Secretary (in 1961 Honorary Chairman) of the Orthodox Doukhobors (later known as the U.S.C.C.) is: Sylvan Kolesnikof → Ilarion Pobirohin → Savely Kapoustin (son of Pobirohin) → Vasily Kalmikof (son of Kapoustin) → Ilarion Kalmikof (son of Vasily Kalmikof) → Peter Kalmikof (son of Ilarion K.) → Loukiriya Kalmokof (wife of Peter K., later second wife of Peter Verigin) → Peter V. ('The Lordly') Verigin I → Peter P. Verigin II (son of Peter V. V. and his first wife Dunia) → (Peter P. Verigin III, dies in Russia) J. J. Verigin (son of Peter P. Verigin II's daughter Anna and I. S. Woikin). Michael Orekoff assumed the name of ('The Archangel') Verigin and Sorokin seems to have claimed to have been P. P. Verigin III at one time.

[11] Holt: 177. Cf. 'Each of us decides . . . things for ourselves. We have no one among us who decides for us' (Wright, 1940: 230). Michael—self styled 'the Archangel Verigin'—claimed leadership through a 'will' of Verigin II; he founded a community of Sharing Doukhobors.

[12] Shulman (in Hawthorn, 1955) p. 130. I give the views of Shulman and some other scholars like Lewis without necessarily subscribing to their views. I would not, for instance, apply the term 'autism' as Shulman does.

[13] Holt, 1964: 11. This is still done at *Sobranya*, see p. 257.

[14] Maude: 312. The modern association of women and literacy in Georgia (USSR), where an epic story is part of every woman's trusseau, is shown by the work of Tamara Dragadze.

[15] Hawthorn, 1955: 15. The relative dominance of women in groups which are 'muted' in relation to another (dominant) group can be documented (e.g. Okely, 1975; Ridd. 1981).

[16] Holt, 1964: 29. Tarasoff (p. 30) states that in 1906 only 211 Independent Doukhobors had registered their households. He notes (p. 14) that by 1907 when the Government enforced evictions from nonregistered lands 5000 out of 8000 were affected, the

other 3000 (Independent Doukhobors) complied with the law. Doukhobors including even the spiritual leader Verigin I, have often cited the precept 'Render unto Ceasar . . .' (though there has been dispute about the limits of Ceasar's rights, compared to duty to God).

[17] Maude, 1904: 215, 224–5; Holt, 1964: 30. Photographs of chains of women pulling ploughs are available.

[18] Maude: 240. Archer, who published various papers on the Doukhobors in the 1890's and who taught in Doukhobor schools, was later burned to death in his log-cabin.

[19] Maude: 19ff. According to Woodcock and Avakumovic (p. 240), 'the Community had its own miniature criminal code for dealing with those who were regarded as disloyal. Public censure was the lightest punishment. More serious offenders could be deprived of their flour ration for anything from three days to a month. The gravest punishment was expulsion from the Community, and few were willing to risk this, since they were turned away without any means whatsoever and lacked the skills or the linguistic ability to live in the outside world as anything better than casual labourers'.

[20] Maude: 241; Holt: 245; Wright: 214–17. It is interesting to note that beating with prickly twigs was a punishment formerly used by the Russians against Doukhobors (*see* Tarasoff).

[21] Quoted in Holt, 1964: 43.

[22] Wright: 217; Holt: 43–4. Malhortov complained of police brutality (Maude: 242); Vasa Popoff complained of Doukhobor brutality following the burning of agricultural machinary (or tarpaulin covering it—Tarasoff) for which he was reported to the police by Peter Verigin (Wright: 216).

[23] Shulman: 145. Woodcock and Avakumovic thought that 'The Doukhobors were astonished at the agitation their nakedness caused among the Canadians' (p. 195). Makhortov is quoted as saying 'It is very strange that these people become so excited when a human takes off cloths' (Wright: 216).

[24] Holt: 70–71. Other Doukhobors claimed that Michael Verigin was opposed to nudity. Witnesses were cross-examined in court on this point. See, for instance, Holt, 1964: 132.

[25] Woodcock and Avakumovic: 10,196. I have no evidence of nudity among the Doukhobors in Russia, so they are probably correct. V. A. Sukhorev suggested that since nudism has no place in earlier Doukhobor tradition, 'the idea may have been introduced by a member of a nudist colony in Oregon who visited the Doukhobors shortly after their arrival in Canada and preached to them the necessity for men to resurrect the original paradise where the fathers of the human race went naked until their innocence was lost. However, the revelation may just as credibly have come to one of the Sons of Freedom in pondering over the enigmatic passages of Verigin's letters ... ' (Woodcock and Avakumovic: 196). Woodcock and Avakumovic's statement that arson was also a new feature, only introduced in Canada, seems to be erroneous, and is contradicted by their own statement on page 26.

[26] Holt: 102. See also school teacher Helen Derhoushoff's testimony: 'A resolution was passed . . . that from then on nudism was not going to be used as a weapon against the government, but just to show our bodies for the purity of the soul and body'.

[27] Shulman: 138. He states that they were usually unaware of the hostility that they expressed.

[28] Quoted in Holt: 227. For the burning of arms on 29th June, 1895 (see Wright: 78–8); for photographs of site and many other excellent illustrations (see Tarasoff, 1969).

[29] Holt: 52. Woodcock and Avakumovic (p. 107) report a small incident of arson in 1903, the first episode in Canada, the perpetrators of which, at the instance of Peter Verigin, were imprisoned. See note 22.

[30] See note 2.

[31] Holt quotes Anuta Kootnikoff: 'When (my son) Harry two years, I burn house. When he five I burn house. Many times I burn house. Police know. I can't remember number times I burn house. Three times I go to jail. Harry two when I go to jail first time, we live many place—Krestova, Goose Creek, Winlaw, Shoreacres, Gilpin—I burn houses. Harry see. He like I should do this. It good Harry should see. This is Doukhobor work. For two hundred years Doukhobor burn churches and guns. I tell Harry this way he should work and live—for Doukhobor' (Holt, 1964: 2).

[32] Holt: 50. For photographs of Doukhobor property and enterprise, see Tarasoff.

[33] For details, see Holt, ch. 4. Peter V. Verigin was succeeded by his son Peter J. Verigin. who died in 1939. Peter Verigin III, his son, was in a Russian prison camp where he died in 1942. J. J. Verigin became active on the death of his grandfather (Verigin II), although Michael (Orekoff) 'Verigin' and S. S. Sorokin also led rivial factions.

[34] There was no prcedure by which a mother could register her child in her own name only and retain its legitimacy, a regulation deplored by the women.

[35] '. . . a box of commerical sandwich cookies appeared in the community. They were passed out by hand to individuals. The message was that these were "spiritual cookies". Some said they came from Sorokin. When the recipients broke them open, they found the distinct and decisive message of the *Spitchka*—an actual kitchen-match—inside' (Holt, 1964: 256).

[36] Holt was given much help by the Canadian Mounted Police and presents them very sympathetically. Their cooperation enabled her to provide detailed accounts of the detection of Doukhobor dynamitists, and of their confessions, which make gripping reading.

[37] Woodcock and Avakumovic: 355. Compare Zubek and Solberg (1952: 236) who imagined that signposts predicted 'complete assimilation in the next few decades'.

[38] Horvath (1972) note 610, summarizing a publication by Peter Verigin of 3rd July, 1913, in New York, says that he found out 'that the solvent action of a democracy is more disintegrating that the oppression of an autocracy.'

[39] It was suggested that some of the strongest feelings were generated in areas of poor agricultural fertility against the relative prosperity of other regions.

[40] Many ideas for migration arose while in Canada—to various parts of Latin America, for example—some of which were tried by some. The pattern came full circle when negotiations abortively began after the Second World War for a return to Russia. The Canadian Government had participated to no avail. In due course, a number of visits were made (see, for instance Tarasoff, 1969).

[41] This paper is part of a wider piece of research into modes of communication by 'muted groups', including those, for example, of nudity, or of vulgarity and other 'disrespectful' expressions (see Ardener, S. G., 1973, 1974, 1975, and work in progress).

[42] The encouragement of 'craft industries' is an attempt to combine both; the definitions involved, however, produce their own problematic.

[43] It was an accepted principle, stated by P. V. Verigin in 1896 (who lifted it from Tolstoy's translation of the W. L. Garrison draft for a peace convection in Boston, Mass., in 1838) that while they could not acknowledge allegiance to any human government; 'neither can we oppose any such government by a resort to physical force' (*see* Wright: 99–100). In the modern period Doukhobors have been very active in the Peace Movements, and have held or attended many rallies (*see* Tarasoff, 1969).

[44] See E. Ardener (1970) for a discussion of 'templates' for thought and action among the Bakweri, which generated new realizations of old patterns.

REFERENCES

Ardener, E. (1970). Witchcraft, economics and the continuity of belief. In: M. Douglas (ed.) *Witchcraft Confessions and Accusations*. London, Tavistock.

Ardener, E. (1973). Some Outstanding Problems in the Analysis of Events. Paper given at ASA Decennial Conference. Published in: E. Schwimmer (ed.) *The Yearbook of Symbolic Anthropology*, 1978. London, Hurst; and in: M. Foster and S. Brandes (eds.) *Symbols as Sense*, 1980. New York, Academic Press.

Ardener, S. (1973). Sexual insult and female militancy. In: *Man* (September, 1973). Reprinted in S. Ardener (ed.) *Perceiving Women*, London, Dent; and New York, Halsted (1975).

Ardener, S. (1974). Nudity, vulgarity and protest, *New Society*, **27**, (598), 704–705.

Cameron, S. (1976). Children of protest, *Weekend Magazine*, Nov. 13th, 1976.

Chapman, M. (1978). *The Gaelic Vision in Scottish Culture*. London, Croom Helm.

Hawthorn, H. B. (ed.) (1952). *Report of the Doukhobor Research Committee*. Canada, University of British Columbia.

Hawthorn, H. B. (1955). *The Doukhobors of British Columbia*. Version of 1952 Report. Canada, Dent.

Hawthorn, H. B. (1955). The Contemporary Picture. In: *The Doukhobors of British Columbia*. Canada, Dent.

Herbison, H. (1955). *Religion*, In: Hawthorn (ed.) 1955.

Holt, S. (1964). *Terror in the Name of God*. Toronto/Montreal, McClelland & Stewart.

Hopkins. T. (1979) Return of the torch and the flesh, *Maclean's* Jan. 8th, 1979.

Horvath, M. (1970). *A Doukhobor Bibliography*. Vancouver, University of British Columbia Library.

Lewis, C. (1955). Childhood and Family Life. In: Hawthorn (ed.) 1955.

Maude, A. (1904) *A Peculiar People*. The Doukhobors. London, Grant Richards.

Novitski. O. (1832). *The Doukhobors: Their Story and Their Creed*. Kiev, University Printing Shop.

Okely, J. (1975). Gypsy women: models in conflict. In: S. Ardener (ed.) *Perceiving Women*.

Ridd, R. (1981). Where women must dominate: response to oppression in a south African Urban community. In: S. Ardener (ed.) *Women and Space: Ground Rules and Social Maps*. (1981) London, Croom Helm.

Shulman, A. (1955). Personality, characteristics and psychological problems. In: Hawthorn (ed.).

Starchnoff, J. P. (1961). *Doukhobors As They Are*. Toronto.

Tarasoff, K. J. (1969). *Pictorial History of the Doukhobors*. Prairie Book Dept., Western Producer, Saskatoon, Canada.

Wright, J. (1940). *Slava Bohu*. New York and Toronto, Farrar & Rinehart.

Wright, J. (1939). The Doukhobors, *Can. Geog. Journal*, **XIX** (5), 300–306.

Woodcock, G., and Avakumovic, I. (1968). *The Doukhobors*. London, Faber.

Zubek. J. P., and Solberg, P. A. (1952). *Doukhobors at War*. Toronto, Ryerson Press.

Author Index

Agnew, J., 181
Agnew, N., 100, 101
Allen, 135
Allport, 7
Altman, 53, 66
Apter, 80, 82, 88, 89
Ardener, E., 261, 262, 266
Ardener, S., 15, 262–266
Argyle, 5
Ashby, 90, 88
Antonovsky, 112
Avakumovic, 245, 256, 262

Ballard, 112
Bancroft, 77
Bannister, 47, 181
Batta, 108, 126
Bavelas, 4
Berger, 3, 120, 121, 122
Berscheid, 56
Biddle, 9
Binder, 163
Binet, 81
Bleuler, 85
Bloom, 69–70
Borrill, 130
Branden, 85, 89
Breakwell, 15, 21, 25, 50, 115, 219
Brehm, 81
Bridges, 81
Burns, 4, 118
Butler, 37
Byrne, 58–59, 60

Cameron, 257
Cattell, 4
Chapman, 91, 92, 96, 97, 98
Clore, 58, 60
Codol, 62
Cohen, 14
Constantinople, 152
Cook, 163
Cooley, 8
Coopersmith, 117
Crawford, 60, 62

De Waele, 43
Denzin, 123
Dodson, 82
Dreger, 4
Dreistadt, 88
Dryden, 65
Duck, 17, 53, 54, 55, 57, 58, 60, 61, 63, 66, 68
Du Preez, 95

Einstein, 94–95
Erikson, 78, 89, 131–133, 146, 151, 152, 160, 163

Featherstone, 250
Foss, 89
Fransella, 4, 151
Frend, 8
Friedman, 152
Fromkin, 62
Fromm, 76

Garfinkel, 50
Geary, 152
Gergen, 12, 14, 117
Goffman, 9, 41, 43, 46, 48, 49, 50, 121
Goldberg, 112
Goldhamer, 115

Goldstein, 65
Graziano, 54
Green, 110–111, 112

Hagestad, 70
Hall, 4
Hampshire, 33, 37, 38
Harari, 111
Harré, 3, 4, 6, 41, 43, 47
Harvey, 68
Hatfield, 67
Hanser, 152, 163
Hawthorne, 239, 263
Hedin, 115
Helling, 36
Herbison, 242–243, 249
Hiller, 121
Hillery, 215
Hinde, 54
Hitch, 14, 111
Hlasny, 63
Holland, 4
Hollis, 9, 11, 12, 48
Holmes, 78
Holt, 239, 242, 244, 245, 246, 247, 248, 250, 252, 255, 262–265
Hopkins, 257
Horney, 131
Horvath, 265
Hume, 39
Hunter, 215
Huston, 70
Hyman, 113

Infield, 94

James, 6, 7, 8, 9, 76
Johnson, 54
Jones, 91, 92, 96, 97, 98

Kelley, 91, 92, 96, 97, 98
Kelly, 47, 92, 94–95, 99, 100, 151
Kelvin, 67
Kerkhoff, 112, 116
Kitwood, 17, 130
Klapp, 78
Kransz, 111
Kuhn, 122

Labov, 46, 48
La Gaipa, 54, 67
Laing, 76, 123, 151
Landfield, 92
Langer, 69
Langford, 40
Lea, 17, 57, 61, 63
Lee, 217
Leed, 85
Lemaine, 218
Lerner, 62
Levinger, 54
Lewis, 244–245, 251
Lindesmith, 120
Lindzey, 4
Little, 174
Lowen, 80
Lyman, 47
Lynch, J. 55, 69, 70
Lynch, K., 215

Mahoney, 93, 102
Mann, 114
Marcia, 152, 163
Mathev-Musser, 54
Matthews, 15, 225
Mande, 239–265
Mawby, 108
McCall, 9, 11, 54, 67
McCarrey, 63
McCarthy, 189
McCormick, 112, 116
McCulloch, 108
McDavid, 111
McCall, 54, 67
Mead, 8, 9, 76, 118, 119–122
Meltzev, 120
Merton, 112, 114–115
Mischel, 5, 6
Mitroff, 93, 101
Morgan, 41
Morris, 42
Miller, 54, 67
Mulford, 119
Murgatroyd, 89

Nelson, 60
Newcomb, 113
Noble, 143
Novak, 62
Novitsky, 241, 244

O'Neill, 41

Osgood, 117

Park, 110, 116
Parks, 54, 67
Perrin, 56
Planck, 102
Polanyi, 93
Pollis, 114
Prince, 35
Pyke, 100, 101

Rahe, 55, 78
Rand, 89
Reeves, 60
Reynolds, 81
Rhamey, 60
Rios-Garcia, 163
Rogers, 77
Rose, 113
Rosenfeld, 65
Rychlak, 102

Salisbury, 119
Schafft, 115
Shapiro, 152
Sherif, 114
Shoemaker, 36
Shulman, 244–246, 250–255, 262–265
Silber, 163
Simmons, 9
Simon, 82
Smith, K. C. P., 82, 87, 89
Smith, N. J., 108
Suyder, 62
Smyder, 70
Soustelle, 44
Stonequist, 110
Strauss, 120
Strawson, 33
Strykev, 9

Tajfel, 21, 23, 43, 45–46
Tarasoff, 240
Taylor, 14, 53, 66
Thomas, 56
Thibant, 61
Tippett, 163
Traupman, 67
Trower, 65, 67
Turner, 9, 10

Vallacher, 133–134
Veblen, 46
Von Cranach, 47

Wallon, 82
Walster, 56
Waterman, 152
Watson, 93
Webber, 217
Wegner, 133–134
Weinreich, 17, 47, 154–155, 160, 164, 172, 177, 178, 179
Weisman, 55
Weiss, 56, 59
Wellman, 122
Williams, 34
Wilson, 109
Wirth, 115
Woodcock, 245, 256, 262
Worden, 55
Wright, J., 243, 262, 265
Wright, P. H., 60, 62

Young, 56

Zukav, 94

Subject Index

Acknowledged identity, 190–192, 193, 197, 210–211
Achieved membership, 20
Ascribed identity, 190–192, 197, 209–211
Ascribed membership, 19–20

Community, 215–221, 223–238
Conceptual groups, 21
Concrete groups, 21
Consistency, 57–59, 76–77

Free will, 6

Generalized other, 8, 120
Group identity, 18–24, 84, 191–192, 197

Hypernegativism, 87–88

Ideal self, 7, 77
Identity conflict, 150, 153, 158, 159, 162
Identity confusion, 107, 129, 130–132, 142–143, 146–147
Identity crisis, 11, 83, 131, 160
Identity diffusion, 160, 173
Identity processes, 12
Identifications, 152–153, 157, 173–174, 177, 181
Implicit self theory, 133
Inertia, 18

Looking-glass self, 8

Marginality, 14, 45, 48, 49, 110–117
Mobility, 17, 18

Negativism, functions 79–80

Orientational other, 122–124

Passing, 121, 124
Personal constructs, 60–61, 91–104, 149–183

Real self, 7, 10, 11
Reconstrual, 17, 151
Relationships, emergent properties, 54–55, 56, 59, 67–69
Reference groups, 113, 119
Resynthesis, 152
Rhetoric, 25, 196–199, 209–213
Role structures, 99

Self-attribution, 133, 143–144, 146–147
Self-devaluation, 154–157, 172–173, 174–175
Self-disclosure, 62–4, 67
Self-esteem, 7, 14, 24, 78–79, 117, 154, 156, 158, 163, 179
Social comparison, 141–142
Stigma, 62
Symbolic interactionism, 119–122